America and the Rogue States

AMERICAN FOREIGN POLICY IN THE 21ST CENTURY

Edited by Thomas H. Henriksen

Published by Palgrave Macmillan:

American Foreign Policy in Regions of Conflict: A Global Perspective
By Howard J. Wiarda

America and the Rogue States
By Thomas H. Henriksen

America and the Rogue States

Thomas H. Henriksen

AMERICA AND THE ROGUE STATES
Copyright © Thomas H. Henriksen, 2012.

First published in 2012 by
PALGRAVE MACMILLAN®
in the United States—a division of St. Martin's Press LLC,
175 Fifth Avenue, New York, NY 10010.

Where this book is distributed in the UK, Europe and the rest of the world,
this is by Palgrave Macmillan, a division of Macmillan Publishers Limited,
registered in England, company number 785998, of Houndmills,
Basingstoke, Hampshire RG21 6XS.

Palgrave Macmillan is the global academic imprint of the above companies
and has companies and representatives throughout the world.

Palgrave® and Macmillan® are registered trademarks in the United States,
the United Kingdom, Europe and other countries.

ISBN: 978–1–137–00639–4 (hardcover)
ISBN: 978–1–137–01999–8 (paperback)

Library of Congress Cataloging-in-Publication Data

Henriksen, Thomas H.
    America and the rogue states / by Thomas H. Henriksen.
        p. cm.—(American foreign policy in the 21st century)
    Includes index.
    ISBN 978–1–137–00639–4 (hardback :alk. paper)—
    ISBN 978–1–137–01999–8 (pbk. : alk. paper)
        1. United States—Foreign relations. 2. World politics. 3. Belligerency.
    I. Title.

E183.7.H43 2012
327.73—dc23   2011050336

A catalogue record of the book is available from the British Library.

Design by Newgen Imaging Systems (P) Ltd., Chennai, India.

First edition: June 2012

D 10 9 8 7 6 5 4 3 2

Printed in the United States of America.

Contents

Note from the Editor   vii

Acknowledgments   ix

Introduction   1

Chapter 1   The Rogue Phenomenon   3

Chapter 2   Iraq: Quintessential Rogue State   29

Chapter 3   Iran: Ace of the Axis of Evil   63

Chapter 4   North Korea: Blackmailing Rogue   103

Chapter 5   Lesser Rogues and Troublesome States   145

Notes   189

Bibliography   213

Index   221

Note from the Editor

The dramatic events of the past several years confirm, if any confirmation were required, that the world has utterly changed from the Cold War era. The fall of the Berlin Wall now appears a curtain-rising for a catalytic drama that is unfolding before our eyes. Among the obvious changes internationally are the economic and political rise of China, the transformation of the Middle East by the Arab Spring, the debt and financial problems faced by Europe, and the diminution of America's sway, in part, from the stalled US economy. Before this era, a number of regional states—such as Brazil, India, and Turkey—received perfunctory attention. Now these states and others are no longer just lumped into blocs of states labeled as pro- or anti-Western. They have emerged in their own right as local powerhouses. Little of this transformed international landscape was predicted with the collapse of the Soviet Union and apparent dominance of the United States in world affairs.

The purpose of this series, American Foreign Policy in the 21st Century, is to describe, analyze, and generally shed light on America's new global role. Interested readers and students, it is hoped, will have a clearer understanding of our emerging global order from reading the series. It is our intention to have volumes that focus on regions, organization, topics, and important individual countries as they relate to the United States.

The series has been launched outstandingly by Howard J. Wiarda's excellent book *American Foreign Policy in Regions of Conflict*. In that work, Professor Wiarda returns the study of international relations to its roots (the fundamentals), relying not on mathematical modeling techniques but rather on a thorough grounding in a region's geography, history, culture, and economics to foster understanding and sound US foreign policy. He provides the reader with background and analysis on which to base America's interest and policy on the important global regions.

The second book in the series is my own, entitled *America and the Rogue States*. In this volume I concentrate on US policy toward a small number of nations, which brutally repress political opponents, deny human rights to most of their populations, export terrorism abroad, and, most significantly, pursue megadeath weapons such as nuclear arms. Although such rogue states were formed during the Cold War, their emergence on the world scene nearly coincided with the collapse of the Soviet Union. The current rogue nations, thus, are very much a product of the post-Soviet era.

THOMAS H. HENRIKSEN
Senior Fellow
Stanford University's
Hoover Institution

Acknowledgments

Most institutions are unique in their own way, but the Hoover Institutions is singularly unique. This volume, like many before it, has been researched and written under its resplendent auspices. Its director, John Raisian, and his able associates David Brady, Stephen Langlois and Richard Sousa, along with their staffs, have provided the fellows the greatest of luxuries to work—unencumbered time so as to search, think, and draft ideas. Hoover's legendary academic atmosphere is conducive to wide-ranging inquiry and productivity. Once again, I am indebted to my colleagues for their stimulation and thought-provoking commentary.

Over the past few years, I have been blessed with many first-rate assistants, who assisted in the research for this volume and read earlier versions of it. They are Hyun-June Chung, Oliver Ennis, Ahkil Iyer, Courtney Matteson, Gabriel Shapiro and Ruth Hall Willson. Their efforts and suggestions were of much help. The errors, of course, remain mine despite their assistance.

Once again, none of my exertions would have succeeded without the encouragement of my wife, Margaret Mary, and our family, Heather, Damien, and Lucy.

Introduction

At the very heart of rogue states—wrapped in dictatorship and belligerence, veiled by secrecy and propaganda, and malevolently framed by terrorism—lay a puzzle for US foreign policy: how to handle these small- to medium-weight states since they first burst on the international scene? This volume strives to set forth a brief account of US policy toward rogue regimes. It concentrates, by design, on the three major rogue powers—Iraq, Iran, and North Korea. But it does analyze, more briefly, American policy toward Libya, Syria, Cuba, and Sudan, which have been lumped into the rogue nation category while posing much less threat to the United States since the end of the Cold War. Other tangential examples of troublesome (but not full-fledged rogue) states, such as Venezuela, Afghanistan, and Myanmar, are noted, too. These classifications are spelled out in the book.

This present volume forms a sort of bookend to my earlier work, *American Power after the Berlin Wall* (Palgrave Macmillan, 2007). That study dwelt on a host of US interventions in such countries as Panama, Somalia, Haiti, Bosnia, Kosovo, Afghanistan, and Iraq (twice). It explored the rationale for military operations, whether diplomatic, humanitarian, or strategic. The prevalence of war-related ventures earned the United States the unwelcome designation as world policeman. That story represents only part of the picture of US policy after the Berlin Wall fell. The other part centered on diplomacy and restraint.

Washington officials were faced with a number of crises for which they did not resort to a military solution. Rogue states, with the singular exception of Iraq, were spared US invasion and pacification. Yet some did provide provocations enough for a conflict. Thus, this current book takes a look at another dimension of American diplomacy. Why the United States did not go to war with bellicose states is one theme. What policies Washington did follow are narrated and examined as well. Indeed, the very nature of the rogue phenomenon itself is described, as is their emergence on the international scene after the Cold War.

The rogue story is far from completed. Adversarial states still pose threats and challenges. But two decades since the Cold War provides enough distance to examine the phenomenon and American reaction to rogue actors. In all likelihood, rogue states will always be with us. Their presence, as noted briefly in this work, has been a matter of the historical record. What gives these contemporary rogue nations their deadly salience today is their reach for nuclear weapons. This ultimate weapon in despotic and perhaps apocalyptic hands arouses legitimate apprehension among other powers.

A word of explanation to the reader: one volume cannot portray definitively America's engagement with several separate players. Interactions between any one of the main rogue nations—Iraq, Iran, and North Korea—could fill a very large book, if every twist and turn were set beneath the microscope. Indeed, there are works focusing solely on each of the rogues—major or minor—that offer fuller (although out-of-date) treatment of the countries themselves. Many of these are cited in this volume's footnotes or bibliography. The claims for this effort are more modest.

This volume, it is hoped, will furnish the interested reader or student of international affairs an assemblage of specific case studies, while setting forth an overview of the rogue phenomenon. It does not purport to be the last word in the history, culture, or policies of each of the rogues themselves. In short, it is an overview and summary of an important aspect of US policy toward adversarial states since the Soviet Union disintegrated in 1991. Thus it covers a significant period for the United States, when it confronted no peer rival but encountered instead a handful of smallish, irascible adversaries. The same historical span saw US power diminished by the costs of overseas conflicts and even higher domestic spending. So, while its military forces remain supreme, the United States enjoys less latitude to confront its rogue adversaries. That trajectory is noted in the discussion as it relates to rogue nations.

CHAPTER 1

The Rogue Phenomenon

The risks that the leaders of a rogue state will use nuclear, chemical or biological weapons against us or our allies is the greatest security threat we face.

—Madeleine Albright

It is better to be feared than loved.

—Niccolò Machiavelli

Who is going to bell the cat?

—Aesop

A small crowd gathered in Baghdad's Firdos Square as US military forces overran Iraq's violent and chaotic capital.[1] Passersby took turns smashing a sledgehammer into Saddam Hussein's statue to no avail. The bronze likeness stood immune to the puny assaults by the Baghdadis. With its right arm raised up as if saluting the future, the hubristic statue built by Hussein to himself defied its would-be destroyers. It was left to the invading military forces to bring down this emblem of the Iraqi dictatorship.

Receiving approval from its headquarters, a tank recovery vehicle rolled up to the monument. The bright sunlight glinted off its narrow windshield. Then, US Marine crewmembers piled out of the H-88 Hercules and placed a rope around the metal casting's head. Next, the giant armored vehicle lumbered away, toppling the statue to the cheers of those ringing the now-vacant pedestal. The flags on buildings surrounding the traffic circle drooped in the breezeless heat. The cheering throng took no notice. The new political winds were enough for them. In retrospect, the event marked the rising curtain on insurgency, sectarian killings, and a bacchanalia of violence, not a final act. The onlookers' joy was brief.

The pulling down of Saddam Hussein's statue in the sun-splashed central plaza represented more than just the symbolic toppling of Iraq's ruthless strongman on April 9, 2003. It denoted the end of a rogue state. During the two preceding decades, Hussein's Iraq attacked its neighbors, sponsored international terrorism, and tried to acquire nuclear arms as well as suppressing much of its population, sometimes with deadly gas. Captured by scores of television cameras, the iconic moment recalled the fall of the Berlin Wall as the precursor to the Cold War's conclusion.[2] That recollection proved fleeting and inaccurate.

The fall of Hussein's statue ushered in neither peace nor relief from the global rogue-state menace. Saddam Hussein's ouster did remove Iraq from the rogue registry and placed it in the column of new and wobbly democratic countries. On the plus side, the American enterprise acted as a midwife to the painful but near-miraculous birth of a consensual government in the Arab Middle East, a fractious quarter of the world devoid of consent-based order at the time. America's occupation-imposed democracy did not trigger the Arab Spring nearly a decade later. But the flushing of Hussein from his spider hole in late 2003 uplifted the prevailing atmosphere. The old air currents at least did not blow against the antiregime windstorm that swept across the Middle East in 2011. On the negative side, the period from the fallen Firdos totem to Iraq's restored sovereignty turned out to be more bloody, expensive, and arduous for the United States than any had realistically imagined at the start. Once bitten, twice shy, the United States was loath to resort again to a military option for dealing with other rogue states, as this volume makes clear.

Even before the United States marched into Iraq, Washington sought repeatedly to avoid war with rogue regimes. Thus, the dramatic and costly Iraqi case has been the exception to American policy vis-à-vis nuclear-threatening states. Chief among the war's mistakes was the grievous intelligence failure that worried the world about Iraq's looming nuclear program. As later revealed, the absence of nuclear arms (or even advanced nuclear-weapons labs) cast a skeptical pall over other findings by US and foreign intelligence agencies. Since the Iraq War, governments have looked askance at intelligence-gathered information about nuclear bomb-making plants within secretive nations. This skepticism inhibits policy making out of fear that decisions premised on intelligence might turn out as wrong as the faulty predictions about Iraq.

Additionally, the intelligence debacle threw doubt on the wisdom of US policy in the wake of the protracted and expensive insurgency in Iraq.

Afterward, no responsible authority seriously advocated another invasion, regime change, and occupation to address dangerous rogue behavior. Yet the threat of force proved a powerful persuader in the case of Libya and Iran, as we shall see. If anything, the Iraq War made the United States more circumspect toward intervening into dangerously unpredictable countries. As such, Washington's anti-Iraq policy offered no replicable strategy to come to grips with a central crisis of the post–Cold War era—the reemergence of renegade states on the world scene.

The balance of this chapter examines fleetingly a few historical examples of rogue political behavior, the part of nuclear arms in heightening the dangers posed by contemporary pariah nations, and the role of the Cold War in breeding rogue regimes. This chapter also includes an investigation into the role Soviet incubation played in the rogues' propensity for exporting terrorism. How the term "rogue" came about in international parlance is also sketched. Washington's official statements defining rogue states are cited to provide an official reference for such countries.

Then the chapter takes up inter-rogue cooperation to circumvent international sanctions imposed by the United States or the United Nations. And it concludes with an overview of the part played by rogue states in the competition among great powers. The purpose of these sketches is to acquaint the reader with the background and foundation for an understanding of the specific rogue states that make up the core of the book.

A Very Brief Historical Overview: Ancient to Modern

Throughout history, minor-league protagonists defied larger powers, empires, or alliances. For millennia, these bit players flouted the major actors' writ by withholding tribute, conducting piracy, or even mounting predatory raids. Acting as free agents or affiliates of larger patrons, these errant entities raised havoc with the established order. Then, as now, wildcard political entities burst on the scene to assault the status quo before succumbing to defeat, imperial incorporation, or the vicissitudes of history. The fate of smallish, militant states, without great-power clientage, is transitory. But not all resisting mini-states were like our present-day rogue nations. Political entities that strove to remain independent of imperial suzerainty must not be lumped into the rogue category.

The classical Greek world bore witness to one of the earliest rudimentary outliers in the international order. The tiny island of Melos in the southern Aegean Sea refused to join the ancient Athenian alliance against its archenemy Sparta. The contemporary historian Thucydides wrote in his famed *History of the Peloponnesian War* how the Melians tried to stay neutral and rejected Athens's demands for tribute. The Athenian army laid siege to Melos in 416 BC for its resistance. After the Melian surrender, Athens killed all the military-age men and sold the women and children into slavery, as was the prevailing custom.[3] The Athenians reasoned that a less harsh resolution risked the repetition of other rebellions. Neither Thucydides nor current political theorists regard Melos as particular hostile to Athens or deserving of its fate. It could be seen as a brave, independent polity like post-1945 Finland struggling against Soviet hegemony to maintain its freedom under threat from an imperialistic neighbor.

Ancient Rome, in another example, imposed its law and order on the Mediterranean world, only to encounter hostilities along its northern frontiers from the wild and unruly Gauls and later Germanic Visigoths and Vandals. Anticipating rogue antics two millennia later, the Gauls allied themselves with Carthage, Rome's foremost rival across the Mediterranean Sea. In fact, the Gallic tribesmen served as auxiliaries to Hannibal, the famous Carthaginian warrior-general, whose elephant-led army crossed the Alps in its ill-fated attack on Rome. In time, these northern barbarian hordes sacked the Roman capital and accelerated the empire's decline, testifying to the anticivilization impulses from undeterrable forces. Well before its extinction, Rome faced piracy in the eastern Mediterranean and renegade behavior from the Kingdom of Pontus in what is today southern Turkey when its king massacred thousands of Roman citizens in 88 BC, setting off a series of military campaigns under Roman commanders. After initial reversals, the empire's renowned general Pompey swept away what Rome perceived as rogue threats from pirates and Pontus.[4]

Other fierce bands, such as the Vikings, pillaged, burned, and shredded burgeoning civilized life in France and the British Isles. Like their future rogue progeny, these longboat warriors demanded payments from their would-be victims. The tenth-century rogue actors compelled the irresolute Anglo-Saxon kingdoms to pay the Danegeld or be battle-axed to death. Eventually, the Viking raids ceased and the former Norse warriors assimilated into Christianizing Europe, no longer posing a threat to the continent. The rogue phenomenon resurfaced in other guises, however.

Violent forays were not confined to Northern Europe. Arab Muslim statelets along the African littoral of the Mediterranean Sea preyed on shipping and the thinly populated coasts of Spain, France, and Italy for booty and bodies almost from the beginning of the Islamic conquest of the Maghreb (meaning the West in Arabic) at the start of the eighth century. From harbors in Algiers, Tunis, Tripoli, and Morocco, the pirate vessels sailed to seize unprotected merchant ships and their cargos. After their depredations, the sea bandits retreated behind their shore guns in the ports. This strategy gave them near impunity from European counterattack.

This early clash of civilizations witnessed Islamic pirates attack predominately Christian victims. The maritime terrorism reached its peak during the seventeenth century. It was a profitable enterprise. Muslim feluccas swept down on European commercial vessels and seacoasts to kill and kidnap victims for slave labor, harems, or ransom. The greatest profits derived from slave trading of the men, women, and children, who were beaten, chained, and transported to lives of hard labor or concubinage or sold at auction.

While justified under Islamic tenets because the hostages were not Muslims, marine marauding offered a handsome livelihood to inhabitants of the parched, sun-blasted city-states along the North African coast. Many European seafaring states gave in and paid tribute to spare their merchantmen from death or incarceration in unspeakable conditions. In their reckoning, it was cheaper to pay protection money than station warships along the Maghreb coastline. Money changed hands between European governments and North African substates in a manner only the twenty-first-century North Koreans could envy in their shakedowns of the West for aid. Following the line of least resistance only abetted the nefarious practices by the Barbary pirates.

These depredations even touched the fledgling American Republic when its sailors wound up in the Barbary Coast's dank prisons or impaled on stakes surrounding the walled forts of their captors. Initially, new American governments sailed in the slipstream of the European powers, which made annual transfers of gold and currency to the Maghrebi coffers. By the 1790s, Washington forked over a prodigious 20 percent annually of the country's revenues in tribute and ransoms to the piratical North African tyrants. The lucrative payments simply whetted the appetite of the self-styled *mujahideen* (Islamic holy warriors), who lived off plunder and payoffs. Goaded into action, Presidents Thomas Jefferson and James Madison dispatched naval frigates and US Marines to attack and to cow the potentates of Tripoli, Tunis, and Algiers.[5] Lasting more than a decade, the US counterattacks won American vessels freedom of the seas from the Barbary Coast raiders. It was America's first overseas conflict after winning independence from Great Britain.

The Barbary Corsairs usually freelanced against legitimate commerce unless the ship owners' governments paid tribute. Thus, Tripoli, Algiers, Tunis, and Morocco constituted the rogue states of their era. Behind the cloak of Islam, the pirates sank merchant vessels, imprisoned crews, and collected protection money for safe passage all in the name of religion. As such, the seafaring thieves seamlessly blended beliefs and business in their piracy. This sea marauding finally ended when France and Italy conquered North Africa and established colonies in the early decades of the nineteenth century. But the piratical practice renewed itself elsewhere in different guises.

Two centuries afterward, African piracy reappeared in Somalia's coastal waters, when local bandits took to speedboats, satellite phones, and GPS devices to hunt down unarmed seagoing vessels, which they boarded, and forced their owners to pay cash ransoms for the release of ships and their crews. By 2009, the Somalia's littoral ranked as the most pirated waters in the world. The reawakened scourge of piracy confounded international shippers, whose supertankers or cruise ships fell prey to boatmen armed with AK-47s and rocket-propelled grenades. Somali pirates seized over 53 ships in 2010, while the North Atlantic Treaty Organization (NATO) flotilla stepped up ocean patrolling to stem the losses. Ship owners usually found it easier to pay the standard $2 million ransom in small-denominated US or European currency than risk the vessel or crew. According the Piracy Reporting Center of the International Maritime Bureau, 1,181 people had been taken hostage and 8 killed in attacks on 445 ships in 2010.[6] At the start of 2011, pirates held 31 ships and over 600 crewmen awaiting ransom.[7]

But rather than protorogue mini-states on the Mediterranean promoting assaults on commercial vessels, the Somali variant springs from a failed nation unable to police its own land let alone its seafront. Piracy reflects a breakdown in territorial order, not a ruler's policy in the anarchical Somalia. This Horn-of-Africa country's descent into chaos opened the door to modern-day buccaneers. Unlike the Barbary pirates, the Somali bands have not signed treaties with foreign governments in exchange for lavish tribute. They operate through clans and local warlords. When the paid-off pirates go ashore, the local Somali population greets them as popular heroes and would-be benefactors. Inland, the country has fallen into disorder and fragmentation, as Islamist groups and clan militias fight for power and influence. Outsiders seem powerless to stem the engulfing anarchy and resurgence of Islamic militias.

Even the briefest of account of rogue Mediterranean players, however, cannot be a black-and-white morality tale of outlaws against law-abiding states. For their own ends, established powers enlisted Maghreb allies against their rivals. Renegade Europeans also transferred state-of-the-art sailing ships to pirates, who had previously gone to sea in galleys powered by oars. Improved ships and seamanship enabled pirates to proliferate terrorism beyond the Straits of Gibraltar to the British Isles and Northern Europe. Their enhanced capabilities also made the pirates effective proxies for European protagonists.[8]

During the Elizabethan "cold war" between England and Spain, Protestant London loosely aligned the Barbary city-states against the Catholic Spanish. At one tenuous point, Morocco turned out to be the supplier of last resort to the embattled English garrison on Gibraltar. Nor were established states averse to falling back on Caribbean pirates during the late sixteenth and early seventeenth centuries to carry out their dirty work by sinking the trading vessels of their competitors. European kingdoms turned a blind eye to their own buccaneers so long as they pounced on their rivals' commerce.[9]

Maritime terrorism was also put to use in the New World. Pirate bands developed large militarized camps on the islands of Jamaica, Guadeloupe, and Hispaniola, which rendered them mini rogue polities. The English governor of Jamaica, in fact, commissioned "Admiral" Henry Morgan, the notorious pirate, to mount military attacks against Spanish holdings in the Caribbean Sea. Spain mostly failed in its counterassaults. This use of proxy forces spared European powers from directly assaulting their international competitors, thereby trigging large-scale confrontations. International law classifies pirates as "*hostis humani generis*"—enemies of all mankind. But seafaring powers were not against diverting the pirate scourge onto their trading adversaries.[10]

This indirect tactic of harming rivals provided a country such as England, or later the Soviet Union, a thinly veiled deniability while damaging an adversary's interests. The model proved viable and applicable in our own times. Small belligerent states still defy great powers while at times casting themselves within the protective orbit of more powerful quasi patrons. Per contra, major powers find it convenient to deploy feisty surrogates to confound their foes, as will be examined in this volume.[11] The consolidation of sovereign states during the eighteenth and nineteenth centuries hardly ended the scofflaw-state phenomenon.

Twentieth-Century Pariahs

The early twentieth century witnessed a form of renegade-state behavior by two major countries. In Russia, the October Revolution ushered the Bolsheviks into power during World War I. This revolutionary party embraced a radical domestic program and clashed head-on with the international order. Internally, Vladimir Lenin's vanguard of the communist revolution executed the Romanov monarchy, confiscated private businesses, collectivized farms, and installed a ruthless secret police to silence dissent against his vision of utopia. Josef Stalin, Lenin's diabolical successor, institutionalized the Soviet Union's reign of terror. Externally, the Soviet Union refuted the global economic system, which they regarded as dominated by imperial states that exploited the world's human and material resources to gain vast financial profits for the imperial West. Little wonder that Bolshevism sent tsunami waves of fear and loathing through the world's financial capitals. Other powers resolved to isolate the radical Bolshevik regime. Not until fears of Japanese military aggression in Asia and the desire to alleviate the economic Depression through expanded trade with Russia did President Franklin D. Roosevelt restore US diplomatic relation with Moscow in 1933. The United States and Soviet Russia cooperated against Nazi Germany during World War II, but later Iran <u>was a den of</u> political intrigue; their relations went into the deep freeze.

Post–World War I Germany slipped into the political outcast category as well. Even though Germany acceded to the terms of the Versailles Treaty and embraced democracy after the abdication of Kaiser Wilhelm II, the unsteady Weimar Republic never won acceptance in European councils. Britain and France concluded that Germany's prewar policies were the main culprit for the start of the Great War. Throughout much of the 1920s, Weimar governments struggled against massive inflation, workers' strikes, left- and right-wing extremists, and political turmoil. By 1933, the uncertainty gave birth to the twentieth century's ultimate rogue-like leader—Adolf Hitler. Coming to power largely through a democratic process, Chancellor Hitler soon revolutionized German society from a quintessential European civilization to a monstrous, militaristic machine bent on conquest, mass murder, nuclear arms, and elimination of Europe's Jewry in the Holocaust.

International ostracism of Bolshevik Russia and Weimar Germany hastened their collaboration before World War II. Excluded from League of Nations membership, the two resentful countries covertly collaborated in military affairs. The terms of the Versailles Treaty demanded that Germany scale back its military forces and dismantle its arms industry. But the Germans sharpened their military technological edge by assisting Moscow in building military factories, which ultimately benefited the Russians with modern tanks in World War II. The colluding of two of the most incompatible societies is hard to imagine, as Soviet Russia professed an abiding hatred for Junker-dominated Germany and its anticommunist persecution. For their part, German aristocrats looked askance at the subversion of the natural hierarchical order, redistributive economics, and inefficiency of collectivized agriculture. The two ostracized pariahs, nonetheless, collaborated because they lacked alternatives. Germany and the Soviet Union even briefly colluded in carving up Poland in the early days of World War II before Hitler turned on his erstwhile friend by sending his armies against the Union of Soviet Socialist Republics (USSR) two years later.

This marriage of convenience saw many similar manifestations in the post–Cold War era, when rogue regimes traded nuclear technologies and missiles among themselves despite their divergent internal political cultures. Although rogue cooperation is nothing new under the historical sun, the stakes are considerably higher when nuclear-related components are being exchanged among problem states. The atomic bomb, therefore, transformed the dynamics of established states versus mavericks. Complacency was no longer a realistic option by great powers in the face of nuclear proliferation among adversarial regimes.

Nuclear Arms and Nonrogue States

From the dawn of the nuclear era during the late 1940s, the principal strategic-weapons states strove to preserve their monopoly of these doomsday arms. The Western nuclear powers—the United States, France, and Britain—resolved to halt the proliferation of atomic weapons beyond China and Russia, which also gained them soon after World War II. America took the lead in convincing allied countries to abandon their nuclear-arms programs. Four aspirant-nuclear nations—Taiwan, South Korea, South Africa, and Israel—embarked on building nuclear arsenals. Each feared the conventional military balance tilting against their viability, especially as the United States appeared geopolitically diminished after its Vietnam War reversal in the mid-1970s. Fed by existential fears for their survival, these states set about nuclear arming.

Taiwan and South Korea, for example, owed their origins to bitter Cold War divisions, and each feared their respective neighbors as well as the ascendancy of communist powers after World War II. Retreating Chinese Nationalists made the Taiwanese island their refuge after defeat by the Chinese Communist Party on the mainland in 1949. Taiwan lived in a shadow of fear cast from the nearby People's Republic of China. South Korea faced an unpredictable and aggressive communist North Korea across a two-mile demilitarized zone (DMZ) after it and the American-led United Nations (UN) forces turned back the 1950 invasion from the north. The Republic of Korea gradually evolved into a democratic nation while its implacable adversary across the DMZ hardened into a doctrinaire Stalinist state. Both Taiwan and South Korea felt gnawing pangs of American abandonment as the United States slipped into a semi-isolationist posture after the Vietnam War. To compensate for their growing vulnerability, they looked to nuclear arms for security.

For Israel, surrounded by enemy states sworn to destroy the Jewish homeland, the nuclear option looked like a necessity for self-preservation. Israel has never publicly acknowledged a nuclear arsenal, but it has become an "open secret" that the tiny country had built an inventory of the dreaded weapons. "By 1970, it became publicly known that the U.S. government considered Israel to be in possession of an operational nuclear weapons capability," according to one leading study.[12] Much later, in the early twenty-first century, Israel resolved that it needed a strong nuclear deterrent against its chief foe—Iran. Along with broadcasting apocalyptic speeches against Israel, the Tehran regime relentlessly pursued atomic warheads and long-distance missiles all the while denying its own nuclear weapons ambitions. Tehran argued that its nuclear reactors were intended for electrical power generation alone.[13] Almost no one outside Iran believed Tehran's peaceful nuclear protestations. Iranian nuclear activities, as will be noted in chapter 3, contributed to the instability and uncertainty in the Middle East.

Of the four aspiring nuclear nations during the 1970s, South Africa constitutes a unique case. Far removed from the global crisis spots in the Middle East or Asia, the Republic of South Africa still captured the world's censorious scrutiny. Pretoria's apartheid policies of white minority domination over the African majority drew international condemnation during the 1970s and 1980s. Regardless of its nominal standing in the Free World against the communist bloc, South Africa offended the West's sense of racial equality and justice. The United States and Europe passed stiff economic sanctions against the apartheid regime. To great effect, they also ostracized South African sports teams and entertainers. Excluded from global participation and beset by guerrilla attacks, the South African government sought security in nuclear arms. As isolated states often do, Pretoria and Tel Aviv reportedly cooperated on conventional military activities and secretly on nuclear capabilities.[14]

History took a decidedly better turn when three of the four nuclear-seeking countries ditched their A-bomb goal. Taiwan and South Korea bowed to American insistence and took shelter under the US nuclear umbrella rather than pursue their own local deterrent. South Africa voluntarily dropped its nuclear dreams in 1993, when the postapartheid government realized that its desire for unconventional arms hindered its pursuit of normal international relations.[15] Only Israel retained and possibly expanded its nuclear armament. Indeed, it may have tested a nuclear device in the South Indian Ocean in 1979.[16]

None of these four nuclear-seeking nations can be classified as rogue regimes. None promoted international terrorism. Each is a democracy. Each wanted to exist peacefully within the world community, although South Africa's racial classifications and imposed segregation made it unacceptable to Western norms. Rather than blustering governments that bellicosely threatened regional order, Seoul, Taipei, Pretoria, and Jerusalem hungered for region-wide peace and stability and for international legitimacy of their respective countries. Their inclusion within this historical sketch is solely to emphasize the linkage between outlier states and weapons of mass destruction. Forsaking nuclear arming (except for Israel), in fact, worked in their favor with world opinion. Each also evolved vibrant democratic governments and globally competitive economies.

Not every country that acquired a nuclear-arms capability over the last half century fell into the rogue category. Both India and Pakistan tested nuclear weapons as late as 1998, but they were not considered rogue nations. The pursuit of the ultimate weapon of mass destruction is not the sole determinate of roguery. Both of these Asian subcontinent states boasted democratic practices, cooperated internationally, and stayed diplomatically connected to the outside world. Pakistan, however, harbored terrorists groups that staged bloody forays inside India, within disputed Kashmir, and across its border against the US presence in Afghanistan after the American-led NATO invasion. Islamabad's working relationship with Washington spared it from the opprobrium heaped on North Korea and Iran. The nuclear arming by opaque, terrorist-exporting dictatorships is a primary characteristic among other nefarious practices for "rogue statedom," as we shall see.

The Cold War Roots of the Current Rogue Regimes

The genesis of contemporary rogue nations stems from Cold War rivalry after World War II. The United States and the Soviet Union competed to hold sway over much of the earth in twin blocs for over four decades. The frosty superpower relations threw a chill over most spheres of international relations. It placed all human endeavors—whether the arts, armaments, diplomacy, human rights, Olympic sports, space exploration, and even chess tournaments—within the framework of the East-West competition.

Each superpower formed and nurtured alliances, blocs, and clients to confront, subvert, or weaken the other superpower and its allies. America, for example, took the lead in organizing NATO so as to check further Red Army advances in Central Europe. It unveiled the Marshall Plan to rebuild west European economies that had been ravaged in the course of World War II. Recovering economic health presented a bulwark against communist penetration. Washington bolstered anticommunist dictators because they held the line against Moscow's encroachments, even though they repressed their own citizens.

The USSR, for its part, countered US defenses with the establishment of the Warsaw Pact to harness its Eastern European satellites into a military alliance against the West. Moscow also aided proxy conflicts against Western interests. It financed, guided, trained, and equipped political movements or liberation fronts in Asia, Africa, and Latin America that employed terrorism and guerrilla warfare against colonial rule or Western-leaning governments. These national liberation movements expanded Soviet leverage and simultaneously eradicated the West's investments and commerce among developing countries in the non-Western world.

The Soviets also sustained unsavory revolutionary regimes. When the USSR disappeared into the scrap heap, it flung these dictatorships on the world stage. In the course of the Cold War, the Soviet outposts received military equipment, economic assistance, and some diplomatic protection in return for the problems they caused the United States and its friends. The USSR's client states did engage in their own aggressive policies. Syria and Egypt went to war with Israel in 1967 and 1973, although Moscow was lukewarm to the idea. Moscow did understand that its client states' local conflicts harmed American interests or allies on the global chessboard. But the Kremlin worried that a client's adventurism might endanger its long-term goals or trigger a direct confrontation with the United States.[17] So it did exercise some restraint on its client allies, which ended in 1991.

Proxy states and indigenous national liberation fronts in the non-Western world furthered the Kremlin's global priorities without triggering a straight-on superpower Armageddon with the United States. A direct clash had the potential to escalate into a nuclear standoff as in the Cuban missile crisis in 1962. A thermonuclear exchange could obliterate both superpowers. Thus, Moscow resorted to backing insurgencies, subversion, and ideological soul mates to advance indirectly the Soviet agenda. Clandestine and low cost, these covert means often proved successful in subverting Washington's partners.

For its part, the United States at times placed bets on ruthless figures such as Mobuto in the Congo, Somoza in Nicaragua, or the Duvaliers in Haiti to fend off the spread of communism. Often the strongmen played the anticommunist card to garner American material and diplomatic support. Serving as bulwarks against communism, autocrats escaped harsh Washington censure for human rights abuses of political opponents in the name of anticommunism.[18] Washington also militarily intervened in the Caribbean nations of Grenada and the Dominican Republic to oust left-wing governments as a means to block the formation of "another Cuba" in the Western Hemisphere. After the Cold War, US interventions were premised on humanitarian and nation-building rationales rather than anti-communist campaigns.[19]

In some respects, the Kremlin seemed more adroit at marshaling others in its cause than the United States. Indeed, Washington's championing of colonial rulers, retrograde dictators, and other representatives of the status quo seemed on the wrong side of history. Moscow leveraged popular discontent against grinding poverty, repressive authority, or colonial rule to its own ends by promoting Marxist governments friendly to the Soviet Union. Its Eastern bloc satellite regimes served as willing accomplices. The East Germans, Bulgarians, and Czechs evolved a division of labor whereby they specialized in training, financing, or arming revolutionary bands. The USSR was ingeniously clever in getting protégés to carry out mischief against the West for its strategic interests.

Foremost among Moscow's protégés stood Cuba as the most committed and energetic in its aiding insurgencies in Latin America and Africa. Fidel Castro, the island's communist caudillo, infiltrated his co-revolutionist Ernesto "Che" Guevara first into a futile guerrilla war in the Congo and then into a fatal insurgency in Bolivia. In the course of these exploits, Guevara became *the* revolutionary icon of the 1960s. Today his bearded image still graces T-shirts worn by youths in Western countries. In actions that fanned revolutionary flames, Havana supplied instructors and arms to insurrections in Guatemala, El Salvador, Nicaragua, and Ethiopia during the 1970s and 1980s. Not content with just supporting roles, Cuba acted as Soviet Russia's Foreign Legion in Africa. Havana dispatched some fifteen thousand ground troops to Angola to reinforce the Popular Movement for the Liberation of Angola's (MPLA's) grab for power against other guerrilla movements backed by the United States and South Africa.[20] Furthermore, Cuba aided the Sandinistas in their insurgency to consolidate control in Nicaragua during the 1980s, which represented another Kremlin priority.

Measured by the metric of countries changing hands, the USSR wound up the net gainer of allies, as the Kremlin pushed a host of countries into its column. From the fall of Vietnam until Ronald Reagan's presidency, ten countries moved into the Soviet orbit. By backing proxy forces or liberation movements, the Kremlin engineered pro-Soviet regimes in Afghanistan, Angola, Mozambique, Guinea-Bissau, Cambodia, Laos, South Yemen, Grenada, Nicaragua, and Ethiopia. Its client states, in turn, furthered their patron's strategy by espousing hard-core socialism and by proclaiming themselves part of the worldwide communist movement.

In Asia, the pro-Soviet country of North Korea kept its southern neighbor, the Republic of Korea (ROK), in a near-constant state of tension. The bellicose propaganda blasts and deadly provocations of the Democratic People's Republic of Korea (DPRK) against the ROK served Moscow's strategy. North Korean antics compelled the United States to station thousands of troops in the south to preserve the peace and protect its ally from a reoccurrence of another North Korean invasion. During the American involvement in the Vietnam War, Pyongyang succeeded in tying down military units needed in the Southeast Asian conflict. After the United States withdrew its military forces from South Vietnam in 1973, the Chinese- and Soviet-backed North Vietnamese armies charged into the country, putting it under ruthless communist domination.

Impressive as were the number of the Kremlin's country acquisitions, the regimes themselves were much less impressive. Communist outposts such as Cuba in the Western Hemisphere or North Korea in the Western Pacific were the Kremlin's natural allies and proxies. Their conversion to revolutionary Marxism and their inherent antagonism to neighboring countries made them willing proxies. Their party-directed economies, nevertheless, lagged in consumer production and wealth creation, making them almost virtual dependencies on Moscow's handouts. Other nations that underwent anticolonial struggles and embraced Marxist economic policies, such as Angola, Mozambique, and Guinea-Bissau, sank further into poverty and underdevelopment.

A second tier of Soviet clients lacked a direct ideological affinity to the Marxist homeland as professed by Cuba and North Korea. But they spouted their own brand of socialism that ended up as little more than veneer laminated over authoritarianism. Akin to their patron, Iraq, Syria, and Libya shared Kremlin attributes—dictatorial rule and antipathy for the United States in particular and the West in general. These regimes as well as others in the Middle East were steeped in a deep hatred of Israel, which Moscow also exploited to its own ends by arming, training, and technically servicing Arab armies. Despite being quasi-Soviet protégés, Iraq, Syria, and Libya pursued their own foreign agenda, without slavish subordination to the Kremlin. But patron and clients shared mutual interests and common enemies, which fostered cooperation from time to time. Sometimes their convergence was merely skin deep and displayed only in propagandistic outbursts against Washington or through votes in the United Nations. Other times, Moscow had to restrain its clients as when Castro pressed the USSR for a more aggressive nuclear posture against the United States during the Cuban missile crises.[21] Their methods more often overlapped. Both patron and client promoted terrorism against adversaries.[22]

Every generalized sketch has at least one exception. This summary, therefore, must note Iran's aberration in not being in league with the Soviet

Union during the Cold War. It was never Moscow's client. Iran, a non-Arab Middle Eastern country, followed a distinct route toward its charter membership in what President George W. Bush called the "axis of evil." Iran, and its predecessor state Persia, had long displayed wariness, if not downright animosity, toward Russia. Whether under the shahs or the revolutionary Shiite ayatollahs, Tehran feared Moscow's long-held ambitions for warm-water ports in the Persian Gulf and claims on Iranian territory. The Soviet invasion of Afghanistan reinforced the Islamic Republic of Iran's apprehensions about the Kremlin's designs. Moreover, the Iranian clerics detested the Soviet Union's atheistic Marxist creed. Both governments shared an abiding hatred for the United States, but they diverged on much else, as will be summarized later in this work. The point to be emphasized here is that not all problematic states came from the same mold. Each rogue regime had overriding internal reasons to make the United States a convenient bête noire so as to consolidate its power.

The USSR, for its part, wooed anti-American states' movements and dictators. In some sense, its modus operandi amounted to little more than the cunning exemplified by the putative-Arabic aphorism "the enemy of my enemy is my friend." In the Soviet rendering, this ran "my enemy's enemy can be my proxy" against the United States. Future rogue states, such as Libya, Iraq, and Syria, received massive armaments during the Cold War. These ruthless dictatorships could be counted on to cause trouble for the United States and its allies, especially Israel, in the Middle East. Moscow, however, sometimes tried to restrain the hostile actions of its Middle Eastern proxies lest they recklessly drag the Soviet Union into direct military confrontation with Washington. Needling and distracting the Americans suited the would-be puppeteers in Red Square, but they wished to avoid open conflict with their American adversaries. For its part, Washington likewise sought to maneuver around steel-on-steel clashes with the Soviets. More clandestine or indirect measures served both superpowers.

The Soviet proxy states actively sponsored or passively enabled terrorism directed at American officials, military personnel, and noncombatants. Here again, not every terrorist plot originated from inside the Kremlin. Nor were Americans the only victims of terrorism. People in non-Western lands died at the hands of terrorists, just as those from Europe or America met death by terrorists' bullets or bombs. One of the most spectacular terror strikes blew Pan Am Flight 103 out of the air over Lockerbie in southern Scotland in 1988, killing a total of 259 people on the plane and 11 on the ground. Ninety were non-Americans. Earlier in September 1989, Libya was implicated in a second downed commercial jet, when an onboard explosion ripped apart France's UTA airliner, killing 177 passengers and crew members mostly from Africa and Europe.

Rogues and Soviet Terrorism

Acts of terrorism formed part of communism's DNA. Vladimir Lenin, the Bolshevik leader, used terrorism to advance the communist revolution in Russia. Lenin's fellow revolutionary Leon Trotsky boldly subscribed to terrorist violence in his book, *Terrorism and Communism*, as means to further the revolutionary process of a state. Together, the Bolshevik chieftains facilitated the initiation of state-sponsored terrorism in the early twentieth century. From Red Square offices, they exported terrorism, along with intelligence and covert operations, through like-minded parties to spread the communist revolution worldwide. "This rage of foreign operations was aimed at weakening 'bourgeois' states and bringing other communist parties to power," wrote one authority on terrorism.[23] The concept, techniques, and objectives of terrorism were rooted in communism's birth, maturation, and propagation. It seemed natural that its protégés would pick up the same political murder traits. Terrorism, it must be emphasized, sprang not just from Soviet example. Killing stealthily outside of war for political reasons has been woven into the historical narrative for eons.[24] During the Cold War, state-sponsored terrorist attacks grew prevalent as an asymmetrical means to assault superiorly armed opponents, such as the United States and Western European states. Libya, Syria, Iraq, North Korea, and Iran engaged directly in terrorist attacks or clandestinely sponsored groups such as Hezbollah, Palestinian Liberation Organization, Irish Republican Army, or the master terrorist Abu Nidal (born Sabri Khalil al-Banna).

Terrorism, therefore, defined one major characteristic of rogue nations. State terrorism as a tool of foreign policy burgeoned during the 1960s and 1970s. In 1979, the US Congress legislated the listing of terrorist states in the Export Administration Act under the Department of State.[25] From that date until the present, the US Department of State released annually a report of terrorist governments; later it also listed nonstate movements that it certified as terrorist networks. The original listing was soon expanded to eight countries as designated state sponsors of international acts of terrorism: Cuba, Iran, Iraq, Libya, North Korea, Sudan, Syria, and South Yemen. These designations held up for many years. The states on the listing also became nearly synonymous with rogue states for a while.

In time, the State Department removed states from the list for various reasons. When North Yemen (or the Yemen Arab Republic), for example, unified with the Marxist-dominated South Yemen (People's Democratic

Republic of Yemen) to create the Republic of Yemen in 1990, Washington delisted South Yemen from the terrorism blacklist. Iraq was removed after the US invasion and occupation in 2003. Libya came off the listing because it voluntary abandoned weapons of mass destruction and opened its territory to international inspections. The George W. Bush administration removed North Korea as part of its negotiations with Pyongyang, which will be detailed in chapter 4. So today, just for four states remain branded as "State Sponsors of Terrorism" by the department; they are Cuba, Iran, Sudan, and Syria.[26] But Cuba's role as a regional troublemaker is much diminished in the wake of the Soviet Union's breakup. Sudan's flagrant human rights violations inside its own territory alone account for its continued classification. Syria, in contrast, has been a launching point for cross-border terrorist attacks into post–Saddam Hussein Iraq as well as serving as a promoter of terrorism and conduit of arms to the Iranian-backed Hezbollah movement in Lebanon, which is to be subsequently analyzed. Of the quartet, Iran is currently far and away the greatest perpetuator of terrorism beyond its borders, as will be taken up later. Terrorism, therefore, is a common thread running through the tapestry of rogue nations, but other threads make up the fabric, too.

Along with the State Department's *de jure* terrorist-state listing, rogues share other manifestations. Dictatorial rule characterizes their form of government. They are flagrant human rights abusers. Their propensity for terrorism, megadeath arms, and warlike threats, if anything, intensified after the Soviet Union's disintegration. The arch rogue nations—Iraq, Iran, Syria, Libya, and North Korea—pursued nuclear weapons to heighten their global status and to intimidate their neighbors. North Korea, for example, routinely hurled threatening hyperbole at the Republic of Korea and the United States. Iran stepped up its sponsorship of terrorism. It utilized its own consulates and its proxy movements to mount terrorist bombings. Iraq attacked Iran, setting off an eight-year war marked by tens of thousands of deaths. It next rattled sabers at Kuwait before invading, occupying, and looting the small Persian Gulf kingdom, even before the Soviet Union completely fell apart. After Iraq's conquest, President George H. W. Bush labeled Saddam Hussein's government a "renegade regime" in an early identification of the emerging rogue phenomenon.[27]

The Soviet Progeny

It is fashionable to conclude that the Soviet Union's dissolution occasioned little more than a series of Velvet Revolutions hopscotching across east-central Europe that restored democracy to the satellite countries formerly held in Moscow's thrall. The mostly peaceful disintegration of the vast landed Soviet empire came with few costs, except for some bloodshed in Lithuania, Romania, and the Central Asian successor republics. Communism's considerable human "expenses" in the millions of deaths from prison camps, famines, and firing squads were recorded well before the fall of the Berlin Wall in 1989 and the Soviet Union's disintegration in 1991.

The intense Cold War competition functioned as the crucible for present-day rogue states that burst forth on the international scene after the Berlin Wall tumbled. The Kremlin managed sometimes to enlist the services of, if not truly control, its non–Eastern European client-states by bestowing Marxist ideological guidance, weapons, and even a measure of protection from the United States. When the Soviet empire crashed, its one-time clients slipped their leash, as will be narrated further on. The one exception to this formulation lies with Iran, which never fell into a patron-client relationship with Moscow. Its fierce anti-Americanism was born of its own history and revolution, as is made clear in a subsequent chapter.

Not all former Soviet proxies embarked on international recklessness. Cuba, hard hit by the stoppage of Moscow's largess, declined into decrepitude. Cuba as well as North Korea clung to the dictatorial communist political and economic model, while other former satellites decided to cast aside their Soviet political trappings and state-directed economic planning. But Cuba eschewed the adversarial policies of its communist brother on the Korean Peninsula. Nor did it follow the east-central European states, which transformed themselves from the Soviet bloc into functioning democracies that looked westward for economic direction. The successor republics in Central Asia, instead, developed illiberal democracies with presidents for life. Yet they, too, stayed off the rogue state path. Once the formidable Iron Curtain fell, Marxist-orientated governments also initially lost power in Cambodia, Ethiopia, Nicaragua, and Mongolia. Vietnam kept its communist rulers in power but adopted the China-type economic liberalization for expanded trade and development. But the rogue states of the post-Soviet period marched in retrograde step.

The Cold War's passing snapped Moscow's clientage system. Arising phoenix-like from the Soviet imperium's ashes was not another formidable titan bestriding the globe but rather a passel of medium- to light-weight aggressive states. In time, these nations' policies and rhetoric earned them the designation of rogue regimes. Their appearance marked the reoccurrence of maverick polities in world history. Instead of tranquility after the East-West competition, America faced fiercely defiant, self-consciously isolated, and truculent states that seemed to have emerged from nowhere and in no time. Dubbed rogue states for their belligerence and waywardness, they stirred fear and loathing among their neighbors.

Since the Soviet Union's denouement passed almost anticlimactically, Washington was initially caught off guard by the recurrence of international dangers, albeit from economically backward, rogue nations. None could come near to defeating the United States in conventional warfare; but they could destabilize their respective geographical bailiwicks and disrupt the globalizing flow of commerce, people, and information that promised to lift nations out of poverty and into an era of peace. Their nuclear-arming, bellicose rhetoric and warlike posture fell at America's doorstep as the sole remaining superpower, now cast in the reluctant role as global sheriff hustling up posses to counter regional threats.[28] Unlike past troublesome states, contemporary rogue players sought nuclear arms—a horrifying prospect for their region and the world. The nuclear threat set them apart from their historical predecessors, with which they shared many features.

Rather than joining international society, the rogues menaced it by exporting terrorism, seeking nuclear weapons, and disrupting the peace in their respective regions. In the eyes of some observers, these pariah regimes simply leapt into the role of irrational actors with almost nihilistic impulses.[29] But there was nothing irrational about the calculations of North Korea, Iran, or, even in the extreme, Hussein Iraq. Their leaders might march to a worn-out drum, but they calibrated their policies on the basis of self-interest. Mistakes they made, but by their own lights the objectives were sound and the policies within rational dimensions.

What outsiders interpreted as irresponsible brinkmanship by rogue regimes was, in fact, rational and self-serving policy. Their saber-rattling pronouncements might strike foreign ministries as unorthodox, but their ends were sensible enough. Externally, rogue regimes competed for influence and interests as did their more conventional neighbors, albeit without saber rattling, risky moves, and outright aggression. Internally, rogue chiefs buttressed their rule by politically rallying their populations and silencing their opposition. By conjuring up foreign demons, the oldest trick of demagogues, a rogue dictatorship justified its legitimacy and its all-encompassing powers among its own citizenry. Far too often, democratic states failed to grasp the domestic angle of the rogue states' international actions. Troublemaking rulers thrived on promoting the protection of their populaces from threats abroad. Their propaganda organs portrayed them as stalwart defenders of the homeland against American imperialism or the "Great Satan," as Iranian leaders characterized the United States for years. Rogue despots wanted their downtrodden subjects to redirect their grievances outward to international bogeymen such as the United States, not toward internal failures and declining economies.

Labeling and Defining Rogues

As the rise of aberrant and aggrieved states became more pronounced in the aftermath of the Soviet Union's dissolution, American policy makers struggled to come to grips with a world profoundly different from the Cold War era. President Bill Clinton's first administration searched for terms to call renegade nations and for policies to deal with the new disorderly post-Soviet conditions and the rising rogue militancy. In a notable speech in September 1993, Anthony Lake, the national security adviser, set out a fresh policy direction on the "enlargement" of democratic states for the still-new Clinton administration. He also grappled with the emerging phenomenon of rogue powers when he termed North Korea and other nations like it as "backlash" states that "sponsor terrorism and traffic in weapons of mass destruction and ballistic missile technology." These regimes, he declared, isolated themselves from the international community. Should they persist in aggressive behavior, then "we clearly must be prepared to strike back decisively and unilaterally."[30] These were bold, even prescient, words in light of US actions against Afghanistan and Iraq after the September 11 terrorist attack on American soil.

President Clinton first officially coined the term "rogue states" at the presidential level when he spoke in Brussels in early 1994. He declared that missiles from "rogue states such as Iran and Libya" posed a "clear and present danger" to Europe.[31] The term "rogue" recalled early usage from the phrase "rogues and vagabonds" as applied in English statutes to less than desirable persons in society. Later, it pointed to the unpredictable and life-threatening behavior displayed by rampaging elephants, which normally had to be killed to preserve life and property in African or Indian villages. Once presidentially uttered, the designation etched itself into diplomatic parlance as well as colloquial conversation. Madeleine Albright, as Clinton's secretary of state, years later tried unsuccessfully to banish it with the awkward and politically correct "states of concern" terminology.[32] Her neologism never took hold, except as coinage for ridicule.

Later, Tony Lake revisited the topic of rogue players and called attention to their alignments in a magazine article. The national security adviser wrote that "backlash states...do not function effectively in alliances." But he correctly noted, nevertheless, the "ties between them are growing" and pointed to "limited cooperation between Baghdad and Tehran."[33] Since the former Clinton official's appraisal, the inter-rogue exchanges multiplied in the intervening years. Even the ultra-isolationist North Korea forged trade ties with Iran, Iraq, Syria, Libya, and others for access to prohibited technologies and for commercial reasons. Trade was vital even among nations that strove for self-contained growth.

The George W. Bush administration issued a succinct summary of the attributes of rogues in its National Security Strategy for 2002. Noting the emergence of "a small number of rogue states" during the 1990s, the official document listed the characteristics. These included brutality toward their own people; contempt for international law; determination to acquire weapons of mass destruction (WMD), plus advanced military technology; sponsorship of terrorism; rejection of human rights values; and hatred for the United States "and everything it stands for."[34] While the document lent official imprimatur to rogue terminology, it is important to comment that like Shakespeare's rose "by any other name," these international malefactors are recognized by their traits as much as by name.

Rogue Interaction

Rogue state cooperation, in part, resulted from a mutual hostility to the United States and the Western world. Despite the differing regimes and wide culture gulfs separating the renegade powers, they shared an antipathy for Washington. Moreover, the outcasts really had no other choice than to interact politically and economically. Sanctions often kept them from legitimate trade with the rest of the world, along with prohibiting the exchange of weapons technology and military hardware. There is no honor among thieves, perhaps, but the international renegades fraternized, swapped missile and nuclear know-how, and traded legitimate goods in contravention of international sanctions. Even implacable foes, such as Iran and Iraq, collaborated in spite of their eight-year bloody war during the 1980s. Iran abetted Iraq's oil smuggling to circumvent the UN-imposed sanctions. Iranian smugglers reaped lucrative profits from the illicit trade. On the surface, Saddam Hussein's Iraq and Slobodan Milošević's Serbia held little in common other than resistance to American censure. Yet Hussein dispatched Iraqi military officers to assist the buttressing of Serbian defenses against NATO bombing during the Kosovo crisis in 1999. A few newspapers printed accounts of an even stranger collaboration between North Korea and Serbia. Belgrade reportedly allowed North Korean officials entry so as to observe the NATO bombardment for advanced preparation of their own defenses should the United States ever attack Pyongyang.

For its part, North Korea served as missile-export central. Devoid of other saleable commodities, it capitalized on its early lead among rogue nations in missile development. Soviet patronage during the Cold War facilitated the transfer of rocketry to the DPRK. After the Soviet Union's breakup, reports surfaced of unemployed Russian scientists and engineers working for North Korean missile factories.[35] Moscow's role in germinating Pyongyang's nuclear capacity will be sketched in chapter 4. It is sufficient to note here that Soviet Russia's assistance was pivotal to the North Korean nuclear inception. Years later, Moscow grew apprehensive of the DPRK's nuclear ambition and acted somewhat to restrain it.

North Korea, Iraq, Iran, and other adversarial nations also traded with major powers. They sought armaments, weapons and missile technology, oil-extracting know-how, and even commercial loans to finance development projects. Companies in Russia, China, and European countries, like France or Germany, looked to sell sophisticated components and equipment to customers flush with cash. Some of the exported items were considered dual-use, either for legitimate civilian application or secret military projects. The dual-use capability made it difficult for governments to police the sales, and they called for tighter export controls on these items. The arms trafficking naturally aroused angst in Washington and allied capitals. The inflow of missiles, tanks, warplanes, and, especially, WMD components to unpredictable and aggressive nations changed the military balance regionally and sometimes internationally.[36] Chinese and Russian intentions, however, were not confined benignly to increasing corporate profit margins; they encompassed designs to expand their influence and disconcert their rival—the Untied States.

Also, China reportedly was instrumental in developing North Korean rocketry, which bore striking similarities to the Chinese missiles that, in turn, were based off earlier Soviet models, when the two communist giants collaborated. These technical origins belie the DPRK's claims of its own missile innovation. North Korea's Taepo Dong-1 missile owed its creation to Chinese rockets. Modified and enhanced by North Korea, it arched over Japan on August 31, 1998. It employed similar design features to the Chinese CSS-3 booster-stage rocket. Liquid hydrogen-nitrogen mixed fuel propelled North Korean and Chinese missiles alike. When Pyongyang lost its longtime Kremlin patron after the Soviet Union's fragmentation, the North Koreans leaned more heavily on Beijing. And the People's Republic of China (PRC) hastened to use the North Koreans as an indirect means to get back at the United States for its support of Taiwan, the island state claimed by Beijing as a mainland province.

The PRC's strategy illustrates, again, the phenomenon of a major power using a rogue to further its own ends. The practice saw earlier application by the Soviet Union as noted in the preceding paragraphs. On the heels of the erroneous US bombing of the Chinese embassy in Belgrade during the Kosovo conflict in 1999, China reportedly stepped up transfers of high-technology components from its state-controlled enterprises to North Korea.[37] The North Koreans insisted that missile breakthroughs were of their own provenance. Their advancing technological capabilities nonetheless served their purpose by turning Pyongyang into an even greater thorn in the side of America and South Korea. The DPRK's missile components and technology sales garnered hard currency and goods. A report from the Center of Nonproliferation Studies at the Monterey Institute of International Studies estimated that the DPRK possessed some 70 missiles and 36 launchers by the end of the 1990s.[38] Developed from Soviet and Chinese rockets, the North Korean variants found buyers in Iran, Iraq, Libya, Pakistan, and Syria.

Rogues in the New Great Power Competition

The Cold War's passing brought an end to the Soviet-American global confrontation, but it did not halt great power rivalry. Such competition preceded the East-West divisions and witnessed small states furnishing the chessboard and pieces while the game was controlled from London, Paris, Berlin, and other seats of power. The post-Soviet era is shaping up to be little different. China and Russia, as emerging and reemerging powers respectively, advance their interests, which at times collide with American goals. They are joined by several rising regional powers to include India, Brazil, and Turkey. Even Western Europe, which shares so many American values, took occasional exception to US initiatives toward rogue nations. Geoeconomic and geopolitical aims, rather than communist ideology, infuse the post–Cold War competition. Anti-Americanism or anti-Western feelings among some ascendant protagonists have never reached the coherence or predictability of the communist ideological onslaught. But the new jockeying for economic and diplomatic interests sees Beijing, Moscow, Ankara, and even Washington resorting to surrogate actors to promote their agendas vis-à-vis other major players. The People's Republic of China, as noted earlier, can see the utility of running diplomatic interference for North Korea, as a reminder to Washington of its concerns over America's backing of the independence-minded Taiwan. Such a policy does not stand in the way of China's encouraging economic reform in the DPRK.

The Russian Federation aided and abetted Iran's nuclear ambitions as means to express its disapproval of Washington's missile defense plans in Poland and the Czech Republic. Moscow's anger had steadily risen during the late 1990s with the West's championing of the Bosnia and Kosovo independence struggles against Serbia—a Russian ally. Independent Russian scientists also further Iran's nuclear arms capacity.[39] Thus, the post–Cold War rogue states, no longer subject to former Soviet Union's restraints, still furthered Russian and, to a lesser degree, Chinese designs. Even Iran, a regional power, used Syria as a proxy for its goals. Students of international relations sometimes missed the connections, believing that rogues and big states operated divergently. Often they do, but sometimes their interests and actions coincide.[40]

Even with their penchant for insularity, rogue dictators at one time or another took shelter under the eaves of a major power. They sought contacts for commercial and security reasons. China and Russia hold permanent seats in the Security Council, granting them veto power to block stiff US-proposed sanctions on adversarial countries. Thus, Washington made direct appeals to Beijing to rein in the North Koreans or to Moscow to cease its nuclear collaboration with Iran. France, though a close US partner, differed with America, particularly in the run-up to the Iraq War. America's diplomatic route therefore met many failures as Washington's influence was circumscribed by the "Gulliverization" of US power by its main competitors along with rotating members on the Security Council. Outside the United Nations, independent-minded government also did not toe the American line because their interests diverged from Washington's view of how to handle rogue powers. American options, therefore, were sometimes limited by other governments' priorities.

Despite the tendency to lump rogue countries together as a group, US administrations tended to treat each state differently, as this book relates. This formula recognized that rogue regimes posed similar threats while possessing different internal characteristics. Cuba and North Korea held fast to the relic of communist political and economic structures. Iran's theocracy increasingly relied on its militant security forces. Iraq was dominated by the dictatorial Saddam Hussein, for whom the Baathist party was merely a political prop for his one-man rule. To recall Tolstoy's observations about unhappy families being different (from the similarity of happy ones), each rogue was a problem state in its own peculiar way. History, culture, geography, political circumstances, and differing agendas contributed to making each rogue unique even if they shared common baleful policies. Thus, each presented a particular challenge to the United States, its allies, and the world at large in the decades after the Soviet Union broke apart.

In summary here, America invaded and occupied Iraq, whereas it entered into arms-control agreements with North Korea. It negotiated with Libya to shed its WMD efforts. It cooperated with European states to present carrots and sticks for Iran to induce it to break off its nuclear quest. Sugar as well as clubs, in fact, formed a fairly consistent component of Washington's approach to adversarial regimes. Circumstances, not a common classification, dictated American responses. Washington's policies did not tumble into a "false dichotomy" because of labeling some regimes under "generic categories such as 'rogue state.'" Its officials rarely called North Korea or Iran rogue nations in public utterances. Nor did US policy reflect rigid categorization that set up "containment and engagement as mutually exclusive strategies."[41] The rogue autocrats held the choice to join with the global fraternity or to resist it. For their own reasons, they persisted against the grain of international society.

Except for the Iraq War, America opted for deterrence and containment toward rogue nations. This approach succeeded against Libya, which set aside its international terrorism and nuclear-arms pursuits before the Arab Spring winds buffeted it. It also compelled North Korea to look toward China to break its isolation. Washington properly brought Beijing into its North Korea initiatives. When it accorded with its own interests, Beijing did act as a restraint on its difficult dependency. More dependably, China served as a model of economic development for its protégé. Iran, as chapter 3 makes clear, is still an intractable case. Strategic patience will not suffice to disarm its growing nuclear and missile capacity. Therefore, Iran's membership in the nuclear club constitutes a defeat for Middle East security and for antiproliferation hopes.

The so-called lesser rogue states, such as Syria, Cuba, and Sudan, suffered setbacks or declined without Soviet aid; they no longer present the threats they once did. Venezuela possesses troublesome tendencies, which might portend a new hostile regime. If that becomes the case, the rogue phenomenon will reoccur as it has in the past. And not once, but like Sisyphus in the underworld, the United States will have to handle again and again these adversarial players or risk catastrophic consequences. Working through the Security Council to craft antirogue sanctions often resembles a Rubik's Cube. Every time all the squares seem right, one pops out and the process continues. So the United Nations is only one option to use against rogue powers.

An examination of these themes—US policies, rogue state actions, and international diplomacy—will form the threads that twist through the brief account in this volume. For the sake of clarity, this book embraces a chronological framework while exploring its themes. It concentrates on the three major adversarial countries—Iraq, Iran, and North Korea—while summarizing lesser rogue nations and the emergence of troublesome states.

CHAPTER 2

Iraq: Quintessential Rogue State

If Saddam Hussein rejects peace and we have to use force, our purpose is clear. We want to seriously diminish the threat posed by Iraq's weapons of mass destruction.

—William J. Clinton

For all who love freedom and peace, the world without Saddam Hussein's regime is a better and safer place.

—George W. Bush

Baghdad is determined to force the Mongols of our age to commit suicide at its gates.

—Saddam Hussein

Before the American invasion into the ancient land between the Tigris and Euphrates Rivers, Iraq constituted the quintessential rogue state. It exceeded each of the established criteria. Externally, its behavior was alarming. Under Saddam Hussein, Iraq attacked two neighbors, threatened others, sponsored terrorism abroad, pursued weapons of mass destruction, and perennially destabilized the Persian Gulf region. Internally, Hussein (a pathological monster) crushed dissent, murdered potential rivals, and savagely exterminated thousands of Kurdish and Shiite citizens, some with chemical weapons. If other rogue regimes did not consciously adopt Iraq's pushing the envelope of accepted state behavior, Hussein did anticipate theirs. Until he tempted fate too far and it bit back, the Iraqi dictator excelled in taunting the United States.

For two decades prior to the US intervention, Iraq blinked on Washington radars. Sometimes its blips illuminated ominously and other times faintly. Although its signal never really left the black screen, Iraq's salience fluctuated alongside more urgent perils from the Soviet Union during the Cold War. After the Berlin Wall fell on November 9, 1989, the George Herbert Walker Bush presidency focused almost exclusively on the fate of Mikhail Gorbachev, Soviet-American arms control treaties, the upwelling of prodemocracy movements in Central Europe, and ending the Red Army's occupation. White House eyes stayed riveted on the unfolding drama east of the Elbe River until early August 1990, when Iraqi tanks rolled into next-door Kuwait. From that time forward, Iraq preoccupied Washington policy makers.

American responses to Iraq's provocations ran the gamut from limited diplomatic feelers to economic sanctions, frequent air strikes, and finally invasion and occupation. After its military defeat, Iraq became the recipient of billions of dollars for reconstruction aid and democracy building. Importantly, American policy underwent a crucial transformation with the adoption of the preventive war doctrine by President George W. Bush. Unveiled a year after the September 11, 2001, terrorist attacks on American soil, the strike-first policy foreshadowed the Iraq War, underpinning the conflict with a doctrinal grounding.[1] Unlike the approaches to other rogue states, American policies toward Iraq embodied all of the instruments of US power, including large-scale military intervention. Iraq's immediate history before the 2003 invasion was turbulent even by Middle East standards. In some ways, its past was predictive of its ultimate encounter with the United States.

Background to a Rogue State

Modern-day Iraq is a recent and anguished state. It rests on lands that cradled the ancient empires of Sumer, Assyria, and Babylon, whose civilizational attainments advanced humankind's progress in art, architecture, crafts, ethical thought, writing, and agriculture. Saddam Hussein, Iraq's former dictator, often boasted in speeches about the past glories and conquests of Babylon in particular. Providential geography favored this cradle of civilization. Human society's birth and contemporary Iraq's flourishing drew from its location at the confluence of two of the world's great rivers—the Tiger and Euphrates, which blessed the riverine with fruit, wheat, barley, vegetables, cotton, and livestock. The preclassical Greeks dubbed this terrain Mesopotamia—meaning "between two rivers." The twentieth century's hydrocarbon-powered economies also favored Iraq because of its bountiful oil and natural gas reserves. Alone among the Arab Middle East nations, Iraq boasted abundant water and oil, endowing it with natural wealth and regional influence. Its star-crossed history and quarrelsome populace negated its providential endowments, however.

For 300 years, the territory that ultimately became known as Iraq lay prostrate beneath the rule of the Ottoman Empire. By the early twentieth century, that empire was a decaying husk. Ottoman governance of the Iraq territory existed in name only. During World War I, Britain invaded, pushed aside the Ottoman army, and occupied the country. After the war, Iraq was declared a League of Nations mandate under British rule in 1920. Over the next dozen years, the British authorities overlay the three former Ottoman-ruled provinces—Mosul, Baghdad, and Basra—with a unitary, central government. These provinces more or less conformed to the homelands of the three main ethno-religious communities, which remained further subdivided into clans and tribes.

The northern Mosul province was home to the Kurds, a distinct people who speak Arabic and practice Islam. For hundreds of years, the Kurds have longed for their own independent state. Making up only about 15 percent of the Iraqi population, they suffered frequent discrimination and persecution at the hands of the larger groups. The Baghdad province sat in the country's midsection and held its eponymous capital. In this middle swath live the Sunni Arabs, who comprised over 20 percent of the country's peoples. Despite their minority status, they controlled the top positions in the government, police, and military until the US occupation. The Sunni lorded over the Kurds and Shia. In parts of the capital and in the southern corner known as the Basra province, the populace adhered to the Shiite branch of Islam. The Shia formed about 60 percent of the overall citizenry. Because of their faith, they often fell victim to the whip hand of Sunni rule. Some Shias looked to Shiite-dominated Iran for protection, inspiration, and even safe havens in harrowing times. Infected by sectarianism and intercommunal clashes, Iraq's political trajectory was anything but smooth.

The British-ruled kingdom moved in stages toward independence, which came in 1932 with an imported monarchy from Saudi Arabia. The British-installed crown presided over the disparate population pulled within borders demarcated by European statesmen thousands of miles away after World War I. The transplanted royal family survived until 1958, when the Iraqi military ousted King Faisal II in a bloody coup. The Iraqi officers decreed a "republic," but it was such a government in name only. The subsequent strongmen ruled with an iron fist and rubber-stamp parliaments. After the coup, Brigadier Abd al-Karim Qasim established a military dictatorship, which was marked by political instability until his overthrow in 1963. More was lost in Faisal's overthrow than just a monarchy. His dethronement abruptly blocked Iraq's path toward democracy that the monarchy charted. It also turned Iraq from a Western ally to a Soviet client and adversary of the West.

After the coup, Qasim withdrew Iraq from the Baghdad Pact, a US-affirmed and anti-Soviet alliance, which had allied the Iraqi government with Britain, Iran, Pakistan, and Turkey. Thereafter, the dictatorial regime drew closer to the Soviet Union. Moscow, in turn, supplied it with weapons. Iraq, like Syria, established a radical socialist Baath Party (which means "renaissance" or "resurrection") in the 1960s. The Iraqi and Syrian parties split, although both attained power in their respective nations. The Iraqi Baath faction ruled briefly in 1963 before returning to power in 1968, where it governed until 2003. Iraq's increasingly totalitarian government cooperated with the Soviet Union, which coveted outposts to contest American influence in the vital oil-producing Persian Gulf.

Coming to power in 1979 as the head of the Baath Party, Saddam Hussein accentuated the party's brutal policies and its ties to Moscow. The Baath Party's anti-Western ideology made Iraq a "logical 'progressive' partner of Moscow."[2]

Once in power, Saddam Hussein quickly displayed the earmarks that identified him as a regional troublemaker. His actions ran the gamut from provoking war with Iran and resorting to nerve agents and mustard gas attacks against Iranian troops and his own rebellious population in violation of international protocols to pursuing nuclear weapons and finally invading Kuwait. The Iraqi autocrat convinced himself that only the use of chemical weapons against Iran saved his nation from defeat and his own rule from removal by disgruntled generals. From that conflict forward, he resolved to seek the insurance of WMD to protect his power from outside forces. In a Shakespearean irony, it was the chase after these megadeath weapons that brought on a collision with the United States and an end to his dictatorship.

America's Engagement of Iraq and Hussein's Response

Toward the end of the Cold War, the United States tried to use Hussein as a counterweight to Iran. It perceived ayatollah Iran as a greater menace than Hussein Iraq. After the ouster of the pro-American shah and the takeover of the US embassy in Tehran, the Islamic Republic of Iran emerged as America's implacable foe in the Middle East. Iran's revolutionary militancy, terrorism, and overt attacks on US interests, as related in the next chapter, aimed to displace American influence with Iranian hegemony from the Straits of

Hormuz to the Hindu Kush. For US policy makers during the 1980s, it was a Hobson's choice to engage Iraq so as to check the Iranian threat. With hindsight, the United States went from the proverbial frying pan to the fire with its courtship of Baghdad. Before that was clear, Washington moved to help Iraq against Iran when Baghdad struck militarily at the Islamic Republic, commencing an eight-year conflict (1980–1988).

Still smarting over the Iranian hostage taking in the American embassy, the new government of Ronald Reagan sought to shore up Iraq, lest it lose its war against a surprisingly strong Iran. The White House removed Iraq from the State Department's list of terrorist states in February 1982. Soon after, it permitted US corporations to sell war-related products to Iraq, such as helicopters, computers, scientific instruments, special alloy steel, and other industrial goods. Next, Washington allowed Egypt, Jordan, and Saudi Arabia to transfer US-manufactured arms, such as howitzers, helicopters, and munitions, to Iraq. The Reagan administration dispatched once and future defense secretary Donald Rumsfeld as special envoy for the Middle East to meet with Saddam Hussein to reassure him of limited US backing. As the Iraq-Iran war ground on, the tide turned against Hussein's forces despite their early victories on Iranian territory. Sunni-dominated countries in the Persian Gulf worried about a possible Iraqi defeat at the hands of the Shiite fundamentalist regime.[3]

By mid-1984, the United States had waived restrictions on "dual-use" (for military or civilian application) exports of hardware and technology to Iraq. The CIA also turned over satellite intelligence to aid Iraqi counterattacks against Iranian ground assaults. Critics of American realpolitik argued that the intelligence sharing made the United States complicit in Iraq's use of chemical weapons, a violation of the 1925 Geneva accords prohibiting gas warfare. Evidence at the time and later surfaced that the Iraqi military desperately turned to nerve gas and blister agents (such as mustard gas) to defeat the increasingly effective Iranian mass suicide offenses in the mid-1980s. Tens of thousands of Iranians died in the Iraqi chemical assaults. An unclassified CIA report observed that Baghdad employed chemical weapons (including nerve agents) as an "integral part" of its battlefield strategy and as a "regular and recurring tactic."[4] Iraq's profligate reliance on these internationally banned weapons constituted one of the reasons that the Islamic Republic finally agreed to the UN-negotiated cease-fire with Baghdad in August 1988. By that time, the Hussein government also had gassed its own restive Kurdish populations. Many thousands of Kurds died in the chemical bombardments, wiping out entire Kurdish villages. Little wonder that the Kurds made common cause with the United States.

Not unlike other rogue leaders, Saddam Hussein operated under the principle that focusing on foreign threats actually worked to consolidate internal support. Hussein, like his fellow rogue compatriots, needed a foreign scapegoat to lay the blame for poverty, poor education, inadequate healthcare, or restrictions on political liberties. America and the West filled this necessity. In explaining rogue states' pugnacity, analysts often underplay the domestic rationale. Dictators depend on foreign enemies for legitimacy, allegiance, and societal cohesion. Hussein had another reason for his international defiance.

Like many of his countrymen, Hussein resented Egypt's preeminent standing in the Arab Middle East. Egypt's universities, historical significance, and centrality in the region's political and cultural affairs were sources of resentment in Iraqi hearts. Much of Hussein's nationalistic bombast as well as Iraq's policies focused on surpassing Egyptian preeminence, despite the fact that (or maybe because) he took up exile there when in 1959 Baghdad authorities pursued him for a failed assassination attempt on Qasim, Iraq's strongman. During his Egyptian stay, he graduated from high school at age 24. He returned to Iraq in 1963, when the Baathist Party toppled Qasim. Almost 30 years later, Hussein's envy of Egypt's status acknowledged no debt for his safe haven and education there. He needed political influence, military success, and funds to displace Egypt from its preeminent standing in the Arab world.[5]

Rather than hunkering down at the conclusion of the war with Iran, Hussein embarked on another reckless course. His ill-fated war against Iran was a disaster for Iraq. Aside from the expenditure of thousands of Iraqi soldiers' lives, it placed the country in grievous debt. The war cost it an estimated $200 billion.[6] Baghdad owed an estimated $60 billion to the Sunni Gulf states, principally Kuwait and Saudi Arabia, which lent funds to Hussein to halt the expansion of Iran's brand of Shiite fundamentalism. Rather than expressions of gratitude, Kuwait insisted on repayment. Hussein was outraged. In his mind, the sheikdom owed him for its safety. Worse, Hussein believed that Kuwait and other Arab oil producers priced black crude too low on the world market. Iraq could not recoup its losses with higher oil revenues from the West. Besides these grievances, Baghdad regarded Kuwait as Iraq's nineteenth province, which had been stolen by Europe's colonial mapmakers who placed it outside Iraqi boundaries. It meant to reclaim its rightful possession.

George H. W. Bush's Olive Branch to Saddam Hussein

The cessation of the Iraq-Iran war nearly coincided with the American presidential election in November 1988. That electoral contest saw Reagan's vice president, George Herbert Walker Bush, succeed him in the White House. The new Bush administration exhibited little initial change in US policy toward the Hussein regime. Both Reagan and Bush interpreted Saddam Hussein as a moderating strongman, who might be turned from Soviet patronage and used to thwart Iranian imperial aspirations. Thus, the Bush White House opposed congressional sanctions against Iraq for its appalling human rights violations against its own citizens. The US engagement of Iraq paid initial dividends, as the country looked to be softening. Iraq, for instance, offered to pay compensation to American families of sailors slain by an Iraqi anti-ship missile fired into the USS *Stark* in the course of its war with Iran.[7] For marginal leverage with Baghdad, the Bush team continued the policy of extending credit guarantees up to $1 billion for American grain exports to Iraq through the Commodity Credit Corporation (CCC) in late 1989. Early the next year, Congress fell in line with the administration's approach and dropped CCC sanctions from pending bills. Secretary of State James Baker recounted that Baghdad's record on repayment was "spotless," that domestic interests lobbied for these loans, and that they were "immensely popular on Capitol Hill and with farm state politicians."[8]

America's "realist" policy toward Iraq came to naught, however. Saddam Hussein was not the man to grasp an olive branch. To him, goodwill overtures signaled weakness. Unlike the run-of-the-mill Cold War dictator, content with his own survival and internal suppression, Hussein exemplified the rogue chieftain who recklessly cavorted on the edge of the abyss. Internationally, Hussein perceived the Soviet decline as both a sign of Iraq's growing vulnerability to a powerful and unchallenged United States and an opportunity to lead an anti-American coalition. The autocrat railed against the American presence in the region. He demanded that the US Navy depart from the Persian Gulf. Hussein called on his brother Arab governments to resume the oil embargo that crippled Western economies in the 1970s.[9]

In the final analysis, the early Bush policy of reaching out to Baghdad was not *the* contributing factor in Hussein's decision to annex Kuwait. The story is much more complicated than the simple, one-sided tale of "it's all Washington's fault." Moreover, everything the world subsequently learned about Hussein strengthens the case that warnings delivered to the Baghdad dictator would in all likelihood have fallen on deaf ears. He misunderstood the consequences of his rash invasion of Kuwait and, more fatefully, his bluff about building nuclear arms years later.

Among the first and clearest messages of impending danger telegraphed from the Iraqi president came in late February 1990. Saddam Hussein correctly gauged the shifting global correlation of forces with the declining

Soviet Union. During an otherwise unimportant meeting in Amman, Jordan, for the first anniversary of the Arab Cooperation Council (Iraq, Egypt, Jordan, and then North Yemen), Hussein delivered a speech that was broadcast by Jordanian television. Laced within bombastic phrases was a pronounced anti-American assessment of Washington's newfound influence in the Middle East. An anemic USSR translated into a predominate US sway within the region. He argued, "This means that if the Gulf people, along with all Arabs, are not careful, the Arab Gulf region will be governed by the wishes of the United States." He opined that oil prices "would be fixed in line with a special perspective benefiting American interests and ignoring the interests of others."[10] Hussein's speech marked a telling break with his previous modulated behavior and announced his quest for mastery of the Persian Gulf.

Hussein's explosive address rippled the political waters in the Middle East. Piqued by remarks, the Egyptian president Hosni Mubarak left the ACC gathering a day earlier than planned. Since the Camp David accords, Egypt had been perceived as pro-American in the Middle East. By receiving some $2 billion annually since signing the 1978 agreements, Egypt appeared to be in Washington's pocket, an impression that Saddam Hussein played up to his benefit among Middle East "rejectionists" of US peacemaking between Israel and Arab states. By championing the greater Middle East cause against the West, Hussein eclipsed Mubarak as the radical torchbearer of the "Arab street."

Hussein hooked his regime's star to the Palestinian cause against Israel in early 1990. By flamboyantly championing the Palestinians, the Iraqi dictator solidified his domestic hold on power and claimed the limelight in the Arab Middle East. Moderate Arab governments denounced Israel but also prized stability in the region. Egypt, Jordan, and Saudi Arabia grew concerned with boisterous anti-Israeli street demonstrations, lest they pose an internal threat to their own governance. Saddam Hussein gloried in the adulation from the streets in Cairo or Amman that his bellicose utterances stirred. On April 2, Hussein outdid himself in fiery rhetoric. He spewed a particularly chilling threat when he declared possession of new chemical weapons "to make the fire eat up half of Israel" if that nation attacked Iraq.[11] His warlike ranting appealed to the Palestinians and their staunchest backers in the Middle East. They also elevated his standing in the so-called "Arab street." Not since Gamal Abd Nasser, the late Egyptian president of the 1960s, had a flag-bearer of Arab nationalism electrified the passions of the humble in the urban Middle East.[12]

The destroy-half-of-Israel comments elicited a stern rebuke from the US Department of State. A departmental spokesman characterized Hussein's speech as "inflammatory, outrageous and irresponsible."[13] Hussein's incendiary language aroused White House suspicions and prompted the Bush team to cancel the CCC credits extended for $500 million in American grain purchases.[14] Washington also foiled an illegal Iraqi scheme to purchase nuclear triggering devices, denied components for a "super gun" artillery piece, and blocked the sale of tungsten furnaces useful for Iraq's illicit nuclear weapons program. The ominous signs of Iraq's sinister designs deepened suspicions among the Bush foreign policy team. It realized that Hussein was abandoning his cloak of moderation. Yet it neglected to embark on deterrent steps, and Iraq pressed ahead.

It must be borne in mind that the Bush presidency was engulfed by a spate of international crises soon after taking office. Senior Bush officials were absorbed by the instability in the Soviet Union, reawakening of nationalism in Eastern Europe, intervention into Panama, and the unexpected massacre in Tiananmen Square, where Chinese authorities brutally suppressed a student protest for democracy in June 1989. Such a full plate led Secretary of State Baker to pen in his memoirs that before Iraq struck at Kuwait, "it [Iraq] was simply not prominent on my radar screen, or the President's."[15] Baghdad took advantage of Washington's preoccupations elsewhere.

Iraq Invades Kuwait

Unperturbed by wartime losses against Iran, the Iraqi despot turned to bite the hand that had fed his war machine against the Iranians. At the summit meeting of Arab League held in Baghdad during May 1990, Hussein returned to a prevalent theme. He thundered against the Gulf minikingdoms, particularly Kuwait, which he faulted for the downward pressure on oil prices by its overproduction in excess of OPEC levels. Each one US dollar drop on a barrel cost Iraq $1 billion a year in lost revenues. Hussein interpreted this as a form of economic warfare. From his perspective, Iraq's stand against the United States as the preeminent imperialist power and Israel as Washington's outpost was a form of "public goods" in which the rest of the Arab world benefited. Thus, effusive deference and monetary assistance were owed Iraq by its neighbors.[16]

A month before Republican Guard armored divisions clanked across the Kuwaiti frontier, Iraq's president denounced Kuwait and the United Arab Emirates for thrusting a "poisoned dagger" into Iraq's back by flooding the oil markets to sustain their revenues amid falling world demand. His Revolutionary Day speech on July 17 sounded, with hindsight, much like the "public case" for invasion that it soon represented. He accused Kuwait of stealing Iraqi petroleum by "slant drilling" under the border into Iraq's oilfields. His fulminations also rekindled the long-simmering border disputes with Kuwait, which he and most Iraqis regarded as the nineteenth province of their country.[17] His claims laid down a pretext for military assault. On July 24, Iraqi T-72 battle tanks barreled up to the Kuwaiti border and stopped.

The Iraq-Kuwait border tension precipitated an unexpected summons from Hussein to US Ambassador April Glaspie, based in Baghdad. At the now-famous meeting on July 25, the Arabic-fluent ambassador spoke alone with the Iraqi leader. After listening to Hussein's hyperbolic exposition about Iraq's grievances and the Gulf kingdoms' injustices to him, Glaspie, to her critics, sounded too sympathetic to the demagogue. The envoy drew no line in the sand. Instead, she uttered "diplomatic speak" by stating, "As you know, we don't take a stand on territorial disputes." By this she meant that the squabble over the Iraqi-Kuwaiti border was not Washington's concern. Her critics argued that such a statement represented a veritable green light to Hussein aggressions. But Glaspie added that "we can never excuse settlement of disputes by other than peaceful means."[18] By her account, she also voiced American resolution to defend its allies and access to oil in the region.[19]

Some commentators harshly indicted President Bush's handling of the pre-invasion diplomacy, as if more determined diplomacy would have forestalled Iraqi actions.[20] Judging from a greater historical perspective two decades after the conflict and with more knowledge of Saddam Hussein, it is far more accurate to place the blame squarely on the Iraqi strongman. Hussein's prewar motives reached beyond intimation for finite ends; his threatening bombast, however crudely delivered, set out the political case for swallowing Kuwait. He misjudged the reaction not only in the West but also in the Arab world, which condemned it and joined in the fight against his gobbling up a neighboring state in early August 1990.

An American Line in the Arabian Sand

The sheer ruthlessness of the Republican Guards' takeover and plundering of the tiny Persian Gulf sheikdom astounded outsiders. On the state level, Baghdad seized a foreign country for its oil resources, which when combined with Iraq's output totaled some 20 percent of the world's proven reserves. It stripped the Kuwaiti government repositories of all essential documents, treaties, and historical papers relating to the country's birth and boundaries. It was a naked power grab for Kuwait territory. On a street level, the Iraqi militarized hordes swept over the capital Kuwait City in a fashion reminiscent of a Viking raiding party, wantonly killing anyone in their sights and looting any valuables not nailed down. To this day, over 600 Kuwaitis remain unaccounted for by the kingdom's government. Marauding troops stole and drove back to Iraq some 29,000 automobiles; they ripped paintings from the walls and looted other artworks. Next, these modern-day Huns turned to the torch and bomb to destroy palaces, museums, power stations, and even oil installations. Almost a year later, Kuwait established in May 1991 a commission, Public Authority for the Assessment of Damages Resulting from Iraqi Aggression, to tally the costs associated with Iraq's "re-annexing" what it termed a breakaway province. It amounted to $173 billion.[21] The brazenness of Iraq's subjugation and rape of Kuwait, akin to something from the pages of the Third Reich, stunned the Bush administration as well as the Middle East.

Taken by surprise, the United States scrambled to respond to Iraq's punitive conquest of Kuwait. Two broad courses of actions presented themselves to the Bush White House. Either the United States could adopt a sanctions policy to hurt Iraq over a long period of time or it could mount a military strike to roll back Iraq's occupation. Embargoes raise havoc with a nation's economy but almost never bring down dictatorships, which deflect the brunt of hardship to the average citizen. Mounting an armed counterassault, nonetheless, risked international opposition, alienation of pro-American states in the Middle East, and American blood and treasures. General Norman Schwarzkopf, commander-in-chief of Central Command (CENTCOM) and the officer responsible for implementing a military response in the Gulf area, briefed the civilian leaders that Iraq's armed forces were large but decrepit. Reflecting America's bitter experience in Vietnam, Schwarzkopf's recommendations were in line with Chairman of the Joint Chiefs of Staff Colin Powell and other top military figures in the Pentagon. They wanted overwhelming force applied against Iraq if any military actions were executed. Their plans envisioned initially 100,000 troops for the mission, a figure later augmented fivefold.

In weighing an apt response, Bush and his top aides had an array of concerns. Strategically, they worried that Baghdad now had dominion over 20 percent of the world's oil reserves and hinted at a further drive into eastern Saudi Arabia, which holds another one-fifth of the planet's known oil deposits. Domestically, the administration was concerned about whether the American public would tolerate a war in light of the fact that much of Saudi oil flowed to Japan. Bush officials also worried that restoring the Kuwaiti monarchy ran counter to American ideals of democracy. Externally, Washington was on the line; as the offshore military heavyweight, it felt an obligation to react forcefully to Iraqis' naked aggression. The heads of Egypt and Turkey telephoned President Bush to express their determination that Iraq's attack could not be left unopposed. The Turkish president Turgut Ozal told Bush that the Iraqi dictator "must go" because "Saddam is more dangerous than Qaddafi," the rogue leader of Libya.[22] On August 5, George Bush uttered what became his most quotable rallying cry for the hawkish approach to the crisis: "This will not stand, this aggression against Kuwait."[23]

The Bush foreign policy team decided that the defense of Saudi Arabia stood out as the key issue. By putting US oil sources at risk, Iraq directly imperiled American vital interests. As he was wont to do again and again, President Hussein overplayed his hand by endangering the security of the desert kingdom. Should Saudi oil and its revenues fall into the Iraqi tyrant's hands, then the strategic balance would be tipped against the United States and its allies in the Middle East. Convincing the hesitant Saudis proved more troublesome than warranted by the imminent peril they faced. Bush feared they would strike a deal with Saddam Hussein rather than accept Washington's offer to defend them militarily by the only reliable means available—ground troops. The Saudi were reluctant to be perceived as Washington's puppets by other Arabs. But the palpable threat posed by the presence of Iraqi armored units proximate to the Saudi border convinced Riyadh of the necessity of American forces to shield it from Iraq.

What also facilitated the US counteroffensive was the joint statement by the Soviet foreign minister, Eduard Shevardnadze, with the American secretary of state, James Baker, in the Russian capital where the two were meeting. To the surprise of many, their statement aligned Moscow with Washington in condemning Iraq for its aggression, isolating that country from its principal backer. This cooperation gave a glimpse of the post–Cold War world, where Moscow and Washington were no long at daggers drawn in their relations.[24] Aside from Jordan, Yemen, and Yasir Arafat's Palestinian Liberation Organization, the Republic of Iraq stood alone. But near-global condemnation did not translate automatically into participation in a military coalition against Iraq.

George Bush's early hesitation soon gave way to forceful diplomacy to forge a coalition of over 30 states to wage a war to expel Iraq from Kuwaiti territory. But first, the White House hammered out a strategy of coercive diplomacy, designed to ratchet up pressure on Baghdad. Tactically, it made political sense to give diplomacy a chance to resolve the crisis. Simultaneously, it strove mightily to build an airtight political case for an armed campaign to eject Hussein's army from Kuwait, even while it pursued diplomacy and sanctions. Working through the United Nations and with foreign governments, the United States lined up international support and gained a global imprimatur for its actions. Early on in the crisis, it obtained

Security Council passage of economic sanctions in Resolution 661, the first in a series of UN resolutions against Iraq. The Bush advisers hoped that an economic embargo and diplomatic isolation alone would induce Hussein to surrender Western hostages taken in Kuwait City and to withdraw his forces back to Iraq. But they realistically prepared for war.

A Desert Shield

The United States sped elements from the 82nd Airborne Division and two US Air Force fighter squadrons to Saudi Arabia in a rush to implant Operation Desert Shield to defend the desert kingdom, lest Iraq make good on its threats. This vanguard was followed by a torrent of heavy armored divisions, bomber squadrons, and aircraft battle groups that were based in facilities on Saudi soil. By the commencement of ground warfare early the next year, US military forces in Saudi Arabia and other Persian Gulf sheikdoms numbered half a million, the largest concentration of armed might since World War II. Allied nations deployed another 300,000 troops against Iraq's half-million-strong armed forces.

The vast military presence, in addition to its defensive role, played a crucial diplomatic function. Since the Saudis approved of this enormous US garrison not far from Islam's holiest sites, they smoothed Washington's coalition building among Arab and Muslim states, which might have been reluctant to join in an alliance against Iraq. Once King Fadh agreed to the US deployment in the Saudi kingdom, Washington fabricated the fiction of a genuine Saudi-American partnership by splitting the command as a sign of unity. The US commander, Norman Schwarzkopf, led the American, British, and other European ground forces, while Prince Khaled Bin Sultan al-Saud led the Arab contingents. The "parallel command," as Prince Khaled wrote, worked well enough for a diplomatic victory to accompany the military one.[25] The rapid and powerful incursion dispelled Riyadh's fears that America's commitment might prove merely transitory. The Saudis worried about Washington's steadfastness if America suffered casualties. They based their apprehension on the withdrawal of US forces from Lebanon in the wake of the Hezbollah attack on the Marine Corps barracks in 1983.

While the buildup of US and allied forces accelerated in the Gulf, the Bush White House worked prodigiously to form an international coalition against Saddam Hussein's cross-border attack—a feat that won George Bush lasting acclaim as a statesman. Having been Ronald Reagan's vice president for eight years and head of the CIA, Bush had met most of the world's prominent leaders. His internationalist disposition prompted him to pursue coalition warfare instead of unilateral hostilities with Iraq. The president diligently "worked the phones" by telephoning his counterparts abroad. Others he met personally within the White House or at his vacation home in Kennebunkport, Maine. Further, he sent Secretary of State Baker on a whirlwind tour of foreign capitals to drum up members for a military coalition and for financial contributions toward wartime expenditures. The US government's exertions paid off, as 34 nations participated in the United Nations–sanctioned coalition. By passing the hat to recoup war expenditures, the Bush administration raised $67 billion from pacifist-minded states such as Japan and Germany toward the final war costs of $87 billion, roughly five-sixths of the total military expenditures.

The Saudi-American partnership enabled Egypt, Syria, and Turkey to join the coalition, although each had genuine enough practical reasons to be worried about Iraq's expansion into Kuwait. Even a majority of the Arab League members condemned Iraq for its invasion. The United States excluded only one state from joining its anti-Iraq operation—Israel. Washington's Arab partnership required the exclusion of its most trustworthy and militarily proficient ally in the region because the Middle East fraternity would never accept Israel as a member. During the Persian Gulf War, the American-Israeli friendship was further tested when Iraq fired Scud missiles at the Jewish state. Washington pleaded with Jerusalem not to respond in kind. The Israelis gritted their teeth and complied with the American request. An Israel counterstrike might well have split the fragile Arab-American wartime alliance. That Arab states stayed committed to the US-led coalition was a testament to George Bush's vigorous diplomacy and to Israeli forbearance under missile bombardment.

Despite diplomatic pressure, numerous Security Council resolutions, and the buildup of warships, warplanes, tanks, and troops in the Gulf bases, Saddam Hussein refused to budge from the armed occupation of Kuwait. In late fall 1990, the Security Council passed Resolution 678, which called for the use of "all necessary means" (i.e., military force) to implement the ten previous resolutions calling for the end of Iraq's occupation by January 15, 1991. Beneath this Damoclean sword, Javier Perez de Cuellar (the UN secretary general), Washington, and foreign chancelleries danced to avoid war. They dispatched emissaries, held meetings, and made offers to Baghdad— all of which came to naught.

For the White House, the outcome was far from certain. Although it had relatively smooth sailing in the Security Council (at least compared to period before the future Iraq War) for passage of the "all necessary means" action, the Republican president encountered stiff opposition from Democrats in the US Congress for any war making. Bush's legislative opponents demanded more time for sanctions to convince Saddam

Hussein to relent. They scoffed at the West Wing's unfashionable notion of rescuing an outdated monarchy and restoring it to the Kuwait throne. They grossly overestimated the casualties that the United States might suffer in a war against Iraq's dilapidated army. On the January 8 vote authorizing the use of force to implement the Security Council resolution, the House of Representatives passed it comfortably; but in the Senate, the authorization squeaked by with 52-47 in favor—the slimmest war vote ever. To jump ahead, because of the Persian Gulf War's resounding military victory, the Democratic opponents found themselves on the wrong side of history. The short, victorious war was popular. Bush's polls surged as a result. Twelve years later, the Gulf war opponents remembered how the Americans lost confidence in them. In 2002, many voted for George W. Bush's call to arms against Hussein—a decision they came to regret when the Iraq War went badly.

A Desert Storm

The US-led multinational coalition let loose a high-tech version of fire and brimstone upon the unwary Iraqi army beginning January 17, 1991. A powerful air assault mercilessly ground up Saddam Hussein's tanks and troops for 39 days. This so-called Nintendo warfare wielded precision-guided bombs and missiles that almost unerringly struck their targets dead center. Likened to the film *Star Wars*, America's advanced technology destroyed Baghdad's military in detail. The start of the US-headed land offense was practically anticlimactic. Indeed, it lasted a mere 100 hours before Powell, the chairman of the Joint Chiefs of Staff, halted it rather than slaughtering the retreating, ramshackle stream of terrified men in headlong flight toward the Iraqi border. An Iron Age military force destroyed a Bronze Age horde.

For all its military savagery and operational mastery, the United States ended the fighting inconclusively. In fact, it simply restored the political status quo ante. The Washington-led coalition expelled Iraqi forces from Kuwait. It fulfilled the letter and spirit of the UN mandate to reinstate Kuwait's sovereignty. Saddam Hussein, despite CIA predictions of a coup around the corner, kept power by harshly suppressing a revolt among the Shia and Kurds that President Bush twice encouraged.[26] The intelligence agency surmised that Hussein's catastrophic military loss automatically entailed his downfall. But the Sunni minority realized that their kinsman's ouster might well end their privileges. So they fought for him by jailing, torturing, and murdering the regime's opponents. The strongman's survival meant nothing changed. Iraq continued to threaten its neighbors.

Most ominously for the United States, dark rumors surfaced about Iraq's nuclear program.

What gave the rumors credence was the inadvertent discovery during the Persian Gulf War that Iraq was far nearer a nuclear weapons capability than the Western intelligence services estimated. Baghdad nuclear ambitions had deep roots. France helped built Iraq's first nuclear venture in the late 1970s. The Osirik nuclear facility aroused acute anxiety in the region. The Iranians bungled an air strike on Osirik, which Israel ten months later saw through to completion. In June 1981, the Israeli air force swooped down on Iraq's nuclear plant and demolished it. Many states, including the United States, publicly criticized the Jewish state; but in reality Israel removed a destabilizing threat in the Middle East. Still, the Iraqis pressed ahead secretly in laboratories at Tuwaitha, Al Athir, and other sites that coalition warplanes bombed during the Persian Gulf conflict.[27] Anxiety also mounted about Iraq's reputed chemical and biological arms as well. The revelations of Iraq's nearness to an atomic capability cast serious doubt on the efficacy of nuclear inspectors from the International Atomic Energy Agency (IAEA) for failing to uncover Hussein's clandestine operations.[28] Soon after the Gulf war, UN inspectors dismantled the nuclear structures. The dream of an Iraqi nuclear bomb nevertheless lived on in the mind of Saddam Hussein, and it contributed a decade later to his undoing.

The IAEA failure to uncover Iraqi nuclear facilities held long-lasting and widespread ramifications. Never again would Washington governments place absolute confidence in IAEA inspections or any non-American arms monitoring. Moreover, in the official mind, the failure to discover Iraq's nuclear headway became linked with other inspections in North Korea and Iran. Doubts about the effectiveness of international inspection teams heightened American anxieties that the North Koreans and Iranians were likely to be secretly producing WMD. This in itself linked Iraq, North Korea, and Iran (and possibly Syria and Libya) in American thinking in what future President George W. Bush characterized as an "axis of evil" in 2002.

In addition to sparing itself a messy and lengthy occupation by not invading Iraq, the Bush administration harbored practical reasons for not taking Baghdad and disposing of Hussein. A greatly enfeebled Iraq could no longer be counterpoised against America's archenemy in the Gulf—the Islamic Republic of Iran. A damaged but still unitary Iraq served US political interests; at the least it was a temporary expedient. The decision did demonstrate that even Washington was willing to manipulate a rogue state—in this case Iraq—against another rogue power, Iran. Such is one function of rogue players on the global chessboard. William Jefferson Clinton, who succeeded Bush Sr. in the White House, walked away from the idea of using Iraq to offset Iran. The Clinton administration treated both Iraq and Iran as pariahs, as will be analyzed later.

From Victory to No-Fly Zones

The US wisdom of depending on a seemingly chastened Iraq to be quasi-counter to Iran proved transitory. Hussein was soon up to his old mischief, threatening neighbors, exporting terrorism, and crushing internal opposition. His Republican Guard attacks on rebellious Shia and Kurds, in fact, made it next to impossible for the United States to extricate itself from the Iraqi quagmire. George Bush Sr. was, in part, culpable for inciting the uprisings. The White House's reactions to the plight of the massacred populations locked America into tense standoff with Iraq through the remainder of President Bush's term, the entire Clinton administration, and into George W. Bush's presidency.

The United States was compelled to act as the afflicted and destitute Kurdish population fled from its northern enclave into Turkey to escape Hussein's barbarous persecution. Something had to be done to save the Kurds, whose exodus, in part, was caused by the White House's egging them on to rise up against their ruler. Also, the Kurdish flight put at risk Turkey's stability, whose southeastern corner had long endured a guerrilla war from the native Kurdish population, demanding autonomy. Onrushing Kurdish refugees into Turkey only stood to intensify their rebellion against Ankara's rule. America could not ignore Turkey, a NATO ally. Nor could the other members of the Atlantic alliance sit idly by as Turkey plunged into turmoil.

Washington, London, and Paris stretched the interpretation of the Security Council's Resolution 688, which called for the Iraqi despot to cease brutalizing the nation's populace. They implemented a "no-fly" zone along the northern tier of Iraq above the country's thirty-sixth parallel. Their aircraft patrolled and blocked Iraqi planes from this so-called northern zone, rending the population safe from aerial assault. Then the Pentagon initiated Operation Provide Comfort in northern Iraq by deploying lightly armed infantry and CIA agents. These actions had the effect of fostering safety and, in time, a measure of Kurdish autonomy within the Republic of Iraq. During the 1990s, the semiautonomous domain strengthened economically and sprouted a fledgling democracy. Kurdistan, as it became called, represented a departure from the planned US disengagement from Iraq after the Gulf war. It also constituted an unsung American success story by nurturing democratic reform and economic development among five million

Kurds. America's Kurdistan policy amounted to a bridge between Bush Sr.'s unsentimental Metternichean realism and balance of power stratagem and Bush Jr.'s sweeping Wilsonian democracy-promotion efforts that came in the wake of the Iraq War.

In Iraq's south, the White House decided against replicating a protectorate among the majority Shia population. But along with Britain and France, the United States did set up a southern "no-fly" zone below the thirty-second parallel in August 1992. Later it extended the zone another degree (to the thirty-third parallel) almost to Baghdad. The Western allied flyovers, nonetheless, lent no protection to the Shiite inhabitants on the ground, thousands of whom were killed by Hussein's soldiers and police or fled to Iran. Tehran, for its part, capitalized on the presence of the Iraqi dissidents by making them beholden to the Islamic Republic. After Hussein was ousted in the American invasion during George W. Bush's presidency, the Iraqi Shia returned home. Some entered politics, and others planted roadside bombs against US and coalition troops.

The twin no-fly corridors culminated in lengthy, expensive, and intrusive operations inside Iraq proper until the start of the Iraq War. Together with British and French warplanes, American pilots flew nearly daily sorties to police the two "no-flight" zones. Later, France dropped out of the aero-triumvirate over the southern zone. Paris disapproved of the Anglo-American air bombardment, Operations Desert Fox, in December 1998. The United States and Britain staged that attack to convince Hussein to halt his obstruction of the UN weapons inspectors, as subsequently will be described. Thereafter, Anglo-American pilots alone carried out the air mission that recorded numerous strafing attacks on Iraqi air defense sites and other targets. No allied planes were lost, but Iraq's missile radars frequently "locked on" in preparation for launching a surface-to-air missile at the aircraft overhead. By the time the flyover operations came to an end in 2003, some 350,000 sorties had been flown at an estimated cost of $11.5 billion in 2011 dollars.[29]

The allied-established air-exclusion strips within Iraq's north and south became the thin edge of a wedge into the Gulf nation. The intrusion was aimed at Iraq's disarmament in addition to protection of Kurds. Operating through the United Nations, the United States and its coalition partners imposed a stringent inspection regime to uncover any WMD sites. The air strikes formed the enforcement mechanism of the UN hunt for Iraq's elicit facilities. Security Council Resolution 687 imposed on Iraq the conditions that it must destroy and remain free of WMD. As the price for the armistice, Iraq agreed to UN weapons inspections, a provision it lost little time in spurning. Because of Washington's disenchantment with the IAEA for its inability earlier to expose Iraq nuclear plants, it turned to the United Nations. Under Security Council auspices, a separate inspection team, United Nations Special Commission (or UNSCOM), was formed. Hussein placed roadblocks to impede UNSCOM, leading to persistent friction with the United States.

To rid itself of the troublesome Saddam Hussein, Washington turned to covert operations to oust the dictator and replace him with an Iraqi president friendlier to American interests, even if not a genuine democratic leader. This CIA operation attempted without success to foment palace coups or outright military-style takeovers. The US Congress appropriated $40 million toward the clandestine effort.[30] Only once did the CIA operatives come close to what might have been a successful plot. But officials in the first Clinton administration pulled the plug fearful of another Bay of Pigs fiasco, which embarrassed President John Kennedy when Fidel Castro trounced the ragtag Cuban exiles on the landing beach in 1961.[31] Internal takeover schemes foundered, too. Unrelated to US intrigues, scores of would-be Iraqi presidents plotted to depose Hussein but wound up going to the wall themselves.

In sum, President Bush put in place a robust containment strategy with four main elements: (1) no-fly zones policed by US, British, and French warplanes; (2) UN-mandated economic sanctions; (3) UN-conducted WMD inspections; and (4) an American-run covert operation to rid Iraq of Hussein. Each failed to chasten or oust the wily Iraqi autocrat. In fact, Hussein tested Bush one last time before the retiring president left the White House. Hussein blocked the UNSCOM inspections as a way to lift the UN embargo. The United States went to the Security Council, which responded by declaring Iraq in "material breach" of Resolution 687, the "cease-fire" resolution embodying the sanction regime. Then, Bush struck back by ordering a large-scale air strike flown by American, British, and French warplanes in mid-January 1993. Following three days of punishing bombardment, Hussein backed down and let the weapons inspectors resume their search. This punitive action along with the elder George Bush's other approaches set the course for the incoming administration.

Clinton's Dual Containment

America was already locked firmly into a hostile containment policy with Iraq when Bill Clinton settled into the White House in January 1989, after defeating George H. W. Bush's reelection bid. President Clinton's secretary of state, Madeleine Albright, later recounted in her autobiography, "Of all the headaches inherited by the Clinton administration, Saddam Hussein was the most persistent."[32] Despite the usual policy reviews ordered up by an incoming administration, the White House stuck to the previous government's line toward Iraq. The Clinton officials concluded that an alternative approach, say engaging the despot in discussions, was fruitless. Hussein was too far beyond the pale of reasonableness.

Indeed, besides just containing Iraq, some top-level foreign policy hands argued that active measures should be advanced to destabilize Hussein. Only an internally orchestrated ouster of the autocrat would solve America's Iraq problem. Since Hussein had sworn internal enemies and envious generals in his entourage, a coup was not out of the question. No one believed a Jeffersonian democrat would take over, but a more stable figure on horseback might be a step toward a less warlike and erratic rogue entity. As time wore on, an assassination or military takeover looked more remote.[33]

Without other options, the Clinton government followed in its predecessors' footsteps. It kept in place the economic and arms control sanctions that denied Iraq international economic and diplomatic intercourse. It backed UNSCOM's weapons inspections. Just like Bush, Clinton continued aggressive air patrols in the no-fly zones and resorted to muscular aerial assaults on occasion. In time, White House labeled this approach as "containment plus," but in reality it copied the Bush initiatives. The Clinton administration reasoned that such a policy might undermine Hussein over time. But if it did not rid the country of its tyrant, at least this posture allowed the Clinton policy makers the freedom to pursue globalization, peace in the Middle East, and strengthening the American domestic economy, while decreasing the defense budget.

By containing Iraq, the Clinton foreign policy team was left with no nearby counterbalance to the Islamic Republic of Iran. As a consequence, the White House inaugurated its "dual-containment" strategy to bottle up both Iraq and Iran with deterrence and sanctions. Unlike the preceding Reagan and Bush administrations, Clinton chose not to use Hussein to check the ayatollah regime. Such a course ensured that the United States must maintain a large military "footprint" in the Persian Gulf with an eye to Iran as well as Iraq. So the US military stockpiled arms and garrisoned bases in the Persian Gulf.

Not long after coming to office, President Clinton faced an acute provocation from Saddam Hussein. According to US intelligence, the Baath Party's General Intelligence Department, the Mukhabbarat, set its sights on assassinating former president George H. W. Bush during a visit to Kuwait to commemorate the second anniversary of the sheikdom's liberation by the US-led coalition. Kuwaiti authorities foiled the car-bombing plot just before Bush arrived in the capital and implicated Mukhabbarat agents in the scheme. The CIA and the FBI later studied the Kuwaiti evidence and concluded they had an open-and-shut case against the Iraqis. Clinton's most senior officials debated the appropriate retaliation.[34] US warships fired 23 Tomahawk cruise missiles at the Mukhabbarat headquarters, razing it to the ground. Since the attack came in the dead of night, wags quipped that only cleaning ladies fell victim to the American projectiles. Given the gravity of the Iraqi attempt, the tepid response betrayed a certain force-aversion stance on the part of the Clinton White House.[35]

The US-Iraqi relations stayed tense after the assassination plot. But the White House was distracted by other crises, such as in Somalia, Haiti, North Korea, and the Balkans. Thus, it placed its chips on sanctions, on UNSCOM to uncover any Iraqi unconventional weapons, and on sporadic air strikes to keep Hussein on the defensive. The far-reaching damage wrought by the internationally imposed economic blockade was not fully comprehended until after the Iraq War. Iraq's infrastructure and oil industry lacked not only new technological investments but also adequate spare parts and maintenance to continue the flow of water, electricity, hospital services, and crude—the country's chief revenue-producing export. Deterioration, underinvestment, and malfeasance together with the international economic sanctions left Iraq impoverished before US troops marched into the country in 2003.

Although beleaguered, Iraq found ways to elude its economic isolation. Entrepreneurial Iraqis managed to circumvent the economic restrictions by smuggling oil northward through Kurdish territory to sell in Turkey or southward down the Shatt al-Arab waterway to the Persian Gulf and over to Iran. Saddam Hussein also cheated on the United Nations with the compliance of at least one of its high officials. To alleviate suffering of ordinary Iraqi citizens, the New York–based organization unveiled its oil-for-food program in 1996. This relief project allowed the Iraqi government to sell oil for funds strictly used to purchase food and medical supplies for its destitute populace. The Iraqi tyrant deceitfully garnered $1.8 billion in kickbacks and surcharges on the oil sales and purchase of humanitarian goods from over 2,000 companies and individuals in 66 countries. The revelations and investigation in 2005 tarnished the UN's reputation.[36]

Saddam Hussein's Resurrection

Years before the UN report revealed Iraq's fraudulent practices, Saddam Hussein established an unenviable record for troublemaking and egregious international behavior. To protest the UN sanctions and UNSCOM's weapons inspections in 1994, he unfurled war flags by barreling his armored tanks right up to the Kuwait border, seemingly in a reprise of his 1990 invasion. When the Clinton White House dispatched 30,000 troop reinforcements, 300 airplanes, and an aircraft carrier battle group, Hussein backed down and returned his Republican Guards to the barracks. Then in 1996, the Iraqi dictator seized on a political division among the Kurdish political movements. He ordered his Republican Guards into the northern reaches of the country. There, they crushed the Kurds' feeble resistance, chased out the CIA operatives, and shot some 200 fighters in an American-backed Kurdish rebel militia before retreating.

President Hussein's boldness strengthened his internal grip and restored his standing in the broader Middle East for having dealt a blow to US prestige by uprooting its toehold in Kurdistan. Like other rogue despots, he resorted to provocations against foreign powers to shore up his internal legitimacy. By standing up to the United States and also championing the Palestinian cause, Hussein deftly turned the tables on the Clinton White House. America appeared the overweening intruder in the Middle East, and Iraq materialized in the popular imagination as its defender. The Washington-pushed UN sanctions were held responsible for malnutrition and even starvation of Iraq's men, women, and children in the hundreds of thousands. Soon, America's applauded liberation of Kuwait was forgotten, as was Hussein's widely unpopular seizure of the Gulf kingdom. Such are the vicissitudes of the Middle East, where heroic and wicked feats flicker and die quickly.

American frustration with Iraq's hamstring of UNSCOM was not confined to the executive branch. The Republican-controlled Congress blamed President Clinton for irresolution and outsourcing American security to the UN weapons inspectors. Taking the initiative, Capitol Hill passed a bipartisan Iraq Liberation Act of 1998. This legislation encompassed four main provisions. It endorsed the removal of Saddam Hussein from power, provided funds to set up a Radio Free Iraq, reaffirmed demands for Hussein's trial before an international tribunal, and authorized $97 million to arm and equip an internal Iraqi opposition to oust the autocrat. The passage of the bill drew vast support in the House and unanimous consent in the Senate. By signing the bill on October 31, Bill Clinton made it the law of the land to oust Hussein; but he had spent less than $3 million (mostly for office supplies) of the legislated funds by the time he left office.

For his part, Hussein was unimpressed by Washington's legislation. The Iraqi president threw up more roadblocks to UNSCOM. Specifically, he expelled American members of the inspection team as spies when it came to light that some cooperated with the CIA. Finally, his on-again, off-again cooperation with UNSCOM infuriated the inspection chief, Richard Butler.

The former Australian diplomat yanked out the UNSCOM inspectors in autumn 1998. Later, his book outlined the UN failures and the likely costs of a nuclear-armed Iraq for world safety.[37]

Fed up by Hussein's cat-and-mouse ploys, Washington and London launched Operation Desert Fox, a four-day heavy-bombing campaign in December 1998. This punishing air attack was the largest such bombardment since George H. W. Bush's farewell military action in mid-January 1993. In the estimation of the commander of Central Command, US Marine General Anthony Zinni, Desert Fox greatly damaged 74 percent of the 111 targets. It unleashed 325 cruise missiles. Anglo-American warplanes flew 650 sorties into Iraq and unloaded ordinance on airfields, barracks, communication centers, and suspected WMD sites.

Speaking from the Oval Office as the allied warplanes struck Iraqi installations, Bill Clinton laid out his reason for the air strike as a defense for UNSCOM. His comments about Hussein's unrelenting pursuit of nuclear, chemical, and biological megadeath weapons presaged his successor's justifications for invasion a few years later. Clinton asserted that "some day, make no mistake, he will use it [WMD] again as he has in the past." Then the American president mentioned the regime-change theme that also formed so much of George W. Bush's subsequent policy. Clinton argued that the best way to eliminate Hussein's persistent threat "was with a new Iraqi government."[38]

Desert Fox marked Washington's most intense militarized putsch to displace Hussein by destroying elements of his armed forces until the Iraq War. Thereafter, President Clinton reverted to containment alone and to working through the United Nations, despite his tough talk. The White House occupant declared that international pressure paired with internal opposition forces would secure "Iraq a government worthy of its people."[39] The presidential bombing and aggressive declaration served to unite the executive and legislative branches in a forward policy pitted against the Iraqi regime. Madeleine Albright selected Frank Ricciardone as the special coordinator for the transition in Iraq. Less formally, the career foreign service officer was dubbed the so-called "czar for overthrowing Saddam." Ricciardone energetically took up his task, but he soon clashed with exiled Iraqi political figures and with resistance from Egypt and the United Arab Emirates. Except for the work of a handful of Clinton's middle-level appointees, the anti-Hussein enterprise languished. Bill Clinton realized that rousing the American people to the task of regime change in Iraq demanded the expenditure of considerable political capital. He decided instead to follow the lines of least resistance rather than rallying the nation for an uncertain course.

Other factors worked for the abandonment of a muscular approach toward the Republic of Iraq. The 1999 bombing campaign against Serbia over the Kosovo province's bid for independence from Belgrade proved prolonged and less effectual than anticipated. It demonstrated the limits of airpower alone to compel Serbia to give up Kosovo. The threat of NATO ground forces finally convinced Slobodan Milošević that his political survival demanded he cut a deal with the United States and its NATO allies. If Milošević could hold out for nearly three months, how much more stubborn would Hussein be? It was a question with an unknown and possibly risky answer. The Kosovo air war gave Clinton officials second thoughts about repeating such an effort in the Middle East.

European goodwill toward the United States, moreover, receded as the 1990s lengthened. The evaporation of the Soviet Union's decades-long threat meant also the rapid dissipation of Europe's gratitude toward and dependence on the United States for its defense. For the first time since 1945, Europeans had the luxury of openly disagreeing with Washington over policy, especially a militarized approach. In the Middle East, the ending of the Soviet presence also allowed moderate Arab governments to breathe easier. Additionally, the buildup of US military might in the Persian Gulf caused unease and problems for governments, whose citizens disliked American forces in close proximity to Islam's two most holy shrines in Mecca and Medina. From many quarters then, the American footprint ran up against firm opposition. To point out one measurable index, the United States mustered an allied coalition of 34 nations against Iraq in the course of Persian Gulf War. But only Britain teamed up with the United States seven years later in Operation Desert Fox.

Domestic considerations also tempered the White House's approach toward the Hussein regime. President Clinton faced opposition from his own party for even maintaining the economic sanctions on Iraq. Seventy-five congressional members wrote the president in early 2000, imploring him to drop the embargo because it deprived ordinary Iraqis of access to food and medical treatments. Clinton was also sensitive to economic concerns. The global economic expansion spiked the demand for crude production. Oil prices jumped upward. The West Wing recoiled at the prospect of a disruption in the flow of petroleum from Iraq and the greater Middle East as a result of US military operations. So the United States stuck with its containment-plus policy toward an increasingly self-confident, even hubristic Saddam Hussein, who believed the political winds blew at his back. The routine Anglo-American air patrols went forward, although as the American 2000 presidential election loomed, the Pentagon reduced the frequency of air-to-ground strafing. It feared the loss or capture of allied crews in the sensitive political environment.

As the national election neared, the Clinton administration also ratcheted back on UN weapons inspections. By the end of August 2000, the White House executed a U-turn in the Security Council by joining the positions of its three main opponents. They opposed vigorous WMD inspections within Iraq. Largely for commercial reasons, France, China, and the Russian Federation had long objected to UNSCOM. After the harassed UNSCOM pulled out of Iraq, the United States insisted on the formation of a new inspection team. Under the former Swedish official, Hans Blixer, the Security Council formed the UN Monitoring and Verification Commission (UNMOVIC). Now, as his presidential term ran out, President Clinton joined with his critics and cancelled the announcement that UNMOVIC was ready to resume inspections. Not until George W. Bush took over the presidency did UNMOVIC deploy to Iraq.

By the time Bill Clinton departed from the White House, Iraq had broken free of its isolation. Hugo Chavez, the populist president of an increasingly troublesome Venezuela, visited Baghdad in his capacity as the chairman of the Organization of Petroleum Exporting Countries (OPEC) in August 2000. Chavez's visit defrosted OPEC's relations with Iraq and shattered the air embargo surrounding Iraq. In his wake, other foreign leaders and international officials flew into Baghdad, inaugurating "air diplomacy." Washington simply accommodated itself to the changed circumstances by letting commercial jets fly through the "no-fly" zones. Arab and European capitals pushed to end Iraq's pariah status.

Washington stood by helplessly while the Middle East states reversed their prior aversion to the Kuwait-conquering Iraqis. Even Saudi Arabia joined Egypt in inviting Saddam Hussein to an emergency summit in Cairo on October 21–22, 2000, to address the outbreak of Palestinian violence against Israel after the collapse of the Camp David peace talks. Including Hussein proved more important to Arab unity than remembering a ten-year-old Iraqi invasion of Kuwait. Hussein's representative conveyed his president's call for a jihad against Israel and reminded his listeners of Iraq's financial aid to the Palestinian cause over the years. By this time, most Arab states had already restored diplomatic relations with Baghdad. Iraq's neighbors also either facilitated or turned a blind eye to the illegal export of Baghdad's oil and the import of goods to the formerly ostracized country. Hussein spent the skimmed-off profits from many crude sales to finance terrorism in Iraq's own camps, among Palestinian groups, and possibly in the Philippines to the al-Qaeda-linked Abu Sayyaf terrorist network.[40]

Keeping Hussein in his box faltered as an American strategy to deal with Iraq. Even the hot containment of air-to-ground missiles seemed destined to fail. The Hussein government claimed American and British warplanes killed some 300 Iraqis in the 18 months after Desert Fox in late 1998. It further charged that pilots deliberately courted radar surveillance and ground missiles for a pretext to return fire disproportionately. Finally, it accused the Anglo-American warplanes of deliberately strafing mosques and people going about their lives. The slippage in oil sanctions, endurance of the regime, and its breakout from diplomatic isolation rendered the air-to-ground strikes as singularly punitive and unmoored to comprehensive and overall effective policy. Indeed, one pundit labeled the practice the "fire-and-forget foreign policy" after the missiles that are satellite guided to their targets after the pilot pushes the button.[41]

Containment plus, moreover, drew ever-sharper protests from European, Saudi Arabian, and Turkish capitals. The governments took issue with the heavy costs to Iraqi civilians by the economic sanctions as well as the air strikes. For the United States, the costs associated with the air war were sustainable but not miniscule; they included $2 billion yearly, 200 aircraft, and 25 naval ships in the Persian Gulf. The presence of US warships in Gulf waters also heightened tensions with Iran. Tehran lashed out at Washington for stationing its navy in what it regarded as a Persian lake.

The air bombardments of a nation not at war with the United States presented one of the rarest examples in history of the pursuit of relentless military operations in the time of nominal peace. For 12 years, American and British jets swept Iraqi planes from their skies and bombed at will a sovereign state in the name of containment and under UN auspices. This policy differed markedly from the Cold War containment doctrine of sanctions, diplomatic pressures, and defensive alliances. Only Iraq's quintessential rogue nature and America's superpower standing lifted constraints on US militarized diplomacy. Conditions within the region and outside, however, were shifting rapidly away from the status quo. By the time President Clinton left office, Hussein was virtually out of his box and containment plus looked as if it was headed for the history books.

George W. Bush and the Iraq War

A shift in presidential administrations in the United States did not initially announce a new strategy to deal with Iraq. When George Walker Bush ascended to the presidency in January 2001, he strode at first in the footsteps of his predecessors on Iraq policy. For instance, the new secretary of state, Colin Powell, went to the United Nations to advocate "smart sanctions" strictly applied to conventional arms and WMD that were less onerous to the average Iraqi. Russian opposition in the Security Council scuttled the revamped sanction proposal. The Kremlin hoped to collect Soviet-era debts from Baghdad, pin down lucrative oil contracts, and resume exporting weaponry to its former trading partner.[42] In her oft-scrutinized *Foreign Affairs* article, Condoleezza Rice wrote that rogue states like North Korea and Iraq lived on "borrowed time, so there need be no sense of panic about them." The soon-to-be national security adviser advocated "classical" deterrence to deal with them, not invasion.[43] Indeed, Rice came to Washington focused on big power relations, not rogue states.

But other self-proclaimed Vulcans (Bush's top foreign policy advisers) in the new government harbored long hostility to Saddam Hussein and insisted passionately on his removal from power. For these officials, Iraq flashed incessantly on their policy radar screens.[44] They along with likeminded commentators wrote and spoke fervently about the shortcomings of the Clinton administration's Iraq policy. Some favored covert operations to subvert the Iraqi dictator, and others advocated more overt means to bring him down.[45] They shared the assumption that Saddam Hussein posed a crystallizing threat to the region and ultimately to American interests. Among the most hawkish was Paul Wolfowitz, the Pentagon's deputy secretary, who cast himself in the reincarnation of the ancient Roman senator Marcus Porcius Cato, who ended his speeches with the phrase "Carthage must be destroyed." Wolfowitz figuratively urged that Iraq be leveled and salted, not Carthage. Toppling the regime came first.[46] Even George Bush spoke out against Iraq in a preinauguration interview: "Saddam Hussein must understand that this nation is very serious about preventing him from the development of weapons of mass destruction."[47]

The Iraq hawks—such as Vice President Dick Cheney, Defense Secretary Donald Rumsfeld, and, of course, Wolfowitz—fed on reports about Saddam Hussein's WMD quest. One of these warnings came improbably from the Clinton administration's outgoing secretary of defense, William S. Cohen. Days before leaving the Pentagon, Cohen released an intelligence report, warning that Iraq had rebuilt its weapons infrastructure and possessed several factories suspected of producing chemical and biological weapons. These plants had ostensibly commercial purposes, but all had been previously involved in producing chemical and biological agents. The January 10 report noted the resumption of work at the suspected chemical and biological plants since UNSCOM left the country in 1998.[48] As the new administration settled into office, this anti-Hussein predisposition initially loomed in the background until after the 9/11 terrorist attacks.[49]

Prior to hijacked-plane crashes into the Pentagon and the Twin Towers in New York, "the Bush administration turned out to be not too dissimilar to the Clinton administration in its final days," wrote Kenneth Pollack, a former Clinton official.[50] Policy differences about how to handle Iraq produced drift as they had in the preceding presidency. Other crises eclipsed the Hussein headache as well. Over the course of the eight months before the 9/11 attacks, the fledgling Bush presidency pushed an active Iraq agenda decidedly to the back burner. The urgent problems—tax cuts, corporate scandal, the Hainan incident with China, and the $8 billion emergency bailout to Argentina's economy—crowded out action on Iraq, even had the foreign policy team agreed on a coherent policy. Since Powell's setback on "smart sanctions" in the Security Council, the White House focused on the tidal wave of other issues until the September 11 terrorist attacks.

The March to War

The horrific 9/11 terrorism transformed the Bush presidency. In slightly over 90 minutes, the al-Qaeda terrorists razed to the ground the 110-storied World Trade Center's Twin Towers, ripped off a face of the Pentagon, and crashed a passenger jet into the Pennsylvania countryside. Nearly three thousand people died as four American commercial planes functioned as high-octane-filled missiles in the hands of 19 Arab suicide bombers. America was under attack by a shadowy terrorist network that professed a hyper-radicalized interpretation of Islam. The overpowering impact of al-Qaeda's "planes operation" revolutionized the White House's thinking about US foreign policy toward Iraq as well as Afghanistan. The American counterattack against al-Qaeda's headquarters in Afghanistan was predictable, expected, and justifiable under established international law. The Iraq War, however, was hatched inside a White House engulfed by a war psychosis that clouded judgments and decision making.

Iraq, for its part, was hardly a pacific actor. Its record of two invasions into Iran and Kuwait made neighbors wary. Saddam Hussein's use of chemical weapons against Iranian troops and his own Kurdish population kept fears alive of a reprise. His lengthy registry of murdered opponents, rivals, and thousands of innocents rendered him monstrously evil.

Three weeks before George W. Bush took office, President Hussein held a provocative four-hour military parade through Baghdad's streets, showing off one thousand new and refurbished Russian-made tanks, new surface-to-air missiles, and jet fighters that flew overhead. In the reviewing stand, the autocrat fired a rifle into the air and uttered inflammatory vaporings.

Not long afterward, Hussein rolled the Republican Guard's Hammurabi Division right up to the Jordan border in an effort to intimidate Israel as it reeled under the suicide bombings of the second *infitada* (Palestinian uprising). But it was in Hussein's flirtations with biological and nuclear weapons that he unwittingly crossed a red line with the Bush administration. He overplayed his hand and virtually invited his own downfall by bluffing Iran and the world about Iraq's WMD capabilities.

Six weeks after the Afghanistan war began with an air bombardment on October 7, 2001, George Bush revealed his warlike intentions toward Iraq to his secretary of defense. After a White House briefing, Bush asked Donald Rumsfeld to start military plans against the Middle Eastern country. From that Thanksgiving order until the Iraq War, the Pentagon laid war plans, prepared military forces, and deployed ships, planes, and army and marine units in the Persian Gulf theater. President Bush, like his father's runup to the Persian Gulf War, barreled down two tracks—one political and the other military. While the military preparations leapt ahead, Washington beat the war drum domestically and overseas. George Bush Jr. reversed his father's political strategy; he built domestic support for a conflict and then tried to nail down international backing rather than the other way around. In his State of the Union address on January 29, 2002, President Bush exclaimed his memorable characterization of the rogue states of Iraq, Iran, and North Korea as an "axis of evil, arming to threaten the peace of the world." He declared, in effect, a call to arms with his pronouncement, "I will not wait on events, while dangers gather."[51]

As military preparations quickened, the White House hammered out a doctrine for preventive war. George Bush unveiled it in his West Point commencement address on June 1, 2002. Facing the graduating cadets, he stressed the danger of waiting while nuclear threats "fully materialize" and avowed that America would take "preemptive action when necessary."[52] His comments presaged the "strike-first" manifesto of his National Security Strategy statement in late September that set forth the formula for preventive war, with Iraq as the first road test for the controversial doctrine. The administration's public case for a ground invasion got a boost from the British as well as the American intelligence communities.

Britain's prime minister, Tony Blair, released an intelligence "white paper" with the sensational claim that Iraq was making progress in developing WMD weaponry. At the end of the report, Blair posited, "The policy of containment is not working."[53] The London dossier backstopped the US National Intelligence Estimate (NIE), which concluded that Iraq had biological weapons and stockpiles of chemical agents. Fears also lurked in the halls of power that Iraq was bent on acquiring nuclear arms. As a summation of the American intelligence community's 16 agencies, the NIE carried great weight in Congress and public opinion. Two years later, the presidential Commission on Intelligence Capabilities of the United States Regarding Weapons of Mass Destruction bluntly stated, "These assessments were wrong."[54] The grossly erroneous reports, however, shaped the national discourse in a prowar direction throughout late 2002 and into the next year. War with Iraq was packaged to the American public as a necessary antiproliferation conflict. Possession of nuclear arms constituted its casus belli.[55]

The White House went on the offensive to gain congressional votes on a war resolution. It briefed House and Senate members. President Bush made the case for invasion of Iraq in speeches to lift poll numbers in his cause. His campaign culminated in a presidential address in Cincinnati that announced that Iraq "could have nuclear weapons in less than a year."[56] The publicity push worked. One poll on the eve of the war reported 71 percent of Americans backed the White House's war on Iraq.[57] Congress joined the bandwagon in authorizing the commander-in-chief to employ military force against Iraq. Later, after the war in Iraq worsened, many representative and senators, particularly those running for the presidency, claimed the White House lied to them. The president's aides maintained that they had the same intelligence as George Bush.

Internationally, the United States encountered tougher sledding to persuade the Security Council to go along with its war plans. Only Britain sided with Washington. The other three permanent members—France, Russia, and China—opposed military action. Each had economic reasons to maintain the status quo with Iraq. But each also genuinely feared the instability that an invasion and ouster of Saddam Hussein would bring to the region. They wanted proof positive of Iraq's cheating on UN disarmament resolutions.

Opposing some of his fellow cabinet members, Secretary of State Powell convinced the president and his reluctant security advisers to endorse a Security Council resolution to send UNMOVIC into Iraq to conduct a weapons search. UNMOVIC entered the Republic of Iraq on November 18, 2002. Until mid-March, it scoured suspected labs and plants for biological, chemical, and nuclear arms. In the end, Powell's compromise settled nothing. No WMD was uncovered. Yet the Bush administration pressed ahead full-throttle for an attack. The Security Council never voted on the second resolution that Powell's negotiations secured. The United States decided that it lacked the needed votes among the members and so never went back to the Security Council for an authorization to use "all necessary means" (i.e., war).[58] With an ad hoc coalition of allies, Washington attacked without a UN resolution.

The End of a Rogue Regime

America embarked on a military invasion, occupation, and regime change in Iraq on March 19, 2003. Operation Iraqi Freedom deployed 137,000 US forces and eventually almost 50,000 troops from a "coalition of willing" international partners. This massive full-scale assault differed markedly from American policy toward the other rogue states, such as North Korea, Iran, or Libya before it surrendered its WMD. Only Afghanistan, which will be discussed in the last chapter, underwent a similar but initially much smaller scale US intervention for its basing al-Qaeda within the mountainous nation. The Bush government premised the Iraqi attack mainly on suspected WMD facilities. No nuclear-arming facilities were found on Iraqi real estate, although speculation still exists that some nuclear equipment was smuggled into Syria just prior to the US invasion.[59] The execution of the antiproliferation campaign, therefore, stumbled badly in the Gulf nation. The Bush administration thereupon emphasized democracy promotion and eradication of suspected but never conclusively proved Hussein links to al-Qaeda.[60]

After the three-week "shock and awe" phase of the Iraq War, in which the US military smashed the hapless Republican Guards to smithereens, the conflict settled into protracted insurgency of roadside bombs, ambushes, and assassinations. It soon became apparent that Washington lacked sufficient boots on the ground to wage counterinsurgency warfare. Rather than a one-on-one guerrilla war between the US armed forces and Iraqi insurgents, the fighting descended to a near Hobbesian state of savage nature of all against all. The collapse of the Hussein police state unleashed paroxysms of hatred and violence across sectarian lines. The three major ethnoreligious communities killed one another in car bombings, suicide attacks, and gruesome torture chambers. The Shia and Sunni populations were the chief purveyors of bloody ethnic cleansing of each other's communities. Up north, the Kurds mostly stayed on sidelines of the Shia-Sunni battle except in the contested northern city of Mosul. The Kurds also cultivated strong ties to the American occupation in hopes of achieving their long-held desire for independence from the rest of Iraq. The Sunni and Shiite militias, when they were not murdering each other, attacked the US-led coalition forces, who attempted to pacify the land. The deaths and atrocities spread across the waist of the country, enflamed by the al-Qaeda in Iraq leader Abu Musab al Zarqawi, who oversaw the deaths of thousands of people.

Zarqawi's suicide car bombers destabilized Iraq as well as pitted Shia and Sunni against each other in a sectarian bloodbath. By late 2006, the Iraq War seemed lost beyond American retrieval.

In one last throw of the dice, George Bush doubled down with a "surge" of an additional 28,500 combat troops in and around Baghdad in a new counterinsurgency strategy under General David Petraeus. The military makeovers succeeded, to the surprise of most observers. The success came from a fortuitous shift within the Sunni community. It had grown weary of the puritanical restrictions imposed on them by al-Qaeda, which forbade alcohol, smoking, dancing, music, and even beard trimming. The constant violence sickened and worried the Sunnis as well. Sunni tribal chiefs also found their business activities crippled by al-Qaeda in Iraq.[61] These sheiks decided to throw in their lot with the Americans. General Petraeus and his local commanders embraced the tribal militias, put them on the payroll, and turned them against the al-Qaeda remnants. Gradually, the extraordinary violence dissipated. By 2008, only sporadic bombings took place.[62] While Americans shifted their gaze to domestic economic concerns before the November presidential elections, a plurality concluded that the Iraq War had been unnecessary or exorbitant in blood, tears, and treasure in the absence of any uncovered WMD stockpiles.

Still, despite all the reservations among the American electorate, the full story of post-Hussein Iraq is still being written. At the present time, some critics hold that Saddam Hussein's removal only strengthened his archrival, Iran, and placed other Arab states such as Saudi Arabia, Jordan, and the Persian Gulf emirates in political jeopardy from Iranian intrigues. There is more than an element of truth to this judgment. Balancing Iraq against Iran had been a Cold War policy practiced by the United States. Before Hussein's eviction, however, Iraq was hardly a reliable counterweight against Iran's Shiite revival and Persian expansion so characteristic of ayatollah Iran since 1979. Iraq was far too aggressive to perform the role of passive counteractor to Iran. Nor was Iraq particularly effective in this capacity. Even while Hussein ruled, the Iranian mullahs financed, armed, and trained terrorist networks such as Lebanon's Hezbollah and exported terrorism against American, Western, and Israeli targets. Moreover, Hussein, an inveterate troublemaker, added to the instability in the Middle East. Hussein's territorial provocations, terrorist sponsorship, and WMD plans stirred deep apprehension regionwide. Now for certain, Iraq is no longer a rogue state bent on manufacturing nuclear arms. In October 2011, President Barack Obama announced the total withdrawal of all US military forces out of Iraq by year's end. The White House decision meant, among other things, that the United States no longer perceived the Iraqi regime as a rogue threat.

President Bush's militarized regime-change and democratization exertions in Iraq will be the subject of future historical studies. Hussein's removal and Iraq's fledgling democracy did not necessarily herald the unmaking of several tyrants during the Arab Spring in 2011. These tyrannies may have fallen under their own deadweight. One fallen domino does not necessarily collapse a row. But the American invasion transformed the dynamics of the Middle East in ways still unknown at the present time. Historians and pundits will debate the relevance of Iraq's democracy in the Arab Spring for a long time. Was Iraq's democratic experiment catalytic? Or would the string of protests that toppled the dictatorial regimes in Tunisia, Egypt, and Libya have taken place anyway? Were the internal dynamics such that popular protests arose foreordained within repressive societies in Syria, Yemen, and Bahrain? The answers to these and related questions will preoccupy Middle East observers for years. Be that as it will, the Persian Gulf arena has been flung open for change by the US intervention.

If democracy triumphs in the greater Middle East over the next decades, then a peaceful and orderly outcome in this tumultuous region may assuage some of the criticism of George W. Bush's Iraq War. But his pugnacious formula is still unlikely to serve as a model for future presidents in dealing with rogue powers. Iraq's costly regime change and pacification almost ensures that similar wars will not be undertaken against other rogue nations. Materially, the Iraq War drained America, costing over 4,400 lives among US forces, 300-plus Coalition soldiers, and some $900 billion. On the other side of the ledger, over one hundred thousand Iraqis died in the American-led ground invasion and occupation.[63]

Some Observations on the Wages of the Iraq War

In spite of the high price paid by the United States and its allies for its pacification, Iraq experienced a rising number of bombings and shootings after the main combat contingent of US troops departed. The Iraq War did not demonstrate the absolute limits of American power to refashion societies, but the postinvasion phase certainly taxed it. It chastened Washington's governing class about the wisdom of large-scale land interventions into foreign lands. The Iraq War strained Euro-American relations and reinforced anti-Americanism among many people in the Middle East. It is argued that the war spared the United States another attack on its soil because would-be terrorists gravitated to Iraqi battlefields to conduct suicide bombings on US and coalition forces. But it is also argued that the Iraqi fighting generated even more converts to terrorism than would otherwise have been the case.[64]

Questions will not haunt just Bush's Iraqi policy. Barack Obama's rapid military abandonment of Iraq before 2012 will also come under scrutiny, especially if things go badly for Iraq or it slips into the center of a proxy conflict between Iran and Saudi Arabia.

In the future, America's policy will, almost out of necessity, revert either to containment, deterrence, and isolation or to diplomacy and engagement of rogue players. Although covert operations, or support for coups and insurgencies, are also an option for regime change in rogue entities, the success rate is too low to make it a viable alternative.[65] Instead, Washington will search for other than direct military operations, such as drone strikes and commando raids, as a consequence of expensive interventions into Iraq and Afghanistan. The Iraq War, while eliminating a rogue regime, imposes restraints on the future exercise of US military power.[66] Ironically, it may have made other rogue nations safer from American attack.

CHAPTER 3

Iran: Ace of the Axis of Evil

Powerful Iran is the best friend of the neighboring states and the best guarantor of regional security.

—Mahmoud Ahmadinejad

Shah is a kind of magic word with the Persian people.

—Shah Mohammed Reza Pahlavi

A decade before the Berlin Wall descended into fragments, Washington and Tehran were already locked into a life-and-death struggle in the Persian Gulf arena. The Islamic Republic of Iran through a blend of shrewd regional strategies, adroit application of terrorism, and religious fervor differed from the decayed communist regimes in North Korea and Cuba or the secular authoritarian governments in Iraq, Syria, and Libya. Except for North Korea, Iran shared a lengthier, more hostile history with the United States than the other major rogue states. But unlike its fellow rogues, Iran interpreted its venomous feud against the United States through a Manichaean prism. Other outlier regimes confronted the United States as a classic opponent to be diplomatically checked, strategically outflanked, and kept at bay in order to preserve their rule from international interference. By contrast, the religious clerics, who ousted the shah in 1979, played a violent chess game against the United Stated as they worked for the elimination of their arch nemesis from the Middle East and for a Pax Iranica over the Persian Gulf region.

Unlike North Korea, Syria, Cuba, or Iraq, the Islamic Republic of Iran was never a client or even semiclient of the Soviet Union. Its relations with Moscow, in fact, were often at daggers drawn. Indeed, until its Islamic revolution, Iran was closely aligned with the United States from almost the start of the Cold War. After the revolutionary birth of the Islamic Republic of Iran, American-Iranian relations soured overnight. Their mutual hostility spread beyond the respective governments to each country's citizenry. Iran's politico-religious revolution against the shah left it a "highly nationalistic country that sees itself as a symbolic beacon for global Islamic enlightenment."[1] Larger in area, more populated, better educated, and wealthier than its fellow rogue states and endowed with bountiful oil reserves, Iran presented a particularly nettlesome problem for the United States. Iran's religious-political revolution culminating in the rule of an Islamic theocracy gave the Persian Gulf nation a fervent dynamism different from its rogue cousins.

Iran's Shia branch of Islam deepened its divide with the surrounding Sunni Arab countries in the region. Not since the Bolshevik revolution in 1917 Russia and the Maoist victory in 1949 China had the world witnessed a similar ideological intensity from a nation's political upheaval. The reverberations from its Islamic revolution are still being felt within and outside the country. Its hegemonic ambitions evoke memories of the ancient Persian Empire among Iranian nationalists and Arab neighbors.

A Thumbnail Historical Sketch

The modern state of Iran is home to many ancient civilizations and empires. The Achaemenid Empire under Darius, for example, conquered Thrace and Macedonia in today's southeastern Europe. The Athenian Greeks defeated the Persians at the Battle of Marathon in 490 BC, but the conflict just marked another episode in the East-West duel.

Later, the Parthian Empire won victories over the eastward-bound armies of ancient Rome, a fact still celebrated by contemporary Iranians. Contemporaries also took pride in their forebears' contributions to architecture, art, and literature, especially poetry. The Arab Islamic conquest of Persia in the seventh century witnessed the displacement of its Zoroastrian religion, but the Persian languages survived. Attempts at Arabization of the Persians failed and catalyzed anti-Arab forces within the country to regain their independence and reassert their own cultural and spiritual identity.

The schism within Islam added to the apartness Shiite Iranians feel toward Middle Eastern states under Sunni domination. The 1,400-year, bitter and at times bloody rivalry between the two sects—tracing its roots to the deadly succession fight after the Prophet Muhammad—impacts the political antagonisms across the current greater Middle East. It plays a major part in explaining the Iraq-Iran War of the 1980s, the Sunni-Shiite tensions in today's Iraq and Lebanon, and the contemporary rivalry between Saudi Arabia and Iran. Iran's historical conflicts went well beyond its Persian Gulf rivals. It fought wars against Afghans, Turks, and Russians over the past hundreds of years.

In the twentieth century, Iran experienced profound modernizing currents leading to societal experiments and uneven advances with constitutional democracy, industrialization, national education, and countrywide railways and roads. Often, the state was at the head of reformist efforts to transform and modernize the society. Throughout Iranian history, outside powers have disrupted internal developments. The chaos following the constitutional revolution at the start of the new century fostered conditions conducive to Britain's interference. Soon after the Royal Navy's conversion to oil-powered warships (from coal-driven vessels) in 1912, the British cast covetous designs on Khuzestan province oilfields in southwestern Iran. Iranian oil, in fact, was the first found within the Middle East. After its discovery in 1908, Britain gradually assumed the position of the most dominant foreign power in Iran, while Russia carried out military operations in its northern belt against rebellious communities. The Iranian central government in Tehran, its capital, often exercised little control beyond its suburbs.

The fighting during World War I spilled into Iran as the Turks and their German allies battled Russians troops. Moscow's actions in northern Iran were terminated when the Bolsheviks came to power after the October Revolution in 1917 and pulled Russia out of the war. Afterward, the tide turned against Germany and Turkey, leaving Britain the predominant force in Iran. But a hard-pressed London lacked the resources or will to impose its rule on the chaotic Persian Gulf country. Instead of trying, the British man-on-the-spot, General William Ironside, handpicked an effective local soldier, Reza Khan, to command the British-trained Persian Cossacks.

It was an inspired decision, for Reza Khan marched 2,500 Cossacks into Tehran in early 1921, where he aided in the formation of a new government. Through a series of savvy political maneuvers and military campaigns against incorrigible tribes, Reza Kahn amassed power and allies over the years. In 1925, the Majles, or national assembly, deposed Ahmad Shah and his Qajar dynasty. Early the next year, the Majles crowned Reza Khan as shah and installed the new Pahlavi dynasty. The former army sergeant took the name Pahlavi because it referred to the Middle Persian language of the pre-Islamic era and thus resonated with Iranian nationalists, most of whom resented foreign meddling. The Majles endorsed Reza Kahn because it perceived him as a force for moving Iran toward "modernization, centralization, and strong government."[2]

America's role in this formative stage of a modern Iranian state was minimal but not totally absent. After the First World War, Woodrow Wilson's clarion call for a new international order based on the democratic principle of the self-determination of former colonies and conquered peoples resonated with Iranian nationalists. President Wilson's declaration of a new dispensation knocked the struts from beneath British and other colonial empires' rule over vast territories in Africa, Asia, and the Middle East. It encouraged Iran to see the United States as a friend among the world powers.

Iran's Reza Shah looked for political guidance from Kemal Ataturk, who transformed Turkey into a secular and modernizing state. Reza Shah set out to build a state-directed economy, centralizing government, modern road and railway network, and strong army, using authoritarian methods. Under his arbitrary rule, Iran's education program expanded with many new schools. Although Reza Shah never carried his Westernizing to the same degree as did Ataturk, he faced opposition from the Majles, which chafed under his high-handed dictates. The religious establishment also despised the shah's rulings for Western dress, which discarded the Islamic practice of women wearing veils. His repression alienated intellectuals and liberal-minded politicians. Reza Shah's need for revenues, however, compelled him to make concessions to the Anglo-Persian Oil Company. This surrender of the country's oil wealth angered nationalistic segments of the population.

The depth of Reza Shah's unpopularity coincided with the start of World War II. When Nazi German armies invaded Russia, the governments in Moscow and London joined briefly together to protect Iran from Berlin's possible subversion or attack. Britain worried mostly about the potential loss of Iranian oil and ultimately the security of the Suez Canal from Germany or the Soviet Union. Since the times of czarist Russia, Moscow held designs on Iran. In August 1941, Soviet troops invaded northern Iran, and British soldiers marched into the country from the south. They linked up in Tehran. The foreign intervention precipitated the abdication of the unpopular shah, who turned over the peacock throne to his son Mohammad Reza.

The Coup That Divided Two Countries

The new shah's enthronement nearly coincided with America's displacement of British and Soviet interference in Iran. The country had resented the inequitable agreements with the Anglo-Iranian Oil Company (or AIOC, renamed from the Anglo-Persian Oil Company), which disproportionately favored Britain. A more pressing predicament at war's end was the persistence of the Red Army on Iranian soil after the British troops departed. Washington and London pressured Moscow to withdraw its soldiers, which it did in May 1946. American influence, as a consequence, stood high among Iranians in the years immediately after the war. The United States cemented ties with the shah's government by training his army and posting technicians to Tehran to assist the country's development.

Increasingly, Iranians grew resentful about what they now perceived as American meddling at the very time when their own politics became wildly unsettled. Strident nationalism, agitation by the communist-oriented Tudeh Party, and assassination attempts on the shah led to political unsteadiness during the early 1950s. The various movements, whatever their place on the political spectrum, had in common a longing for a strong, vibrant Iran independent from foreign control. Iranians were particularly irked by the unfair distribution of oil monies under the AIOC arrangement and by the company's virtual state-within-a-state status in their country.

The Majles voted to nationalize Iranian oil and named Mohammad Mossadeq, a long-term proponent of Iran's national integrity and democracy, as prime minister in 1951. Once in office, Mossadeq moved to seize control of Iran's oil production. The British government retaliated by imposing economic sanctions, by reinforcing its naval squadron in the Persian Gulf, and by boycotting the sale of Iranian oil. When the United States joined with Britain in the boycott, it propelled the Gulf country into a financial crisis. Mossadeq stood his ground on the nationalization. Next the Majlis granted Mossadeq emergency powers to rein in the shah's prerogatives, place the army under parliamentary control, and redistribute land and wealth held by the upper classes. These measures alarmed Iran's privileged elite and army generals. Without subsidies from oil revenues, prices for basic items rose, and unemployment spread. As a consequence, Mossadeq lost support among average people along with governing strata. As Mossadeq's fortunes faltered, the political tide swept toward the Tudeh Party. All these political developments alarmed military officers, a group of which established a secret council to plot the ouster of Mossadeq and restore royal authority.

Before Mossadeq's ascendancy, America's role had been confined mostly to keeping the Soviet Union sidelined from Iran. Viewing the Tudeh Party as a Soviet front organization, President Dwight Eisenhower slipped CIA agents into the Iranian officers' council to help plan a coup against Mossadeq. These operatives gave out some advice and spent about $10 to $20 million that helped bankroll the overthrow, which initially failed. Three days after an abortive coup attempt, the Iranian military establishment struck again, this time successfully. The generals captured Mossadeq on August 19, 1953. The populist leader's removal enabled the shah to consolidate his reign and to entrench a royal dictatorship.

America's role in what was known as Operation Ajax was initially praised and damned as the first "United States paramilitary victory" in the Cold War era.[3] But many historians and neutral writers now conclude that Washington's part was more of a well-heeled but minor producer of an already underway show rather than that of an arch-director, as is so often depicted.[4] The Iranian generals hardly needed US coaching in how to rumble tanks up to the prime minister's residence. Besides, they had the backing of the *bazaaris* (merchants) and clergy. Reassurance from the United States and Britain to the coup's ringleaders provided them breathing room, but it was insufficient alone to motivate the plotters.[5]

Iranian reaction toward America's role, however murky, constituted another matter entirely. Animosity and humiliation burned deeply into the Iranian psyche. America's hand in the dispatch of Mossadeq and the strangling of his revolutionary program assumed an overarching dimension in the country's history with the passage of time. It is the origin of much of the "down with America" rhetoric that pulses through demagogic speeches at massed rallies convened to denounce the "Great Satan." In the minds of many Iranians, that American interference still lies at the root of all the country's problems over the past half century.[6]

From Policeman to Pariah

Before the vitriolic anti-US brew seeped into Iranian-American relations, the two countries forged exceedingly close bonds during the shah's reign. Mossadeq's unseating displaced the Soviet Union's influence in Iran and solidified American buttressing of the Pahlavi monarchy. But in the eyes of many, the United States resembled Britain's colonial interference. In the words of one historian, "The United States was Prince Charming no more."[7] For his part, Mohammad Reza Shah installed safeguards against a repetition of political dangers to his throne. He jailed, tortured, and executed members of the Tudeh Party and other radical opponents. His internal intelligence and security organization, widely known by its English-language acronym SAVAK, became a byword for repression. The shah entered into new business relationships with foreign companies to gain a larger share of the oil profits. His petroleum revenues rose hugely over the years, enabling him to buy weapons from abroad and to Westernize the ancient land, while also pocketing funds for his family and cronies.

From the US viewpoint, the shah was not a Prince Charming but rather Prince Valiant battling for the Western camp against the Soviet Union and its Middle Eastern allies. When the British withdrew from "East of Suez" in 1968, the United States filled the politico-military vacuum with a reliance on the peacock throne. A growing cross section of Iranians resented the shah's Western alignment and the large presence of American military experts to train his US-equipped armed forces. Conservative clerics and anti-Western circles detested the alien intrusion of some sixty thousand foreigners into Persian cultural and national life.

An even greater sense of alienation arose from the shah's pell-mell race toward modernity with a Western face to attain a "great civilization" and to reposition Iran among the world's front-rank states. Announced in 1963, his White Revolution initially concentrated on education and land reform. The redistribution of large landholdings to peasants fulfilled the political objective of reducing the power of the landed elite and introducing central authority into the countryside. Literacy also spread beyond urban centers. Female education, suffrage, and employment opportunities were expanded. The Iranian economy, fed by massive oil revenues, leaped ahead and with it rapid Westernization. But the top-down changes never reaped the political legitimacy that the shah pursued. Extravagance, corruption, and maladministration sapped his political standing. The shah and his family raked off the government revenues for private use. His officials also siphoned funds from businesses that needed licenses and contracts. The corrupt cronyism, political suppression, and objectionable reforms unsettled society and generated resentment, which the opposition tapped into to bring him down.

The United States unwittingly played a part in the downfall of its staunchest ally in the Persian Gulf. Washington leaned too heavily on its slender reed in Tehran to safeguard American interests in the Persian Gulf at a time when the shah faced an increasingly restive population. After the US military withdrawal from the Vietnam War in 1973, President Richard M. Nixon struggled to protect the country's growing dependence on Gulf oil. At the same time, America looked inward following the exertions in the controversial Southeast Asian conflict. In what became known as the Nixon Doctrine, Washington policy makers "reexamined the nature and extent of America's obligations under existing security agreements abroad" to determine whether others could share the burden.[8] Even though it was a global doctrine, the ramifications for pro-American Iran were devastating. To secure its energy interests in the Gulf, Nixon resorted to a "twin pillar" policy of relying on Iran and Saudi Arabia and selling them military hardware to guard against the Soviet Union's encroachments. To his own undoing, Mohammed Reza Shah reveled in his role of Gulf "policeman" for the United States.[9]

Accumulating grievances brought down America's stalwart regional cop. This fragmented anger and alienation from the monarchial regime were channeled into a political revolution by the rhetoric and charisma of Ayatollah

Ruhollah Khomeini. His uncompromising stand and skillful manipulation of the antishah sentiments united the opposition movements against the monarchy. Often exiled for his antishah stance, Khomeini gained credibility and loyal followers. One of his persistent themes was that the shah sold out the country to US interests. Without the Americans, Khomeini argued the shah would have fallen instead of Mossadeq. The shah's betrayal was seen as "tantamount to destruction of Iran's Islamic identity," as one scholar described.[10] Khomeini revolutionary tirades resonated among the population. He declared that an Islamic republic modeled on the Koran must be created and ruled by clerics. From Paris, the exiled ayatollah called for the toppling of the shah and the institutionalization of a government run by the *ulema* (the community of the clergy) in Iran.

Antiregime currents formed a powerful tide in 1978. The shah's half-hearted attempts to suppress street protestors backfired and strengthened the opposition. At the same time, President Jimmy Carter pressed the shah to relax his repressive measures. The monarchy complied, and Iran saw the opposition triumph.[11] By this time, the shah's prestige had reached a nadir. His policies alienated the *ulema*, the *bazaaris*, the educated middle class, and left-wing fronts, all of which reviled the monarchy. Muhammad Reza Shah abdicated in early 1979 and died a year later from cancer in Egypt. The Pahlavi dynasty was consigned to history and with it the close US alliance of over a quarter century.

The Iranian revolution then swerved from a budding democracy to a militant anti-American theocracy. Khomeini rushed from exile to fill the political vacuum. The religious establishment's consolidation of its power took the next two years and cost thousands of lives. In the end, the forces of extremist Shiism destroyed the constitutionalist movements bent on restoring a democratic parliamentarianism to the chaotic country. Khomeini's adherents formed an Islamic Republic Party. With its paramilitary Islamic Revolutionary Guards Corps (IRGC), the theocracy liquated its rivals. The radicals marginalized the moderates, shut down dissenting newspapers, and flipped SAVAK into the new regime's own repressive agency. By 1982, the ayatollahs and their military wing were ensconced in the near total power that they hold to this day. Afterward, the theocracy turned to the Islamization of society and the rupture of the country from international society. The Khomeinists envisioned the restoration of an Islamic society and hostility toward the United States, its way of life, and even the philosophy of the Enlightenment with its crass materialism, vulgar values, and secularism.

The Iranian religious establishment touted its theological-political revolution to Muslims around the world. For them, it provided an example of how to expunge Western culture through institutionalizing Khomeini's interpretation of Koranic teachings. According to Khomeini and his acolytes, the Shia branch of Islam, long persecuted by the larger Sunni community, revived at a propitious moment in Islamic history to confront the illegitimacy of secular governments. Internally, Khomeini's doctrine for the guardianship of the jurist (religious establishment)—*velayat-e faqih*—implied the recognition of him as supreme leader of the Shiite branch of Islam and of the Iranian people. Externally, the Khomeinists interpreted their revolution as the genesis of a broad Islamic revival with pan-Muslim objectives of revolt against secular Muslim rulers. Their appeal also incorporated the resonant themes of anti-Americanism and anti-Zionism.[12]

The Embassy Takeover and the Last Straw

America's "twin pillar" defensive strategy crashed after the shah departed from his throne. Iran fell precipitously from the American column of close allies to Washington's most venomous enemy. The precipitating action came with seizure of the US embassy in Tehran in November 1979. Radical Iranian students, blessed by the authorities, stormed the embassy and took hostage most of the staff. Ostensibly, the takeover of the American diplomatic mission stemmed from the Carter administration's granting the ailing shah entrance to the United States for cancer treatment. America, however, had been a target of Iranian protestors of many stripes since the Mossadeq coup. Weeks later, the hostage takers set free 13 women and the African American staff, but they kept the balance of the contingent. Their Iranian captors subjected the Americans to psychological torture and to the mental trauma of mock executions.

The lengthening standoff dismayed Washington, which looked impotent at home and abroad. The Iranian government's complicity in the capture of diplomatic property and abduction of the embassy staff members constituted a gross violation of international law. The Carter government protested far and wide but to no avail, revealing a defining castration for all to see. For Americans, the embassy takeover and hostage drama was one of the most wrenching episodes in the nation's history during the last quarter of the twentieth century. They were at once humiliated and outraged by the violation of the centuries-old principle that embassies enjoyed territorial sovereignty and diplomats benefited from immunity granted under international law.

The Iranians felt the seized embassy and hostages were a justifiable payback for America's role in the ousting of Mossadeq and in propping up the shah. Khomeini called the embassy an American spy den, where the United States was planning another coup to restore the shah. In reaction,

Washington applied sanctions on Iranian oil imports and froze the country's $8 billion in financial assets within the United States. As the hostage crisis received more distraught media coverage than any other event since World War II, it eroded Carter's political fortunes.[13]

The beleaguered Carter desperately rolled the dice on a military rescue mission, Operation Eagle Claw, on April 24, 1980. It failed abysmally, leaving the United States even more disgraced and pusillanimous. The US aircraft flew to a remote site, Desert One, where a helicopter crashed into a C-130 tanker plane, killing eight American servicemen and wounding several others. Additional mishaps marred the operation, and Carter abandoned it at the suggestion of the military commanders.[14] The failed raid represented a stinging setback for US prestige. It permanently blemished Carter's presidential legacy. The hostage crisis even played a part in Carter's loss to Ronald Reagan in the November 1980 presidential election. The Islamic Republic held 52 Americans in captivity for 444 days, finally freeing them on the day President Reagan stepped into the White House on January 20, 1981.

The Iranian hostage crisis marked *the* turning point in American-Iranian relations. It constituted a watershed demarcation that to this day afflicts the policies of both nations. The embassy takeover ushered in Iran's extreme hostility to the West in general and to the United States in particular. The upheaval also starkly dramatized the elimination of Tehran's dependence on Washington—one of the key goals of the Islamic revolution. Unlike Cuba, North Korea, or Iraq, the Islamic Republic of Iran eschewed the Soviet Union's circle, too. In the words of Khomeini, Iran's foreign policy was to be "neither East nor West."[15] The Islamic Republic's religiously inspired revolutionary fervor held no grace for the Soviets' godless communism. Iran's abundant oil wealth and its imperial impulses toward the Persian Gulf also made it an unlikely Soviet surrogate.

US-Iranian Skirmishes

The United States feebly retaliated against Iran. Yet the cycle of action and reaction that followed the hostage crisis deepened the two countries' mutual suspicion and antagonism toward each other. When Iraq started an eight-year war against Iran in September 1980, Washington gave modest backing to Saddam Hussein, who hoped to take advantage of Iran's internal divisions and capture its Khuzestan province's oil wealth. Instead, Iraq's invasion boomeranged. It inflamed Iranian nationalism, allowing Khomeini to cement his grip on power. The long war, in fact, drained both combatants in blood and treasure. For Iran, it fused the Shiite branch of Islam with Iranian patriotism and ensured the regime's survival.

The Iran-Iraq War also brought the United States into a shadowy conflict with Iran. Four years into the fighting, Saddam Hussein decided to expand military operations to the sea by closing off Tehran's oil shipments through the Persian Gulf. In March 1984, Hussein's air force began striking Iranian ships and foreign-flagged vessels carrying Iran's oil in order to strangle his enemy's economy. Iran counterattacked against oil tankers arriving and leaving Kuwaiti and Saudi Arabian ports, which transported Iraqi crude. Iran's IRCG prowled the Gulf and the Strait of Hormuz in small speedboats. They stopped and searched ships to uncover war materiel bound for Iraq. On other occasions, the Iranian crews launched outright rocket bombardments of suspected cargo transports. As its own tankers came under increasingly frequent assault, Iran retaliated against Kuwait's oil fleet because the small sheikdom financially backed wartime Iraq. The Kuwaiti government also opened its ports to Soviet weaponry destined for Iraqi forces.

The Kuwaiti emirate requested American assistance to fend off Iranian interference. In response, the Pentagon steamed warships to the Gulf and reflagged Kuwaiti vessels with the Stars and Stripes to afford them US protection. The Iranians were not deterred. They harassed oil tankers and American naval ships with go-fast boats that recklessly provoked incidents. From their shore, the Iranian gunners fired Chinese-made Silkworm missiles at patrolling US destroyers—an act of war that demanded the American Congress declare hostilities against Iran, had it known about the actions at the time.[16]

The naval engagements became known as the Tanker War. The United States and other oil importing states maneuvered warships into the Gulf to protect their oil tankers. The Reagan administration announced Operation Praying Mantis in early 1988 after an American missile destroyer struck an Iranian mine in international waters. When the Iranian navy opposed US warships, it lost a frigate, several smaller vessels, and two oil plaforms. It was the largest naval battle since World War II. Provoked by Iranian gunboats in July 1988, the USS *Vincennes*, an AEGIS-guided missile cruiser, aggressively steamed into Iran's territorial waters in the Straits of Hormuz. Sensing his ship under attack on July 3, the US commander ordered the firing of two missiles at what was perceived as an approaching Iranian warplane. In fact, the US missiles struck an Iranian commercial airliner, killing all 290 passengers on board. Needless to state, the Iranian government and people never accepted the United States' official explanation of the mistake. Indeed, the Iranian government and some independent observers charged that Washington deliberately covered up the shooting down of the Airbus A300 airliner by the "disastrously gun-ho commander" of the *Vincennes*.[17]

At the start of the Iran-Iraq War, the United States had first tried to dry up the supply of armaments to both sides in its Operation Staunch. But as the tide of battle seemed to flow toward Iran, Washington felt compelled to engage in a "limited form of balance-of-power policy" or "watch the Khomeini revolution sweep forward" to dominate the Persian Gulf.[18] The Reagan government extended $210 million in credits for Iraq to purchase American wheat and other foodstuffs. It also passed on satellite intelligence to Iraq, enabling it to anticipate Iranian ground attacks. While the United States harbored residual resentment against Iran for the embassy crisis, it also received fresh impetus for its anti-Iran stance from events within Lebanon.

Two attacks on Americans in the Levantine country deepened Washington's anti-Iranian outlook. First, Lebanese Shiites carried out a bombing of the US embassy in April 1983 that claimed 63 lives. Next, a martyrdom operation struck the US Marine Corps base in Beirut on October 23, 1983, that killed 241 US servicemen. President Reagan had deployed American troops in Lebanon as part of a multinational UN peacekeeping force along with French and Italian soldiers at the request of the Beirut government after Israel invaded the country in mid-1982. Washington perceived itself as a peacekeeper; but Iran, its coreligious surrogates among the local Shia, and other Lebanese parties believed the United States was anti-Muslim and pro-Israeli. The Iranian clerics appealed to their fellow Shia in Lebanon to resist the Israel presence and the US-led peacekeepers, even if under the United Nations flag.[19]

A US commission investigating the Marine barracks assault called it an "act of war" and largely held Iran responsible, as well as for the earlier American embassy bombing.[20] Afterward, the elusive factions that carried out the Marine truck bombing coalesced into Hezbollah (meaning "Party of God"). Hezbollah was formed with Iranian training, arms, and financing in southern Lebanon in the early 1980s after the Israeli army invaded the country in pursuit of Palestinian terrorists.[21] American officials discerned Iranian and Syrian hands in the marine barracks blast, which was the largest single loss of American troops since World War II. Iran and Syria denied it, as did Hezbollah. The barracks catastrophe was added to the litany of American grievances against the Islamic Republic of Iran; but it was not to be the last on the list. After the Israeli intervention into Lebanon, a series of kidnappings took place in which American and other Westerners were swept up by spectral Lebanese Shiite groups linked to the Iranian-supported

Hezbollah. More than a dozen hostages were grabbed from 1982 to 1992, five of whom died or were executed in captivity. Foreign experts offered several tactical motives for hostage taking, but anti-American and anti-Western feelings lay at the core.[22]

Hezbollah, Iran's proxy, eventually wore down the 18-year Israeli occupation in southern Lebanon until Tel Aviv pulled out its troops in 2000. As a result, Hezbollah's prestige in the Middle East soared even among the Sunni populations. It solidified the basis for an alliance among Hezbollah, Syria, and Iran that exists to this day. The military breakthrough announced, as one scholar wrote, "a Shia front cutting through the heart of the Arab world" and "connected Iran and Lebanon, as something like two wings of the Khomeini's project."[23] Iran's backing of Hezbollah and later Hamas, the anti-Israel movement in the Gaza Strip, advanced Tehran's regional interests and gave it a presence on the Mediterranean Sea.

Iran-Contra Scandal: Another Sour Note in a Bad Melody

The Lebanese hostage issue stood at the heart of another chapter in the history of Irano-American animosity. Washington's anguish over Western captives in Lebanon altered America's diplomatic tilt temporarily away from Baghdad and toward Tehran during the Iraq-Iran War. To spring the hostages, officials in the Reagan White House embarked on a high-stakes, high-risk surreptitious operation with elements of the Iranian regime. Days before the November 1986 midterm elections in the United States, the story exploded in the media that the Reagan administration had conducted a clandestine weapons swap with Iran for the release of hostages. The deal violated federal statutes, established policies, and principles of a sitting government. At a minimum, exchanging arms for the hostages' freedom simply encouraged terrorists to abduct other Americans and contravened President Reagan's stated policies. More broadly, since Iran was listed on the US Department of State's terrorism listing, it could not be sold or receive arms from America because it violated the country's laws.

The preposterous scheme and the desperate cover-up nearly toppled Ronald Reagan in the worst scandal of his presidency. He had signed the intelligence "finding" authorizing the sale of antitank missiles to Iran.[24] But he denied knowledge about the transfer of funds to American-backed guerrillas, the *Contras*, in Nicaragua against a Marxist-oriented regime. As such, the *Contras* formed the third corner in the complex triangular scandal. For months, Reagan's political fate hung in the balance as information leaked out to the media and congressional investigators about using the funds from the arms-for-hostage exchange to finance US proxy forces operating in Central America. The president survived the crisis, but some of his aides were convicted.[25]

This "Irangate" affair exacerbated the mutual distrust between the Islamic Republic of Iran and the United States. Along with generating funds, the sale of hundreds of antitank missiles was intended to further a rapprochement with purported moderate Iranian politicians, such as al Akbar Hashemi Rafsanjani (the Majles speaker), in order to pave the way for release of the Western hostages held in Lebanon. The scheme utterly flopped.

When a Beirut newspaper revealed the arms sale, it ignited a political firestorm not only in Washington but Tehran. Thereafter, the United States resumed its tough stance toward Iran in the so-called Tanker War, as previously discussed. Retrospectively, the Iran-Contra scandal marked another failing episode in America's search for Iranian "moderates" with whom to work toward normal diplomatic relations. It was not the last such hunt by Washington, which invariably ended in rejection, failure, and bitterness.

For Tehran, the fiasco deepened its distrust and suspicion of perfidious Washington. Besides, the political pillar of anti-Americanism meant too much to the clerical rulers and their acolytes of the Islamic Republic to dismantle it just for restored ties with the United States. Hatred of the United States and the internal power it gave the ruling clique was their raison d'être. Just as for other rogue nations, the United States was a vital prop for Tehran. Opposition to Washington justified repression, hardship, and dictatorship. In short, it ensured legitimacy for rogue regimes no matter how poor their domestic economy or bad their human rights record. The United States was always at fault for everything, a very convenient bogeyman. In time, anti-Americanism waned within certain sectors of Iranian society. University students and other youth warmed to the popular culture and freedoms of young Americans. Educated, professional, and many middle-class Iranians hungered for the liberties enjoyed by their counterparts in America. Still, the ayatollahs could rely on the urban poor, rural folk, and regime hangers-on to take to the streets and chant death to the Great Satan.

The most concrete and immediate fallout for Irano-American relations came from fresh anti-Iranian sanctions. In 1987, Reagan imposed bans on imports of Iranian carpets, pistachios, caviar, and dried fruits. Although specialty items, these exports to the United States totaled about $85 million in 1985 and accounted for 8 percent of all Iran's exports at the time.[26] This embargo and later restrictions added to the enormous damage done to Iran's economy by the clerical regime's policies on the heels of the Iraq-Iran War.

Living standards and employment fell. Additionally, the Reagan sanctions served as forerunners to more severe economic boycotts of subsequent US administrations and allied governments.

The United States, Iran, and the Persian Gulf War

The incoming president, George H. W. Bush, took up office in January 1989, just six months before Ayatollah Khomeini's death. But the president's focus settled elsewhere than on Iran. Almost from the start, President Bush was preoccupied with the falling Berlin Wall and the faltering Soviet Union. The end of the Cold War, the four-decade competition with Moscow, was an epochal transformation in world politics. Little wonder the White House fixed on the disintegration of its nuclear-armed nemesis.[27] Only the Persian Gulf with its strategic energy sources ultimately succeeded in redirecting America's attention back to the Middle East's turgid history and then solely to avert a regional shift in the balance of power that threatened its access to oil. Saddam Hussein was responsible for compelling the United States to switch its attention back to the Middle East. Iraq's conquest of Kuwait initiated the Persian Gulf War and the interjection of American military power into the turbulent arena, where it remains today on an even larger scale than in 1991. Iraq's threat to Saudi Arabia as well as the bloody subjugation of Kuwait triggered the UN-blessed armed coalition to drive Hussein from Kuwaiti territory, as narrated in the previous chapter.

America's thrashing of Iraq benefited Iran by damaging its chief rival. The frigid Irano-American relationship, however, thawed not at all from the US-led coalition's destruction of Hussein's military during the Gulf War. In this case, the Middle East axiom proved inaccurate: the enemy of my enemy was not a friend. Instead, Iran stayed neutral while condemning both combatants. It called for Iraq to evacuate Kuwait and denounced the American military intervention. But it did not materially aid its old foe. The Iranians did allow Hussein to park about 150 warplanes on their airfields to escape harm from the coalition air forces. Yet they never returned the aircraft to Iraq, thereby weakening their adversary without firing a shot. Tehran denied the use of its territory or airspace to the US-orchestrated coalition against Iraq. Indeed, the newly installed ayatollah Ali Husseini Khamanei exclaimed that those who resist "America's aggression, greed, plan and policies aimed at committing aggression in the Persian Gulf region will have participated in a holy war in the path of Allah and anybody who is killed on that path is regarded as a martyr."[28]

Tehran cashed in strategically from Baghdad's defeat. It raised its political profile in the Middle East by condemning the Western military assault.

Iran's stature rose in Muslim minds as a bulwark against American aggression. Its oil profits skyrocketed after the start of the Gulf war as the price of crude jumped three times out of fear for its possible interruption. All in all, Iranian savvy was on display for all to see.

Beneath the surface, the ayatollah regime redoubled its exertions to drive the United States out of the Gulf so that Iran could play its "natural" role as regional hegemon. Iran-American relations remained at crossed swords even after most US troops left the Persian Gulf following the lopsided defeat of Hussein's Republican Guards. America's expanded defense bases in Kuwait infuriated the Iranian regime, which wanted to cast its own shadow over the oil-rich pocket.[29] By this time, the mutual antagonism was set in stone. Even the electoral defeat of George H. W. Bush and the entrance of William Jefferson Clinton into the White House in 1993 did not set things right between the two foes. If anything, the new Washington administration codified America's estrangement from the Islamic Republic. The Clinton government moved to bottle up and to isolate both Iran and Iraq in its policy of "dual containment."

Dual Containment and the Khomeinist Response

Dual containment derived from "an assessment that the current Iraqi and Iranian regimes are both hostile to American interests in the region."[30] The disappearance of the Soviet power in the Middle East meant that the United States no longer was forced to balance Iran with Iraq or vice versa. After its projection of power into the Gulf, the United States no longer needed Iraq as a counterweight to Iran. In May 1993, Martin Indyk, special assistant to the president on Near East and South Asian affairs, delivered a speech that explained the pillars of the dual containment doctrine as envisioned by Bill Clinton:

> As long as we are able to maintain our military presence in the region; as long as we succeed in restricting the military ambitions of both Iraq and Iran, and as long as we can rely on our regional allies—Egypt, Israel, Saudi Arabia, the GCC [Gulf Cooperation Council], and Turkey—to preserve the balance of power in our favor in the wider Middle East, we will have the means to counter the Iraqi and Iranian regimes.[31]

President Clinton adhered to the dual containment policy during both of his presidential terms. Copying the Bush policy, he went along with the previous administration's coercive instruments to constrain Iraq; these included air strikes, abortive covert operations to oust Saddam Hussein, no-fly zones, economic sanctions, and UN arms control inspections as outlined in chapter 2. Nevertheless, Clinton continued them under the rubric of "containment plus" until its will began to flag in the last two years of its tenure.[32]

The dual containment agenda of the Clinton years failed to restrain Iranian rogue propensities. The Islamic Republic carried on a range of terrorist acts and clandestine operations against the United States and its allies. It reinforced its assistance to Hezbollah in Lebanon. It amplified its secret nuclear program, which was unexposed until the next decade. The Iranian clerics persuaded themselves that the Islamic Republic "inherited the mantle of the Soviet Union as the principal challenger to the global system created by the West."[33] They preached hellfire and damnation against this international society as decadent, hedonistic, materialistic, and godless. To them the West went wrong with the Enlightenment, which stripped religion from daily life. They championed a restoration of "the Islam in its Khomeinist version" to serve as the organizing principal of their "born-again" society.[34] America was seen in existential terms, as in the chant "Death to America," and not in a wish just for "Yankee go home" by other anti-American voices around the world.

In spite of its declared policy of dual containment, the Clinton White House did episodically consider diplomatic engagement of Iran, whereas it never seriously contemplated a similar approach to Iraq. Saddam Hussein's antics placed his regime beyond reasonable interaction with outside powers during the 1990s. His lingering threats to neighboring countries, to his minority Kurdish population, and to go nuclear—all cast Hussein as beyond the pale of productive negotiations. Per contra, Iran's Islamic revolution seemed to have entered a Thermidorian phase. Seemingly a moderate, Mohammad Khatami won the presidency in May 1997, heralding a reformist period in Iranian politics and society. Although ultimately outmaneuvered by hard-liners in domestic policies, Khatami made statements suggesting openness to reconciliation with the United States. Iran's relations did improve with Britain by mid-1998, possibly cracking the door ajar to a similar rapprochement with Washington. President Bill Clinton and his secretary of state Madeleine Albright reciprocated with conciliatory statements toward Iran in the last years of their tenure.[35] Nothing of substance came of these fleeting diplomatic flirtations, however. The moment lapsed as Clinton left office, only to reascend fleetingly in the wake of the 9/11 attacks, when American and Iranian interests overlapped in Afghanistan.

Washington and Tehran in the
Post–Sept 11 Environment

Unexpectedly for American observers of the Islamic Republic, Iranian officials condemned the terrorist assaults on the Twin Towers and the Pentagon. Knots of Iranian citizens held candlelit vigils in Tehran's streets expressing sympathy for America—a response much different from celebrations of US pain in the Arab streets. Even more concrete actions flowed from Iran after the United States counterattacked the terrorist mastermind Osama bin Laden's lair in Afghanistan. President George W. Bush's military intervention went exceedingly well in displacing al-Qaeda bases in the mountainous country. Washington engineered a United Nations conference in Bonn, Germany, in December 2001 to set up an interim Afghan government, as US military operations relentlessly battered retreating Taliban militias. For a time, things also went well with Iran.

The United States reached out to Afghanistan's neighbors to stabilize the war-torn Central Asian nation. Secretary of State Colin Powell oversaw a diplomatic coup in gaining much postinvasion assistance from the three major allies of the Northern Alliance, which fought the Taliban before and after the US-led NATO intervention. The Russian Federation waived concerns about the American military presence in its backyard. India looked past its usual animosity toward Pakistan, which was now allied with the US military incursion. Iran worked with Washington, too. Tehran prevailed on its main protégé, Ismail Khan (the key Afghan warlord close to the Iranian border in Herat), to cooperate during the Bonn conference. Khan, in fact, went along with the choice of Hamid Kerzai to be the interim president until elections could be held. Later, the Iranian government pledged $500 million in Afghan reconstruction aid at the Tokyo donors meeting.[36] Iran also passed information to the United States about Arabs fleeing Afghanistan when the United States invaded. These actions coincided with American policies.

Iran's clerical rulers, therefore, were not simply reflexive in their hostility to the United States. When it was in Iran's national interests, Tehran pragmatically cooperated with Washington. As an illustration, Iran had long set its lance against the Sunni-dominated Taliban regime in Afghanistan. Thus, Tehran supported the Northern Alliance's insurgent struggle against the Taliban regime because of its anti-Shia violence. The Taliban militias killed and oppressed Shiite communities in Hazarat region of western Afghanistan. When the Taliban took control of the mountain-laced country's northern city of Mazar-i-Sharif in September 1998, they found 11 Iranian "diplomats" working with the anti-Taliban forces. The Taliban militia summarily executed them. Many Iranians wanted to invade Afghanistan out of revenge, but the government concluded it lacked effective ground forces for the task.[37] Alternatively, Tehran gave assistance to the Northern Alliance. Then, it backed and funded the post-Taliban government of Hamid Karzai because it lay well within Iranian international priorities to help the successor to the Taliban regime.

The propitious convergence in Irano-American interests during immediate post-Taliban Afghanistan was a short-lived moment in the history of the two countries. Soon afterward, Iran was once more enmeshed in its schemes to expand its reach through subversion. At the start of January 2002, Israel's naval forces intercepted and boarded the cargo ship *Karine A* in the Red Sea. The vessel carried an Iranian arsenal of arms that the crew intended to hand over to the Palestinian Authority in the Gaza Strip for use against Israel.[38] Furthermore, disputed evidence came to light at about the same time that Iran opened a sanctuary on its territory to fleeing al-Qaeda officials from Afghanistan right after the US invasion. Finally, initial reports of Iran's nuclear headway had surfaced in late 2001.[39] This alarmed the United States.

Washington's tough reaction came in a speech on January 29, 2002. President George W. Bush in his now-famous State of the Union address lumped Iran with Iraq and North Korea into "an axis of evil, arming to threaten the peace of the world."[40] This gauntlet thrown at the feet of the irked Iranian mullahs was answered in typical fashion—a tit for tat delivered in a cold, calculated manner. Initially, they released from custody Gulbuddin Hekmatyar, an Afghan Sunni extremist who fled to Iran to escape the US intervention after the 9/11 terrorist attack. A free Hekmatyar presented the fledgling Karzai government with another headache, as the onetime Soviet resistance fighter organized an anti-Kabul insurgent militia. This was only an opening shot, however.

Proxy Movements in Iran's Service

The Islamic Republic of Iran powerfully confronted the United States indirectly, through proxy movements. Tehran's resort to secondary agents stemmed from its comparative military weakness vis-à-vis the United States. Realpolitik calculations, not religious fervor, dictated its instruments. In its immediate postrevolutionary period, Iran failed to export its brand of radical Islamic faith. Sobered by the experience, it now turned to subcontractors to hit back at its perennial adversary. Iran gave funds, arms, and training to both Shiite and Sunni groups so long as they were sufficiently anti-American. Working through proxy forces, it moved to create a string of sympathetic forces and regimes in the Middle East. Its prototype and later model for this outsourced policy was Hezbollah, the Shiite militant and social welfare organization in Lebanon. Iran also worked to spread instability, neutralize opposition, or even "Finlandize" Arab regimes in Oman, Bahrain, Qatar, and Yemen so as to keep these small states from entering the anti-Iran bloc headed by the US-allied governments in Saudi Arabia and Egypt. Tehran sought to intimidate these ministates or to undermine their Sunni rulers with restive Shiite populations.

The Islamic Republic also held very divergent strategic views from those of other rogue states. North Korea, Syria, and preinvasion Iraq interpreted the United States as a hostile power to be outmaneuvered and kept at arm's length. But Iran's outlook, like that of the Soviet Union, envisioned a different world order without the presence of the United States, its secular ideology, and military outposts within the Middle East. Also echoing Moscow, Iran organized and sponsored networks to carry out its political and terror missions rather than directly attacking the United States. The mullahs relied on their chess pieces—Hezbollah, Hamas, Syria, and Shiite militias in Iraq—to advance their game against Washington and its regional allies. On occasion, the Islamic Republic did sponsor terror strikes from its own embassies and consulates. It even turned to Iranian companies and sympathetic individuals to spread terror worldwide.[41] This below-the-radar surrogate warfare enabled Iran, militarily overmatched several times by the United States, to commission terrorism with the reduced risk of retribution from Uncle Sam.[42]

Iran's machinations with Shiite communities in the Gulf triggered a not-unexpected reaction. The Gulf Arab monarchies first felt threatened by the furies unleashed by the Shiite revolution in their neighbor. Then, Iran's Islamic internationalism unnerved them. In 1981, the nearby states closed ranks and formed a defensive alliance in the Gulf Cooperation Council (Bahrain, Kuwait, Oman, Qatar, Saudi Arabia, and United Arab Emirates). The GCC bought military equipment from the United States, raised small armed forces, and yet remained dependent on Washington for defense against their powerful neighbor. These sheikdoms also dispersed subsidies and made minor internal policy changes to placate internal dissent while repressing any would-be rebels. Iran, nonetheless, kept fishing in troubled waters amid Shiite populations abroad, which formed natural constituencies for Tehran.[43] In Kuwait, a closely aligned US ally, Iran reportedly implanted a spy network to incite civil unrest and provide support for illicit economic endeavors.[44]

Similar motives prompted Iran to mobilize Shiite communities in Bahrain and Saudi Arabia. On the smallish island of Bahrain, the Sunni-ruled kingdom peers apprehensively toward its eastern neighbor Iran. The

Shiite government of Iran poses a danger to the monarchy and the Sunni minority by provoking the Shia majority to destabilize the island nation. Even without Iranian meddling, the Shiite population feels discriminated against by the Sunni minority. At 70 percent of the population, the Shiite populace feels economically disadvantaged and politically disenfranchised by the promonarchy Sunni minority. From time to time, the Iranian mullahs have stirred the passions of the Bahraini Shiites for equal political treatment by the island's rulers. They have also issued veiled threats to the sovereignty of Bahrain. In a February 11, 2009, speech commemorating the Iranian revolution, for example, an official close to Supreme Ayatollah Ali Khamenei declared that the Arab Gulf state was "our 14th province and had a representative at the [Iranian] parliament."[45]

In 2011, the Arab Spring political winds unsettled Bahrain. Anxious about Shiite protests in the island country, Saudi Arabia deployed military units to quiet the antimonarchal demonstrations. The Obama government muted its objections to Saudi interference, lest it lose a vital base. The Persian Gulf nation is a regional financial hub and headquarters of the US Fifth Fleet, which safeguards the flow of oil in the Persian Gulf and contains Iran's regionwide ambitions. For these reasons, the stability of the Bahraini polity is prized by Washington, which does not lack for reasons to oppose Iran.

An even greater international prize, which also fears Iranian intrigue, is Saudi Arabia. The desert kingdom is home to the largest proven oil reserves in the world. It exports daily 10 million barrels that are consumed by Western and Asian countries. Despite its immense wealth, Saudi Arabia has experienced turbulence from time to time by extremists within both the Sunni majority and the Shiite minority. Before his death, Osama bin Laden pilloried the ruling House of Saud for its religious laxity. Bin Laden broke with his homeland when Riyadh opened itself to thousands of US troops during the Persian Gulf War. The Saudi terrorist believed the stationing of infidel soldiers in the Land of the Two Holy Places (Mecca and Medina) amounted to sacrilege. His appeal resonated with likeminded Sunni purists, who have staged several terrorist attacks in the kingdom.[46] The Saudi security establishment has paid close attention to the activities of the Sunni-dominated al-Qaeda, monitoring cells and arresting suspected militants.[47]

Saudi officials eyed with particular alarm, though, the restiveness among the country's minority Shiite peoples, who made up between 10 and 15 percent of the population. Saudi authorities blamed Shiite terrorists for the 1996 massive truck bombing of Khobar Towers close by King Abdul Aziz Air Base in Dhahran, in which 19 US airmen died and over 500 suffered wounds. The Saudis refused a request by American investigators to interview the suspects, leaving them frustrated and doubtful of the kingdom's anatomy of the attack.[48] Later, in the official report on the 9/11 terrorism, the commission hinted at Iranian and al-Qaeda complicity in the Khobar attack.[49] The Shiites' presence in the eastern part of Saudi Arabia, where most of the state's oil is found, compounded the feelings of insecurity in Riyadh.[50] Iranian influence seemed to rise temporarily during the 2011 popular revolts across the Middle East, something that signaled a decline in Saudi Arabia's regional standing.[51] More significantly, America's withdrawal of its military forces from Iraq at the end of 2011 opened the way for a Saudi-Iranian proxy war in the Middle East. Conflicts already flared between Sunni and Shia factions in Iraq, Bahrain, Lebanon, Syria, and Yemen.

Farther to the west, the Islamic Republic reached the shores of the Mediterranean by relying on a blend of sectarian tensions, organizing skill, and anti-Western and anti-Israeli sentiments.[52] Foremost among its instruments was Hezbollah in Lebanon. Within Lebanon, the Shia have their own local political ambitions; they are not just a blind instrument of Tehran. But their sectarian bonds and shared impulses—opposition to the United States and Israel—made for a tight alliance, because of which outsiders interpreted Hezbollah as simply Iran's foreign legion. Hezbollah has worked to broaden support beyond the Shiite community. It makes up at least an estimated 35 percent of Lebanon's population, which is deeply fractured among 17 religious sects or subsects.

As a tool of Iran's muscular policy, Hezbollah often did function as the spear point of the Iranian lance, while working as well to secure its Lebanese political base. It carried out many terror assaults while often protesting its innocence. The movements' spokesmen deny that it played a direct role in the kidnappings of the Westerners during the 1980s. It rejected American and Israeli intelligence findings that Imad Mugniyeh, long considered a terror mastermind to rival Osama bin Laden, held membership in Hezbollah. The shadowy Mugniyeh had been linked to violent attacks, including the 1985 hijacking of TWA Flight 847 during which a US Navy diver was murdered, his body tossed onto the runway of the Beirut airport. Hezbollah and Mugniyeh were also bound up with the 1992 Israeli embassy bombing and that of the 1994 Jewish Community Center in Buenos Aires that claimed 144 lives.[53]

During the past quarter of a century, Hezbollah evolved from an insurgent-terrorist force to a politico-military movement that also functioned as a charity providing money, food, medical treatment, and educational benefits to its constituents.[54] After the 2006 Hezbollah-Israel War, it handed out cash to rebuild houses and businesses damaged in the fighting. Politically astute, the Party of God sought to widen its appeal beyond just the Shiite community to other sectarian groups so as to further its Lebanon-wide electoral goals. In 2011, Hezbollah attained a tight hold on the Lebanese government with threats to send its feared militia into the streets, adroit political maneuvering, local alliances, and backing from Iran and Syria.[55] Despite its political progress, Hezbollah persisted in amassing arms, particularly longer-range rockets and guided missiles, which threaten the Levantine military balance. Its leadership also missed few opportunities to hurl taunts and rattle sabers at Israel and the United States, keeping the area unsettled.[56]

Iran also turned to assisting non-Shiite forces to bedevil the Middle East and to undermine pro-American governments. It channeled arms, trained cadres, and funneled cash to Hamas, the radical Sunni movement that fought both Israel and its political rival, the Fatah party, for the overall leadership of the Palestinian cause. Operating in Gaza, Hamas fired Qassam rockets into southern Israel, killing unarmed people. Although a Sunni organization, Hamas attracted Iranian sponsorship because of its militancy and terror attacks on Israeli targets. Working through its Hamas proxy, Iran spread its tentacles into a non-Shiite arena, garnering the Arab street's accolades for hitting the Jewish state while their own regimes lined up with Washington.

Before the tumultuous prodemocracy protests toppled Hosni Mubarak in early 2011, Iran's agents were at work in Egypt. In April 2009, Egyptian authorities revealed their uncovering of an Iranian proxy unit from arrests made the previous November. This Hezbollah ring of over 40 members allegedly plotted terror strikes at tourist destinations in Sinai and in Cairo. Tourism is Egypt's leading industry, and one only recovering from the 1997 killing of 58 tourists at Luxor by the Egyptian Islamic Jihad. Hassan Nasrallah, the leader of the Lebanese branch of Hezbollah, acknowledged that he had dispatched agents to Egypt but only to facilitate assistance for Hamas across the border in Gaza.[57] In late April 2010, an Egyptian court found 26 men affiliated with Hezbollah guilty of plotting attacks and sentenced them to varying prison terms.[58]

Iran employed surrogate movements against US troops with deadly effect in Iraq after the American invasion in 2003. America's ouster of Iran's archfoe Saddam Hussein and its Iraqi occupation blew open unanticipated opportunities for Iranian interference. Iran initially held its fire. After all, US power dealt the ayatollahs a very good political hand. They feared and hated Hussein for his eight-year war against the Islamic Republic starting in 1980. They long despised him for his persecution of their coreligious brethren inside Iraq. He was an impediment to their regional expansion. With Hussein out of the picture, the majority Shia stood to rule a democratic Iraq through the ballot box. At first, Iran chose to exert its influence through

Shiite political movements within Iraq, such as the Dawa Party and the Islamic Supreme Council of Iraq.

In time, Iran reassessed its military's neutral approach in Iraq. No longer would Tehran just provide funding to pro-Iranian political movements and limited arms shipments to rabble-rousers such as Moqtada al-Sadr, who lorded over the Shiite slums in Baghdad during the years immediately after the US intervention. By 2006, the Iranians were becoming a force to reckon with in eastern Iraq. They turned the Iraqi strip abutting their border into the main battle zone for indirect warfare against US and other coalition forces in the ethnically torn land. They grew to fear American proximity and fought to expel US forces.

The Islamic Republic of Iran poured an array of arms into the hands of Iraqi Shia, notably the EFPs (or explosively formed penetrators) that smashed through the thickest armored vehicle. Its operatives recruited Shiite Iraqi youths for insurgency training in Iranian camps. Beyond that, Iran insinuated members of the IRGC into Iraq to coordinate and train Shiite militants in cells resembling Hezbollah in Lebanon. Terrorist facilitators from Iran's Ministry of Intelligence and Security fanned out throughout southern Iraq to instigate bombings and killings. The IRGC-Quds Force, along with the Lebanese Hezbollah, conducted advanced instruction in military camps inside Lebanon. These foreign-trained militias, known as "special groups," returned to their homeland, where they took a deadly toll of US troops with EFPs and ambushes.[59] By late 2008, the Iranian-fueled insurgency temporarily quieted as Iraq's Shiite majority consolidated its political control. As Washington prepared to remove its remaining troops from Iraq at the end of 2011, the Quds Force resumed arms transfers and training missions to Kataib Hezbollah (Brigades of the Party of God) and other Shiite militias to attack US soldiers, killing record numbers.[60] Reacting to the US sanction policy in still another way, Iran aided the Sunni-dominated al-Qaeda by allowing the terrorist network to use its territory for transferring arms, money, and militants to Afghanistan and Pakistan from Arab nations. Fed up by Iran's deadly proxy war in Iraq, Washington formally accused Tehran of forging an alliance with al-Qaeda in mid-2011.[61]

In nearby Afghanistan, American and other NATO forces watched warily as Iran strengthen its foothold in that country's western reaches, which bordered the Islamic Republic. Around the provincial town of Herat, Tehran paved a 75-mile stretch of highway, built a dozen schools, and electrified communities. Known for its mosques and minarets, Herat had long felt the pull of its coreligious Shia in Iran. But Iran's presence stemmed from a desire for a stable and peaceful border with its war-engulfed neighbor. Economic development of Afghanistan's west also alleviated Iran's burden of around two million Afghan refugees by inducing them to return to a developing strip across the border.[62] By May 2010, General Stanley A. McChrystal (the commander of US and allied forces in Afghanistan) commented that Iranian subversive operations, such as training and arming insurgents, were "not enough to change the basic calculus of the fight at this point." Moreover, the four-star officer noted Iran's assistance had positive ramifications for Afghanistan, too.[63] Once more, American and Iranian interests overlapped in Afghanistan, if only tangentially.

Finally, in reaction to Iran's political meddling, provocative naval maneuvers in the Gulf, and growing nuclear capacity, the United States established a "listening post" in Dubai of the United Arab Emirates and set up a dedicated Iran desk at the Department of State in 2006. Both endeavors aimed to enhance information about Iran. About 100 miles from the Islamic Republic, the Dubai station was located at a nexus of Iranian expatriates in the UAE and business contacts with Tehran. Dissident American-Iranian organizations trained opposition movements there to force political change within Iran. State Department officials likened the Dubai office to that of Riga, Latvia, after the Bolshevik Revolution and before the United States and Soviet Russia restored diplomatic relations. The Riga station helped American officials understand what was happening within the Soviet Union. Amid some 200,000 Iranians living in Dubai, American diplomats monitored activities and improved their knowledge of developments in the country across the Persian Gulf.[64] There was much in Iran to transfix American attention.

Iran's Nuclear Weapons and Long-Range Missile Quests

None of Iran's rogue-state behavior so blacklisted it among respectable powers as its relentless drive toward nuclear mastery. Iran aroused hostility among its neighbors with its export of terrorism, espionage, and sponsorship of militant movements, such as Hezbollah and Hamas. But the prospect of the revolutionary Islamic Republic with its mixture of militant theology, theocratic dictatorship, police-state repression, and apocalyptic rhetoric in possession of the ultimate weapon filled states near and far with anxiety. Membership in the nuclear-arms club stood to elevate Iran's standing as the regional hegemon. Little wonder that a regime that looked to its imperial Persian past and to a future of Islamic revolutionary inroads strove mightily to obtain these catastrophic weapons. Iran's nuclear confrontation with the world outside served as well a vital purpose for its leaders. The showdowns with the West kept alive the country's theocratic ideology and preserved the rulers' power base. The "us versus them" antagonism consolidated Iranian nationalism and backing for the regime among its population.

Under international law, Iran was entitled to build a civilian nuclear capacity to meet its energy needs. Tehran made much of its guaranteed rights to construct nuclear plants under the 1968 Nuclear Nonproliferation Treaty (NPT), which it ratified along with more than 185 other states. This landmark international agreement aims to limit the spread of nuclear arms and to promote nuclear disarmament among all nations, including the five recognized nuclear-armed states (Britain, China, France, Russia, and the United States). But the NPT allows for peaceful nuclear development and even cooperation among treaty signatories in the civil production of nuclear energy.

A legality rube arises from the difficulty in verifying the difference between uranium enrichment consistent with civil production and that at higher levels for weapons. For reliable results, outside inspectors must depend on the genuine openness and cooperation from local scientists and engineers. The NPT mandated inspections by the International Atomic Energy Agency. The IAEA was required to check for compliance of the treaty's provisions concerning the exclusive civil application of nuclear facilities. Iran's interaction with the IAEA consistently fell well short of forthright compliance and genuine openness vis-à-vis the nuclear watchdog agency over many years.

The shah initiated Iran's nuclear quest with plans to build 20 nuclear-power reactors in the 1970s. Two reactors were partially constructed in Bushehr on the Persian Gulf coast with French and American cooperation. They suspended assistance after the 1979 revolution. Saddam Hussein's air force bombed the Bushehr complex during the Iran-Iraq War. Following the conflict, Tehran contracted for Russian fuel and expertise to restore Bushehr as the country's first commercial reactor. During the 1990s, Iran received Chinese as well as Russian technology. Iranian engineers trained in Russian labs. Like most plutonium production, the Bushehr plant generated spent fuel, which could be diverted to making plutonium bombs. Hence, there was a need for international verification. Tehran permitted only limited IAEA inspections since 1992. Even though it secretly pursued a nuclear-arms capability, Iran could not hide from outsiders its work on missiles for airlifting nuclear bombs to targets.

The clerical regime embarked on building, testing, and perfecting missiles. Foreign observers worried about Iran's growing advances in rocketry as noted by their lengthening flight range, enhanced telemetry, and nosecone capacity for greater payloads. The growing sophistication in ballistic missile technology formed a significant component in a credible

Iranian nuclear threat. Missiles are the best delivery system for an atom bomb.

The George W. Bush presidency took note of Iran's missile threat by proposing to erect a defensive missile shield in Eastern Europe. In 2007, Washington announced plans to install ten antimissile interceptors in Poland and a battle-management radar system in the Czech Republic to counter Iranian missiles. Agreements with Warsaw and Prague were followed by implementation steps by the Pentagon despite Russia's steely opposition. Moscow perceived the proposed American antimissile shield as a threat, especially since President Bush pulled the United States out of the Anti-Ballistic Missile Treaty with Russia in 2002.[65]

The Oval Office stated that the 1972 treaty restrained research and development of antimissile launchers in the post–Cold War world, where rogue states, such as Iran and North Korea, presented a real risk. The Bush White House struggled to allay Russian fears that its new policy posed threats to their intercontinental ballistic missiles (ICBMs). It argued that the limited missile defense would provide for America's European allies against Iranian projectiles. Some European capitals, nonetheless, objected to the emplacement of the US air defense system on their continent.[66] When President Barack Obama took office in 2009, he scuttled the Bush plan because of Moscow's objections. He replaced it with a naval antimissile defense whose short-range interceptors presented little danger to Russian ICBMs. This phased adaptive approach called later for a land-based antimissile system placed in Romania and Poland, with a radar installation in Turkey. Despite its growing diplomatic assertiveness toward Washington, Ankara announced its intention in late 2011 to allow a US radar system to be installed on its territory as part of a NATO shield against Iran.[67] Other phases were to follow with upgraded capabilities. Before Obama's arrival in the West Wing, the Iranian nuclear danger had grown apace and so had Western concerns.

Iran's Nuclear Arms Exposed

No major Iranian violations of the NPT were made public before 2002. In August of that year, a shady dissident Iranian movement, the Mujahideen-e Khalq (MEK), revealed that the Islamic Republic had two secret nuclear facilities. The MEK exposed a gas centrifuge plant at Natanz, which enriched uranium by high-speed centrifuges. The Natanz facility possessed the capability for enriching uranium for electricity-generating plants or at a higher level for nuclear arms. In central Iran, a uranium-conversion plant at Isfahan could also refine uranium to differing levels of potency. Another installation at Arak produced plutonium from a heavy-water production facility, constituting another method for bomb making. American intelligence soon confirmed the revelations. Over the years, the sizeable Iranian nuclear effort had benefited from the rise in oil prices to generate funds to pursue enrichment activities and from the black-market availability of components and technology sold by A. Q. Khan, the Pakistani scientist, who acted with official complicity.[68]

After the MEK pulled back the curtain on Iran's secretive enrichment activities, the United States accused the Islamic Republic in December 2002 of pursuing weapons of mass destruction. The IAEA stepped up its inspections. The United Nations' nuclear agency confirmed the MEK leaks and uncovered a pilot program of over 100 functioning centrifuges used for uranium enrichment at the Natanz facility. It also located components being assembled for some 50,000 centrifuges that when up and running could produce enough highly enriched uranium (HEU) for between 25 and 50 bombs per year. Additionally, the nuclear inspectors found refined uranium (the so-called yellow cake) imported from China and Pakistan. These discoveries led the Iranians to divulge that they were completing a facility in Isfahan to convert yellow cake into uranium hexafluoride for preparation of HEU. This revelation and others led the IAEA to conclude that Iran violated the Safeguards Agreements to the NPT.[69] The IAEA called upon Iran to cease its uranium enrichment enterprises. It requested frank answers to questions about its nuclear program. It also demanded Iran sign the Additional Protocol to the NPT that required reports on nuclear activities and accepted surprise international inspections at any site. Iran never signed the Additional Protocol. The IAEA also set an unmet deadline of October 31, 2003, for compliance or it pledged to refer the violations to the UN Security Council, which it did.

Iran's nuclear and missile programs prompted deep apprehensions. George W. Bush refused to enter into direct negotiations with Iran until it ceased all nuclear-arming activities, to be verified by the IAEA. He also pushed for sanctions until Iran closed down all its nuclear efforts. Washington, however, approved of the European Union's initiative to engage Iran in substantive talks. Germany, France, and Britain, known as the E-3, entered into talks with Iranian diplomats. These European states worried about not only nuclear proliferation but also its impact on possible UN resolutions, which might harm their extensive commercial and trade business with Iran. In November 2004, the reformist Iranian president, Mohammed Khatami, reached an agreement with the E-3 to suspend temporarily Iran's uranium enrichment. The deal eased European fears that Iran was building a nuclear weapon—an accusation that Tehran always denied. The country's supreme leader, Ayatollah Ali

Khamenei, approved this accord because it temporarily spared Iran from UN sanctions. Iranian accommodation was brief, however.

When Mahmoud Ahmadinejad, the former mayor of Tehran, assumed the presidency in 2005, he labeled his predecessor's agreement "disgraceful" and announced the resumption of Iran's enrichment program. Thereafter, Iran merely disclosed partial information on its nuclear enterprises. At the same time, Iran cleverly let it be known that its atomic endeavors were spread furtively around the country. If Tehran kept the outside world in the dark about the extent and location of its nuclear industry, then neither the United States nor Israel could strike preemptively to cripple the entire nuclear project. Reports also circulated that Iran had hardened some of its underground nuclear plants with concrete layers as added protection against conventional penetrating warheads. Obviously, Iran's hidden capabilities to complete the fuel cycle (the ability to manufacture fissile material) and its bomb-resistant shields to safeguard nuclear plants only further unsettled international society about Iran's real intentions.

The Iran-Iraq Link

The United States unexpectedly adopted a restrained approach to the unfolding nuclear drama in Iran and the European Union's plodding steps to address it. Condemned for its Iraq War, the George W. Bush government now embraced a cautious, multilateral course toward Iran. It relied on Paris, Berlin, and London to pull the laboring oar on a necessary hardnosed policy toward Iran, for which they undeniably lacked the resolve. There was no lack of unanimity about Iran's growing technical and industrial competency for turning out bomb-grade uranium. By 2005, American, Western European, and Israeli officials believed that Iran was within a short timeframe (two to eight years depending on the estimate) for manufacturing highly enriched uranium—for bomb-grade fissile material. Yet the Bush government demurred despite its tough verbal utterances. The White House also rejected its own internal hawks, who advocated an air strike. It temporarily sidelined Israel's request for bunker-busting bombs to hit Iran's nuclear complex as well.[70]

Washington's paralysis stemmed mainly from America's worsening circumstances in Iraq, where US and coalition troops were bogged down in a fierce insurgency by late 2004. With the Oval Office increasingly preoccupied with the fighting within the Persian Gulf country, the United States possessed neither the military resources nor diplomatic latitude to launch a ground attack against another country in the Middle East.

Finally, the Bush government was internally divided by a dove-hawk split over its policy toward Iran. Hard-liners favored aggressive initiatives to overthrow the ayatollah regime by covert operations or to bomb the country's burgeoning nuclear installation before it went completely online.[71] The more dovish advisers leaned toward UN-approved sanctions matched with enticements. They mused about such sweeteners as American diplomatic recognitions and US-sponsored membership in the World Trade Organization in exchange for Iran's compliance with its nuclear treaty obligations. This softer course of action received a boost from events inside Iraq as the wave of roadside bombings and guerrilla ambushes crested in the war-torn country. US policy mandarins discerned Iranian hands in the falloff of attacks on coalition troops. In the eyes of these officials, Iran seemed to be the ultimate foreign arbiter of political actions within Iraq, where Tehran exercised considerable influence.

Desperate for a way out of the deepening Iraqi morass, the US Congress formed a bipartisan blue-ribbon commission, the Iraq Study Group. This ten-person panel recommended engaging Iran and Syria "in diplomatic dialogue, without preconditions," for help with Iraq. Specifically, it advocated persuading "Iran that it should take specific steps to improve the situation in Iraq" by curbing its flow of military instructors and arms to violent Iraqi Shiite militias.[72] Of all its 79 recommendations, the report's advocacy of engaging Iran was one of a half-dozen proposals that garnered serious attention, even months after it was released in late 2006.[73] Ultimately, the operational "surge" of an additional 28,500 combat troops and a refined counterinsurgency strategy in Iraq brought stability to the convoluted country, obviating the Iraq Study Group's findings. Diplomatic engagement of Iran, America's archfoe in the Persian Gulf, therefore gained only temporary currency in Washington circles.

Iranian actions soon disabused Washington officials of reaching out to Tehran. In 2006, Ahmadinejad restarted Iran's centrifuges at the Natanz nuclear facility after nearly a three-year suspension. Later that year, the Iranian president announced that the Islamic Republic had produced its first batch of enriched uranium, which was condemned by the United States and other powers for defiance of the United Nations' rulings. Despite the European Union's package of enticements to Iran to halt its uranium enrichment, the Tehran government pushed ahead. In December, the UN Security Council voted new sanctions against Iran, which, in turn, labeled them illegal. In March 2007, the Security Council approved additional arms and financial penalties against the recalcitrant regime. None of these punitive measures induced Iran to abandon its enrichment activities, which enjoyed broad popular support among the country's population.

Iran's demagogic president, Mahmoud Ahmadinejad, added to the gnawing foreboding about Iran's mounting nuclear capability. He astounded the international community with his genocidal outbursts calling for the destruction of Israel. At the "World without Zionism" Conference held in Iran in late October 2005, Ahmadinejad thundered, "This Jerusalem occupying regime [Israel] must be erased from the page of time."[74] He blared that the "Israel regime is on the verge of disappearing" or would be "wiped off the map."[75] It was not unusual to see missiles or vehicles in Iranian military parades draped with banners advocating, "Israel should be wiped out of the face of the world."[76] Iranian leaders persisted in this bellicose vein into 2012, referring to Israel as a cancer that must be removed from the Middle East.

Despite Iran's incendiary words and nuclear deeds, American perceptions took an unexpected turn because of a grossly inaccurate estimate of Iranian capabilities. On December 3, 2007, the US director of National Intelligence, who served as the head of the American intelligence community, issued a startling retraction from the past National Intelligence Estimates on Iran's intentions and capabilities. The new NIE now concluded with "high confidence" that "in fall 2003, Tehran halted its nuclear program." The 2007 report, therefore, reversed the NIE assessment two years earlier. In 2005, the NIE advised that "Iran currently is determined to develop nuclear weapons."[77]

This new NIE assessment halted any planning for military action against Iran. Some voices inside and outside the Bush administration speculated that the US invasion of Iraq had frightened Iran into UN compliance in 2003—the year Iran reputedly stopped its nuclear arms activities to escape an American attack.[78] But the NIE report, nonetheless, attributed the alleged suspension to "increasing international scrutiny and pressure resulting from the exposure of Iran's previously undeclared nuclear work."[79] Tehran later complained that the United States ignored its offer of a Grand Bargain in spring 2003. This diplomatic package supposedly offered a "resolution of the nuclear issue and de facto recognition of Israel."[80] Was Tehran's Grand Bargain dictated by fear of the US military intervention extending its operations from Iraq to Iran? It coincided with the NIE's reckoning that Iran suspended its nuclear arms activity. Was it just another wily Iranian stratagem, of which there had been many? We may never know the rational behind the offer. Given the mutual animosity, it remains highly unlikely that any positive outcome could have developed from the putative Grand Bargain talk, however.

Many independent analysts and foreign intelligence agencies, nonetheless, greeted the NIE estimate with deep skepticism. Some distrusted the NIE, pointing out that it was packed with anti-Bush officials from the State

Department. They resented the West Wing's dismissal of their views that preinvasion Iraq posed no serious WMD threat.[81] Other skeptics argued that the NIE had simply been duped by Iranian scientists, who used secret facilities. Other disbelievers argued that the nuclear arms stoppage was temporary or irrelevant so long as Iran pursued uranium enrichment on a vast scale. Going to weapons-grade uranium from civilian reactor–grade material presented no real obstacle to a determined government. During the next presidential administration, most observers concluded that any Iranian stoppage, if it occurred at all, was a thing of the past.[82]

The 2011 NIE report, which was the first full, new analysis since the controversial 2007 report, observed that Iran resumed nuclear-weapons research. The Iranian leadership, however, were locked in debate about how far to proceed toward nuclear arms, suggesting that the stringent international sanctions was sowing discord.[83] In spite of the whitewashing 2007 NIE report, Bush stuck to his theme that Iran remained "a threat to world peace."[84] His warning proved accurate. As of this writing, Iran's ongoing nuclear program keeps the world on pins and needles.

Unclench Your Fist

Barack Obama moved into the Oval Office determined to turn the page on his predecessor's international policies even toward regimes that "sow conflict." In his inaugural address of January 20, 2009, the new president offered an olive branch to authoritarian figures who cling to power through "silencing of dissent" by extending a hand to them, "if you are willing to unclench your fist."[85] No rogue adversary would test the new commander-in-chief's outreached hand as Iran did. He dropped George W. Bush's precondition for talks that Iran first suspend its nuclear program.

In May, Obama got his response. The Islamic Republic test-fired a solid-fuel Sajjil-2 missile capable of striking Israel. Before an applauding crowd in Semnan, the site of the rocket launch, Ahmadinejad linked the missile firing and Iran's nuclear program: "In the nuclear case, we send them [those who oppose it] a message. Today the Islamic Republic of Iran is running the show."[86] Iran's famed Shabab-3 rocket was known to have a range of 1,250 miles, allowing it to strike not only Tel Aviv but also Cairo, Athens, and New Delhi.[87] Earlier in 2009, Iran fired a missile into outer space, placing a satellite in orbit. Iranian engineers earlier profited from North Korean technology and missile components passed to them in exchange for commercial benefits. But they surpassed their tutor, alarming neighbors and the West.

Six months into his still-young presidency, Barack Obama delivered a speech in Cairo, Egypt, directed, in some part, toward Iran. He announced his overriding goal in speaking at the ancient Al-Azhar University as "to seek a new beginning between the United States and Muslims." Along with calling for a fresh start based on "mutual interest and mutual respect," the president tried to clear the air with Iran by acknowledging America's 1953 "role in the overthrow of a democratically elected Iranian government." The Mossadeq coup still angered Iranians, and the new US president tried to make amends for an action five decades earlier. His June 4, 2009, plea to Iran offered the peace pipe—"My country is prepared to move forward" rather than remaining "trapped in the past" in confronting the new issue of nuclear weapons.[88] The Iranian leader, Ahmadinejad, lost little time in condemning his American counterpart.[89] The Islamic Republic's tangible response to the American conciliatory démarche spoke louder than words. Tehran simply raced incessantly ahead with its nuclear and missile development.

Nothing the United States tried—whether sanctions, threats, or diplomacy—warmed the iced heart of the Iranian regime to negotiate. Nuclear and long-range missile capacity became the full-on sine qua non of all Iranian aspirations. The nuclear dream enjoyed approval across the political spectrum from the religious hierarchy in the capital to villagers living in the backcountry. Even the antiregime Green Movement backed their government's nuclear program, which became an Iranian expression of nationalism. Polls showed that two-thirds of the Iranian populace favored a peaceful nuclear quest, despite economic hard times brought on by international sanctions.[90] This unity did not extend to all political questions. When divisions burst in full view, the United States missed its one and only opportunity to obtain a less belligerent and, perhaps, denuclearized Iran through a new government.[91]

The pivotal juncture arrived with the disputed Iranian presidential election on June 12, 2009. President Ahmadinejad's fraudulent reelection touched off raucous prodemocracy protests in Tehran and other Iranian cities. Thousands suffered injury, torture, and death or imprisonment at the hands of the IRGC and its auxiliary goon squads, the Basij militia, over the next several months as the country erupted in turmoil. The opposition Green Movement took root within Iranian society. The new media—mobile phone cameras, YouTube, Twitter, bloggers—amplified reportage across the globe and heightened the demonstrators' courageous stand against club-wielding thugs. Bloody images of street confrontations between reformers and their tormentors circulated within Iran as well as around the world.[92] The regime hurled invectives at its detractors and accused the United States and Israel of fomenting a "velvet coup" against Ahmadinejad's antidemocratic rule. Backed against the wall of rising protest, the Iranian president cleverly signaled more cooperation with the IAEA to buy time and stave off any potential American lifelines to the reformers.[93]

Tragically, Washington let slip an opportunity it had long desired in Iran—a grassroots upwelling of a secular, democratic movement. As the regime teetered on the edge, Obama hewed to his realist approach of noninterference internally and proengagement stance with Tehran, easing international pressure on the hard-pressed regime.[94] Unlike his predecessor, George W. Bush, who stood up for freedom in the Ukraine, Kyrgyzstan, Lebanon, and the Republic of Georgia during their internal crises, President Obama placed his bet for denuclearization on a grateful Iranian regime.[95] He cautioned against "meddling" in the sham Iranian election, while members of his own party along with the political opposition criticized his cynical realism.[96] By early 2010, the moment had passed for any effective American counteraction to facilitate the transfer of power to a reasonable government. The Oval Office's forbearance earned no gratitude from Ahmadinejad, who pressed ahead with his nuclear program after turning down a US offer to allow Iran to swap its enriched uranium for medical isotopes.

Sanctions Again but Tougher

Although the Obama administration first tried to engage Iran in nuclear diplomacy, it later sobered and turned to additional, far-reaching sanctions against the Islamic Republic. The White House had a willing helper in the US Congress. The legislative body passed new unilateral sanctions to clamp down on Iran's energy and banking industries in June 2010. Eleven months later, Congress blacklisted its twenty-first Iranian bank as a WMD proliferator. In June 2011, Washington announced sanctions against the IRGC and associate domestic security forces.

In reaction, Iran was nothing if not inventive in circumventing earlier UN embargoes. Reports surfaced of elaborate subterfuges it enlisted to acquire sophisticated technology from China, Germany, and even the United States. The Persian Gulf port of Dubai, with its many Iranian expatriates, evolved into a clandestine market to acquire electronics and computer equipment for Tehran's nuclear agenda. Dubai-based companies purchased high-grade German technology by using false end-user certificates for Asian companies. Once goods were in Dubai, unscrupulous intermediaries and shell companies transferred the items to Iran.[97] Similarly, Malaysian middlemen bought Chinese or American goods and sold them to Iranian front companies linked to nuclear and missile programs.[98]

At home, the Islamic Republic of Iran Shipping Lines (IRISL) renamed vessels, set up front companies, and changed owners and operators to escape the US Treasury's blacklist of the IRISL fleet. Blacklisted ships were re-registered to companies in Cyprus, Hong Kong, Malta, and the Isle of Man.

The shell game extended to the replacement of IRISL itself by other Iranian companies, named Hafiz Darya, Sapid, and Soroush. Their managers and stockholders often came from the original firm's ranks.[99] This legerdemain enabled Iranian scientists and engineers to construct nuclear plants and missile systems despite sanctions. Together with fraudulent export companies in Asia, the reflagged blacklisted vessels secreted prohibited nuclear components to Iranian facilities. By guile and subterfuge, the non-Iranian flagged cargo containers also transported small arms, ammunition, and Katyusha rockets to Hamas in Gaza and Hezbollah in Lebanon.[100] As the US Treasury and the United Nations cracked down on intermediaries, the shippers moved elsewhere or to different vessels.

The United States struck back with countermeasures. It cobbled together a sanction resolution that China and Russia, as permanent members on the Security Council, grudgingly approved in June 2010. This new UN sanction regime imposed a limited embargo on Iran's energy sector. It called for asset freezes on 40 companies not included in previous blacklisting. It also reinforced previous appeals for UN member states to board Iranian ships suspected of transporting contraband to or from Iran.[101] Days later, both the United States and the European Union added additional sanctions; this time penalties fell on companies, transport services, and banks, some of which were unconnected to Iran's nuclear program.[102] Ahmadinejad dismissed the Security Council resolution. He snarled, "These sanctions are like used tissues which should be thrown in the trash."[103] Moreover, the Islamic Republic forged ahead with its nuclear plans without skipping a beat.

Thus, the Obama presidency swung back partially toward the harder line of preceding American governments. Along with enticing a handful of Iranian nuclear scientists to defect and reveal the extent of the Ahmadinejad regime's uranium enrichment progress, Washington unveiled initiatives to sap further the dictatorship's eroding legitimacy. It looked belatedly to helping the suppressed Green Movement. It stepped up Persian-language radio and television broadcasts into Iran. It facilitated the transfer of computer hardware and software to help antigovernment protestors evade Tehran's electronic censors, who jammed their opponents' communications and access to foreign news.[104]

The administration, however, held back on what is termed a "nuclear option" in the financial war against Iran. Despite the urging of US senators, it balked at implementing sanctions on Iran's central bank, the Bank Markazi, which would effectively freeze Tehran out of the global financial system. Such a step would make it extremely difficult for Iran to clear billions of dollars each month in oil sales. The clerical regime declared that such a measure was an act of war. American allies in Europe and Asia also counseled against blacklisting, for it would inhibit their ability to buy oil from Iran, the third-largest exporter in the Organization of Petroleum Exporting Countries.[105]

The Obama administration also powered down the US military focus on Iran's growing strategic-weapons threat. Israel, by necessity, stepped into the American-opened breach. With doomsday threats emanating from Tehran toward the Jewish state, Israel cranked up its defensive preparations. Beginning during the last years of Bush's term and carrying over into the Obama presidency, the Israel Defense Forces (IDF) conducted air exercises in preparation for a preemptive attack on Iran. President Obama also went along with Bush's decisions for the transfer of "bunker buster" bombs to Israel to penetrate Iranian concrete underground nuclear factories.[106] While Obama spoke of the need to avoid "major conflict in the Middle East," US Air Force pilots staged aerial drills with their IDF counterparts.[107] Rather than camouflaging its preparations, the Israeli Defense Forces let it be known that it clearly had Iran in its crosshairs.[108] Israel also announced that it planned on deploying at least one of its three submarines at a time in the Persian Gulf off the Iranian coast, bringing the ships' nuclear-tipped cruise missiles in range of any aiming point within Iran.[109] Rumors of an Israeli attack on Iran's nuclear facilities ebbed and flowed during much of Obama's presidency. In late 2011, the speculation spiked when Israel test-fired a ballistic missile that could reach Iran and the IAEA released a report pointing to Iran's design and development of nuclear warheads.[110] Both deepened anxiety in Washington policy circles.

Pebbles on the Nuclear Path

Then almost out of a spy novel came a deus ex machina: a "Black Swan" catastrophe for Iran's nuclear program. Revelations of a mysterious computer worm surfaced in late 2010. The Stuxnet software code infected the spinning centrifuges at Natanz for almost 17 months before the outside world learned of the devastating damage to the equipment manufactured by the German conglomerate Siemans.[111] Although Iranian officials denied the presence of the sophisticated malworm, they stopped feeding uranium into their main plant. Speculation about the malicious Stuxnet program turned toward the United States or Israel as the provenance for the mysterious cyber-attack.

The antinuke campaign shifted next toward the human dimension of Iran's frenzied race for weapons of mass destruction. On November 28, 2010, during the morning rush hour, attempts were made on the lives of two

Iranian scientists in Tehran. One bombing killed a nuclear physicist in his car. The other assassination plot narrowly failed to blow up a scientist whose name had been listed among those in the UN sanctions. Earlier that year, another of Iran's scientists met death by an exploding motorcycle. Then in July 2011, a physicist, who crafted high-voltage switches for nuclear detonations, was shot down by motorcycle-riding gunmen. Once again, suspicion fell on Israel and its Mossad intelligence agency. But some of the targeted scientists sympathized with the Green Movement. Therefore, they might have been singled out by the IRGC for disloyalty to the regime. The attacks and finger-pointing among capitals as to the responsibility recalled the "wilderness of mirrors" during the Cold War, when intelligence agencies denied knowledge of assassinations or intrigues. Despite these shadowy episodes, the Stuxnet software remained the most damaging breach of Iran's nuclear program. Outsiders estimated that Stuxnet's damage set back the Islamic Republic's nuclear arming by several years, easing temporarily rumors of an air strike on its atomic facilities.[112] This estimate proved far too optimistic.

The nuclear program went ahead. Iran declared the start-up of its Fordo facility to inject uranium gas into sophisticated centrifuges in January 2012. Tehran also took steps to protect this nuclear fuel production in fortified underground military bunkers outside the city of Qum. It hoped to thwart any American or Israeli air attacks on its nuclear facilities. By this time, the Iranian government also had broken off negotiations to import nuclear fuel rather than produce its own. Fereydoon Abbasi, the head of Iran's atomic energy agency, stated, "We will no longer negotiate a fuel swap and a halt to our production of fuel." The twin decisions pointed toward the inevitability of an Iranian nuclear weapon, if the country's scientists chose to move toward that goal.[113]

The popular uprisings throughout the Middle East in early 2011 returned Washington's worried focus toward Iran. When the street demonstrations led to the toppling of the pro-West strongmen in Tunisia and Egypt, the antigovernment fervor spread to Libya, Yemen, and Syria as well as to other countries. But the protests in Bahrain, with its large Shiite majority, turned attention back to Iran, which stood to gain by the unrest if it toppled the island's pro-US Sunni monarch. Fearful of expanding Iranian influence, Saudi Arabia briefly rolled in 2,000 troops (800 were from the United Arab Emirates) and armored vehicles into Bahrain to suppress a revolt that endangered the Sunni monarchy and its own hold on the region.[114]

As the military force moved across the narrow causeway connecting the Arabian Peninsula to the island, the Obama government uttered oblique criticism of the Saudi-led intervention. Tensions between Washington and Riyadh worsened in the wake of their different approach to the regionwide upheaval against old-line dictators from Tunisia to Egypt and to Libya. Angered by America's handling of the ouster of Egyptian president Hosni Mubarak, the Saudi rulers made clear their displeasure over what President Obama called "universal values," including peaceful protests and consensual government. For its part, the US government pressed for political reform in both Sunni-ruled kingdoms to avert unrest. Beneath the surface friction between the two long-term allies, there lurked the deeper apprehension of Iran, which waited to capitalize on the tumult within the Arab world.[115]

By the start of the second decade of the twenty-first century, Iran seemed well positioned to prolong its protracted hostility to the United States and its regional allies in the Middle East under evermore favorable circumstances. The Arab Spring revolts upturned Egypt and displaced it as a staunch ally against Iranian espionage. Iran's nuclear program proceeded steadily. The political turbulence from the Straits of Gibraltar to the Straits of Hormuz propitiously laid the lands in between open for religious extremism, al-Qaeda-inspired terrorist networks, and even Iranian intrigue. For their part, new and old Arab governments grew apprehensive of Iran's schemes. Egypt turned toward an economically and politically resurgent Turkey for friendship and for a counterweight to Iranian assertiveness.

In keeping with the historical arc of rogue states, Iran has moved beyond its solitary posture toward friendly affiliations with Russia and China. All three share an abiding hostility toward the United States and its muscle flexing in the Persian Gulf. For their own ends, Moscow and Beijing blocked repeatedly American diplomatic exertions in the Security Council to tighten the UN economic sanctions on Iran. Of the two extraregional powers, Tehran gravitated much more toward Beijing than Moscow. Russian territorial ambitions, stemming from its czarist days, always loom large in Iranian thinking. Besides, China's economic emergence and thirst for oil made it an ideal trading partner and counterbalance to the US presence in the Gulf and Afghanistan. As for China, it recognizes the strategic location of Iran and its animosity toward the United States. Iran is a potential partner against China's democratic rivals such as America and India. The Chinese government notes that Iran is the only Gulf oil supplier that it can reach by land-based pipeline and by sea routes. Beijing's trade with Tehran reached $30 billion in 2010 and is projected to reach $40 billion in 2011. Iran purchased Chinese conventional arms, such as antiship cruise missiles, sniper rifles, rocket-propelled grenades, and explosives used in roadside bombs; some of these weapons found their way into the hands of militants operating in Iraq and Afghanistan against US troops. Beijing transferred nuclear technology and materials used by Iran in the development of nuclear-capable ballistic missiles. Its UN representative can be counted on to thwart Washington's Security Council measures against Iran for its nuclear arming.[116]

Within Iran, its nuclear plants accumulated more than enough low-grade uranium for several atomic weapons, if it further enriched its accruing 3.5 percent uranium stockpile. Its Stuxnet hiccup passed, and it reportedly possessed 9,000 centrifuges at Natanz.[117] In July 2011, the United States for the first time formally accused Iran of facilitating al-Qaeda's terrorism by serving as a transit point for the flow of arms, fighters, and money to the terrorist network. Iran had granted sanctuary to al-Qaeda operatives since at least the 9/11 attacks on the United States. Under Iranian auspices, material assistance originating in the oil-rich Persian Gulf sheikdoms passed through its territory to al-Qaeda allies in Afghanistan and Pakistan. The Islamic Republic moved to take advantage of the turbulence in the Middle East and of the planned US and NATO withdrawal from Afghanistan by the end of 2014.[118]

It did not wait until that date, however, to pursue its lethal chess match against its archenemy Saudi Arabia. In a plot right out of a spy thriller, elements of the IRGC's Quds Force schemed to assassinate Riyadh's ambassador on American soil. Washington revealed the penetrated murder plan in mid-October 2011. Tehran denied the accusation, but Washington held substantial evidence.[119] Besides, Iran had a nefarious record of exporting terrorism and killing its opponents.[120] Tehran also dispatched advisers to assist its Damascus client in staving off antiregime protests in many Syrian cities, as noted in chapter 5. It backed proxy movements in Iraq that resembled its allied Hezbollah party in Lebanon to spread Iranian political influence in the former Baathist state.

The Obama administration focused primarily on Iran's nuclear program, even in the wake of the foiled Iranian plot to murder the Saudi Arabian envoy in Washington. It imposed restrictions on Iran's Central Bank, which stymied the country's trade. Hurting Iranian oil exports, however, would raise fuel prices at time when Western nations opposed constricting crude exports because of the adverse impact on their struggling economies mired in the global recession. As it stands now, Iran is the most sanctioned member in the United Nations. The Security Council targeted it with five resolutions since 2006 to get Iran to suspend its uranium enrichment program.

Fearing a military conflict in the Persian Gulf that would disrupt its oil shipments, the European Union got on board with America's stepped-up sanction policy toward the Islamic Republic. The EU initiated a phased ban on oil purchases from Iran. This measure called for a cutoff of future oil contracts while ending the existing ones on July 1, 2012. Tehran retaliated by curtailing oil sales to Britain and France. Both the US and EU governments worried about an Israeli air strike on Iran's nuclear sites that might inflame the region. Their joint economic penalties lacked visible impact on Iran's crash nuclear program, although the Iranian economy took a severe hit.

Meanwhile, the world waited and worried about Tehran's nuclear decisions and its deadly machinations in the region and beyond. In late 2011, the IAEA released a report that UN inspectors found a "credible" amount of evidence that "Iran has carried out activities relevant to the development of a nuclear device."[121] The reported envisioned a nuclear-armed Iran just over the horizon. Additional Security Council sanctions seemed remote as Russia and China opposed them in early 2012. Both developments intensified speculation that Israel might preemptively strike Iran's nuclear plants. But US officials cautioned against such an attack, making it likely that Iran would attain the capability to fashion atomic weapons.

If the political divisions between Ahmadinejad and Khamanei fail to disrupt the theocratic state of Iran, then the future as of this writing looks comparable to the 1930s. Iran's pursuit of nuclear arms could be likened to Germany's military policies of that era, which culminated in World War II. There were instances then when resolute British and French intervention would have halted the German march from rearmament to remilitarization of the Rhineland and from Austria's takeover to Czechoslovakia's dismemberment before Poland's invasion, which precipitated the conflict. It is painful to record that the appeasement of Iran as it gains nuclear weaponry and then commits a horrific calamity has been trod before by humanity—and not that long ago.

CHAPTER 4

North Korea: Blackmailing Rogue

The most important thing in our war preparation is to teach all our people to hate U.S. imperialism. Otherwise, we will not be able to defeat the U.S. imperialists who boast of their technological superiority.

—Kim Il Sung

When you examine the nature of the American security commitment to Korea, to Japan, to this region, it is pointless for them [North Korea] to try to develop nuclear weapons, because if they ever use them it would be the end of their country.

—William J. Clinton

The United States' decades-long engagement of North Korea yielded little beyond Pyongyang's broken promises, frustrating artful dodges, and its relentless pursuit of nuclear weaponry. Far more than any of the other post–Cold War rogue states, the Democratic People's Republic of Korea (DPRK) practiced brinkmanship, broadcast saber-rattling threats, and yet scored a series of diplomatic successes against the United States. Washington and its close ally, the Republic of Korea (ROK), or South Korea, many times worked for accommodation with the DPRK. The two allies frequently offered Pyongyang inducements, which seemingly reinforced its bad behavior. Washington donated food shipments through the UN's World Food Program, which delivered the relief packages to the North. The ROK repeatedly turned its cheek to DPRK slaps while it offered generous aid to Pyongyang. It financed an industrial zone, ran tourist excursions into the North, and donated mammoth food and humanitarian assistance—all for naught. The DPRK refused to halt its nuclear arming or to open itself entirely to international arms inspections. In fact, its belligerency intensified over the years.

American entreaties met with implacable hostility punctuated occasionally by brief thaws in Pyongyang's colorful but clichéd Soviet-era rhetoric. Always the consummate poker player, the opaque North Korea bluffed, blustered, and patiently played a poor hand well enough to avoid an American attack, as had happened to Iraq. Four American presidents have been compelled to take notice and to deal with the rust-bucket country that is the last Stalinist state on the planet. It seemed to play Russian roulette with a half-loaded revolver, which unnerved US policy makers. It ranks among the most impoverished in the Third World in every category but armaments and canny deal-making skills. Waiting for its predicted political collapse has enabled Washington to make a string of concessions while sticking with a form of containment strategy to keep the peace on the peninsula.

North Korea's History in Brief

North Korea came into existence as a consequence of the Cold War competition after World War II. As the Japanese imperial edifice crumbled on the Korean Peninsula in 1945, the Soviet Union carved out a sphere of influence north of the thirty-eighth parallel, and the United States assumed a loose guardianship over the southern half of the peninsula. That demarcation lasts to this day, as does the respective political and economic systems that grew from the bifurcation of the country. The division became hard and fast because of the Korean War, which broke out when the DPRK leader, Kim Il Sung (with the concurrence of Josef Stalin), invaded the South. America led a UN-sanctioned multilateral force to repel the North Korean attack. When advancing US soldiers and marines neared the Chinese-Korean border, the People's Republic of China (PRC) unleashed a massive human wave of nearly one million troops to toss back the American advance. Subsequently, the war descended into a stalemate near the original boundary.

Occurring at one of the iciest points during the Cold War, the Korean War (1950–1953) claimed 33,000 American lives, three million South Korean deaths, and hundreds of thousands of Chinese troops. Politically, it froze the peninsula into two sectors—North and South. As part of the armistice (no peace treaty was ever signed), both sides agreed to a two-and-a-half-mile demilitarized zone almost along the thirty-eighth parallel dividing the peninsula nearly in half and separating the two states. Although the DMZ is a weapons-free corridor, both North and South Korea built elaborate military fortifications along the 155-mile strip, making it the most heavily armed and politically tense border in the world. To this day, the United States maintains 28,500 troops in South Korea to guard against a reprise of the DPRK invasion.

Equally frozen was the political and economic apparatus within the DPRK. Despite the intervening half century and the collapse of the USSR, North Korea is still bound in a Stalinist time warp, where the 1930s Soviet Russia model of totalitarianism remains entrenched. No other state, even a communist one, retains the same level of mass terror, prison camps, regimented indoctrination, national starvation, and cult of personality. Its reigning ideology, nevertheless, is not an exact replica of the former Soviet Union's Marxist and Leninist dogma. Under the inspiration of the Great Leader, Kim Il Sung, the DPRK concocted its own political gospel, known as *juche*, or "spirit of self-reliance."

The *juche* philosophy spells out an elaborate case for national self-sufficiency, a case borne of necessity. Its unyielding orthodoxy precluded Western-style economic development and international trade, which might undermine the hold of the Korean Workers' Party on the population. Further, the secretive nation curdled into an increasingly distrustful island isolated from the outside world. *Juche* justified deprivation and hardship for nonparty members. In fact, dire necessity demanded time and again that North Korea accept international handouts of food, fuel, and other assistance from its sworn enemies—South Korea, Japan, and the United States, plus supplies from the fraternal PRC. Except for the top ranks in the Korean Workers' Party and the Korean People's Army (which includes the navy and air force), the mountainous country of 23 million people suffered severe privations and even starvation. Their plight was brought on by collectivized agriculture and rigid economic policies that periodic floods and droughts exacerbated.[1]

American relations stayed testy with the heavily militarized Northeast Asian country after the war. The so-called Hermit Kingdom provoked clashes along the DMZ, shot at planes it claimed crossed into North Korean airspace, and even hijacked an American reconnaissance ship, the USS *Pueblo*, on the open seas in 1968. The ultimate provocation came with US detection of North Korea's nuclear-arming capabilities in the mid-1980s. The rogue communist state's nuclear quest, nevertheless, dates back decades. The longevity of its nuclear program should caution anyone against the facile notion that the DPRK will easily relinquish a military trump weapon. Its dream of atomic weapons started shortly after the Korean War.

Being under the wing of Soviet power at the time, the DPRK prevailed on Moscow for technical assistance. The Soviet Union trained North Korean engineers and in 1965 transferred a small, two- to four-megawatt reactor to

Yongbyon, some 60 miles north of Pyongyang. Later, Chinese scientists joined Russian technicians to assist North Korea's fledgling nuclear program. During the Reagan presidency, US spy satellites beamed disturbing images to the National Reconnaissance Office of a possible nuclear "breakout" by the North Koreans. As a consequence, Ronald Reagan pressured the Kremlin to persuade its protégé to enter into the Nuclear Nonproliferation Treaty. This landmark treaty mandated its signatories to construct only peaceful, civilian nuclear reactors for energy, not atom bombs. The NPT bound its signers to allow the UN's watchdog agency, the International Atomic Energy Agency, to conduct inspections. The DPRK signed the treaty in 1985 but paid it only lip service before openly flouting the provisions.

The Emergence of a Rogue State

The USSR's dissolution in 1991 transformed North Korea's nuclear policy. As with other ascending rogue players, Pyongyang no longer felt bound by its former patron. For all its ills, the Cold War did serve to check the spread of nuclear weapons. Neither the United States nor the Soviet Union saw it within their national interests to shed the nuclear monopoly. They shared in this exclusive capability with smaller nuclear powers, such as Britain, France, and China. The two-superpower world saw each of the principals hold in check its alliance partners. Moscow kept nuclear arms out of the hands of North Korea and the members of the Warsaw Pact. Washington compelled Taiwan and South Korea to forego these awesome weapons as spelled out in the first chapter. South Korea did develop its own nuclear-power industry for electricity with over 20 reactors, a feat that the North envied. Seoul, however, deferred to Washington's demands that it abstain from developing nuclear warheads. Instead, the ROK remained under the American nuclear umbrella. The disintegration of the Cold War's Pax Atomica gave free rein to despotic governments to pursue nuclear ambitions unhindered by their former Soviet protector.

Before its end, the Soviet Union played an outsized role in North Korea's missile development. Pyongyang developed five separate missile systems between 1987 and 1992. The transfer of technology, missile components, and human expertise came from the declining USSR. North Korean technicians adapted, reverse-engineered, assembled, deployed, and sold mid-range missiles based on their Soviet mentor's rocketry. To compete with its communist rival, China also furnished rocketry to Pyongyang to win its affections from Moscow. In DPRK laboratories, scientists and technicians eventually built missiles with a range that might reach the US naval and air base on Guam Island some 1,800 miles from the Korean Peninsula.[2]

Even before the USSR slipped into oblivion, DPRK officials signaled ominously that they were free of Moscow's restraints on building atomic arms. In reaction, President George H. W. Bush postponed the planned withdrawal of 6,000 US troops until it was clear about the North Korean nuclear intentions. Colin Powell, who served as chairman of the US Joint Chiefs of Staff, uttered an uncharacteristic warning to North Korea: "If they [the North Koreans] missed Desert Storm, this is a chance to catch a re-run" of the 1991 blitzkrieg that pulverized Iraq's Republic Guards.[3] American military prowess stood nearly omnipotent after the first Persian Gulf War. With the Soviet Union slipping into the historical dustbin and Iraq crushed in a resounding defeat, the United States appeared unchallengeable. Such unrivaled supremacy did serve to sober North Korea's posturing.

US military prowess and Powell's tough talk convinced the DPRK to permit international inspections of its nuclear facility as it had agreed to in the NPT. The IAEA team, led by Inspector General Hans Blix, visited the Yongbyon nuclear site in May 1992. The weapons search at the North Korean nuclear site, in effect, was a second chance for Blix. He had been roundly criticized for failing to uncover Iraq's nuclear plants before the Persian Gulf War. Because Blix felt embarrassed by the Iraqi disclosures, the former Swedish foreign minister resolved to press doubly hard in his North Korean inspections.

Blix's determination was rewarded when North Korean technicians inadvertently turned over self-incriminating documents. The evidence revealed that Yongbyon technicians had reprocessed some 90 grams of plutonium in 1990. From these documents, the CIA deduced that North Korea in all likelihood extracted between 8 and 16 pounds of plutonium from spent fuel in its reactor. This amount could produce one or even two nuclear bombs. Thus Blix's inspection raised concerns about North Korea's possession of plutonium-fueled weapons and its warlike intentions that persist to this day.[4]

The United States reacted with restraint to the flushed-out clandestine plutonium-reprocessing scheme. Several reasons account for the moderate reaction. The collapse of communism in Eastern Europe as well as the Soviet Union convinced policy makers and academic observers that the Marxist-Leninist model was doomed. It was just a matter of time—and not long either—before rigid North Korea would also implode. More specifically, the United States, in the North Korean case, went along with the ROK's urgings for restraint. As a consequence, President Bush packed up and sent home all the US nuclear bombs and artillery shells based in the South. Next, Bush suspended for one year the 1992 Team Spirit military exercises jointly held between American and South Korean forces that Pyongyang deemed a pointed dagger.

Seoul hoped for reconciliation with its prickly adversary across the DMZ following a series of agreements with Pyongyang. North and South Korea had signed the Joint Declaration on the Denuclearization of the Korean Peninsula at the end of 1991. It banned all nuclear weapons, plutonium reprocessing, and uranium enrichment in either country. The accord was hailed as a stunning breakthrough for intrapeninsula relations. This treaty, in reality, was too good to be honored by North Korea; and it, plus the NPT, were violated by Pyongyang, as time would soon tell.

At the end of the Bush administration, the White House received intelligence from orbiting US satellites that North Korea was reprocessing plutonium, despite its treaty assurances. Bush officials passed the intelligence to the incoming president, William J. Clinton. It fell to the incoming government, the first elected since the end of the Cold War, to take on the international scofflaw.

Bill Clinton and a Blatant Nuclear Rogue State

North Korea figured not at all in the young Arkansas governor's election to the residence at 1600 Pennsylvania Avenue. During the presidential campaign, Bill Clinton never discussed North Korea at any length. In his Inaugural Address in late January 1993, he passed over South Korea when he praised "the brave Americans serving our nation today in the Persian Gulf and Somalia."[5] At that time, 37,000 US troops stood on guard along the DMZ in "eyeball-to-eyeball contact" with a bellicose foe, whose armed forces were ranked as the world's fifth-largest standing army. The incoming president was equally unprepared for the white-hot tension with North Korea over its nuclear goals.

Not long after settling into the White House, Clinton was confronted by the North's nuclear plans. A US satellite's detection of plutonium reprocessing also alerted the IAEA's Hans Blix to a possible infraction. He requested another sweep of two DPRK nuclear sites in mid-March 1993. The timing coincided with the reinstated Team Spirit military maneuvers that had been annual American–South Korean defense exercise since 1976, except for President Bush's 1992 suspension. The exercises deployed both America's B-1B bombers (rigged to carry nuclear bombs) and US troop reinforcements to South Korea. The twining of the two activities proved alarmingly provocative to an aggrieved North Korea, which never passed up an opportunity that a crisis afforded to advance its agenda. First, Kim Il Sung, known domestically as the Great Leader, dismissed the IAEA's inspection request and revoked North Korea's participation in the Nonproliferation Treaty after the lapse of the required 90-day grace period. His son and "crown prince" in the DPRK dynasty, Kim Jong Il, mobilized the country's military forces for war as their newly installed supreme commander.

Pyongyang's actions and declarations jolted Washington and other capitals. The Clinton government sought China's assistance with its opaque neighbor. Although the PRC had remained a North Korean backer since the Korean War, Beijing begged off American requests for diplomatic leverage with the DPRK. China implausibly declared that it lacked sway over the North Koreans despite its lifesaving shipments of fuel oil and food to its fellow communist regime. Although US officials did not take these disclaimers at face value, they were reluctant to offend Beijing publicly.

The new presidency scrambled to craft a policy. Rather than a tough, military posture, it settled initially on negotiations with the Kim regime. Clinton officials met several times with their DPRK counterparts in Beijing, Geneva, and New York City to halt Pyongyang's scheduled departure from the NPT. Tension stayed high on the peninsula. It was in this atmosphere that the savvy North Korean negotiators refloated a proposal previously spurned by the George H. W. Bush administration, for it regarded the proposition as one of rewarding blackmail. Pyongyang's interlocutors replaced on the table an offer to suspend plutonium reprocessing and stop new construction of outmoded graphite reactors. In return, the DPKR envoys demanded that the United States furnish up-to-date light-water reactors (LWR). The LWR possessed several advantages. Unlike the 1950-vintage heavy-water reactors (that used deuterium oxide), the LWR ran on ordinary water, produced more energy for greater electrical output, and employed "proliferation-resistant" technology that inhibited the siphoning off of plutonium for arms production.

Washington surprisingly accepted the North Korean offer. But actual codification of the proposal drifted for over a year. The Clinton foreign policy team had several reasons for the decision. The LWR, while vastly expensive, came with safeguards against bleeding off bomb-making plutonium. Moreover, installing the modern reactors presented a way to engage the reclusive North Koreans in hopes of opening the country to outside influence. Mainly, the proposal could defuse the peninsular antagonism. Finally, it seemed the only viable option to a risk-averse White House. It ruled out war or sanctions.

Neither the Oval Office nor the Pentagon desired an encore of the 1950s conflict. Economic sanctions, as Pyongyang menacingly warned, constituted an act of war. In addition, the PRC's steadfast opposition to an embargo meant certain failure at the United Nations to secure its passage in the Security Council, where Beijing held a veto. A military option was tentatively explored in spring 1993. Midlevel officers at the Pentagon mapped out surgical strikes on the known nuclear reactor at Yongbyon. They concluded that a bombing run on the target before the technicians carted off the spent plutonium fuel rods presented the optimum window for air strikes. The Pentagon chiefs shelved the plan because they lacked absolute certainty that a bombardment would eliminate all of the North's nuclear capacity.[6] The DPRK had burrowed hideouts and bases deep within the country's mountainsides. One or more of these fastnesses might house a secret nuclear facility. No clean sweep, therefore, could be guaranteed by air operations. Even a destructive onslaught on Yongbyon would throw up clouds of nuclear particles that would spill across South Korea, Japan, and the East Asian region. Showers of atomic dust promised horrendous side effects for the region and the US image abroad. An aerial attack in all likelihood would spark another Korean War, something that Defense Secretary William Perry and his military commanders wished to avoid.

What complicated the military picture even more was the fact that the heavily militarized DPRK also fielded deadly conventional forces along the DMZ. Its army had entrenched long-range artillery and multiple rocket launchers to a gun density that approached the Soviet defense of Stalingrad against the Third Reich's Wehrmacht. This combat "punch" gave Pyongyang a land-based lethality that confronted the US and South Korean militaries with hard choices. A DPRK shelling of Seoul, a mere 40 miles from the North Korean barrels, would cause an estimated million casualties within a few days and the destruction of South Korea's capital city. The two allies possessed the wherewithal to defeat the North over an extended period. But the heavy costs might result in little more than a Pyrrhic victory. Estimates predicted some 50,000 American casualties and several hundred thousand ROK soldiers before the North could be stopped in its tracks. In the last analysis, the DPRK's conventional force posed an inhibiting deterrent to any American preemptive aerial strikes on Yongbyon.

The Two-Simultaneous-Conflicts Dilemma

To understand the US response to North Korea and other rogue nations during the 1990s, it is important to explain the two-major-threat scenario on which the United States based its war planning. The Pentagon assessed the likelihood of war with North Korea and Iraq as higher than any other hot spots. Both dictatorships blew war trumpets and made ominous gestures. What caused sleepless nights among US military planners was the prospect of a war on two fronts at the same time. Saddam Hussein's Iraq, as is described in chapter 2, kept the Middle East on edge after the Persian Gulf War by blocking UN arms inspections, backing terrorism, and repressing his own Kurdish population that enjoyed limited US protection. The Kim dynasty in North Korea, likewise, aroused unease in the Pentagon corridors with its inflammatory pronouncements and nuclear arming.

America's military brass, as a consequence, war-gamed a two-conflict scenario on fighting simultaneously "two major-regional-contingencies." War planning, a necessity even in the post–Cold War era, took into account the grim fact of hostilities in battlefields half a world apart. The exigencies were intensified by the knowledge that America's military downsized 40 percent during the decade after the Soviet Union disintegration. These large-scale reductions compelled the top brass to pare down their projections and adjust the timing to read *"nearly* simultaneously" waging two conflicts. The Defense Department, if called on to fight in two different theaters, planned engaging either Iraq or North Korea first with knockout blows and then shifting forces to the other battlefront. Both Presidents George H. W. Bush and Bill Clinton had a hand in shrinking the US Army from 18 regular divisions to 10 divisions, the US Air Force from 28 Fighter Wing Equivalents (FWE) (roughly 72 planes per FWE) to 13 Air Force wings, and the US Navy from almost 600 ships to around 350 naval vessels. Later, the navy lost another 100 vessels, as retired warships were not replaced with new ones. Because of the possibility of another conflict with Iraq, the Pentagon had reservations about getting into a pitched land conflict with North Korea. Containing and deterring Pyongyang were believed to be the best approaches for US interests.

Bargaining with North Korea

As always in dealing with rogue nations, the United States held neither all the cards nor all the chips. North Korea often stole a march on or maneuvered forcefully against its American opponent, as was the case in 1994. The apparent breakthrough in the US-DPRK negotiations in mid-1993 had dissipated by the end of that year. Nineteen-ninety-four witnessed a supercharged showdown. Angered by what it perceived as America perfidy for not following up on its offer to provide light-water reactors and by IAEA demands for treaty-mandated access to Yongbyon, the DPRK regime reacted belligerently. It refused inspectors entrée to its nuclear facilities. It fulminated at the US Army's fielding of Patriot antimissile batteries in South Korea as a defense against its rockets. It sounded the war tocsin when the US commander in the ROK, General Gary Luck, got the extra American troops he wanted for the 1994 Team Spirit military exercises. Pyongyang claimed that the military buildup was a prelude to an attack. One of its officials threatened that if war broke out, "Seoul will turn into a sea of fire."[7] South Korea's population panicked. They hoarded food. They voiced their war fears on televisions and in newspapers. Their stock market plunged. East Asia braced for another Korean War.

The resumption of the light-water reactor negotiations calmed the roiled seas. It was former president Jimmy Carter, serving as the Clinton administration's envoy to Pyongyang, who resurfaced the talks on the LWR. He met with Kim Il Sung in Pyongyang in June 1994. Together they defused what had become a North Korean–created crisis. Carter's role was controversial in that he stole the limelight for the peaceful resolution of the tension from Clinton.[8] Without his intercession, Washington might have pressed harder for coal-fired generators instead of the LWR. Coal-consuming generators held several advantages. Cheaper to build and maintain, these electrical producers could use North Korea's abundance of coal deposits for power. Small coal-fueled plants could be scattered in several locations, eliminating the need to erect a nationwide modern electrical grid to carry electricity far and wide. As it were, the old power lines (many built by the Japanese occupiers) stood to be vaporized with a sudden surge of electricity from a powerful nuclear generator.

None of this practical logic registered with the North Koreans, who wanted their own nuclear reactors to compete with their South Korean cousins, who already had built more than 20 nuclear facilities for electrical power. The construction of one or more LWR, well beyond the North's technical capacity, would keep Pyongyang in the atomic game to boot. Belonging to the nuclear club can be irresistible for desperate regimes, whose dictatorships conjure up foreign enemies to maintain their power and utilize the prospect of fabricating nuclear arms to bolster internal support.

The Clinton administration saw the LWR as a panacea. It averted conflict, conciliated the DPRK, and quieted war fears on the peninsula. But giving into Pyongyang's demands for one or two LWR prompted accusations of Bill Clinton's appeasement by his political opponents, independent analysts, and some foreign countries, such as Japan. It harbored deep resentment against North Korea for its continual threats to the Japanese islands. Tokyo governments also were castigated for not doing enough to secure the freedom of Japanese citizens (at least 13 and possibly more) abducted from coastal areas and taken to North Korea in the late 1970s and 1980s. Any perceived compromise, as Prime Minister Junichiro Koizumi's deal of rice and medicine for the release of children of some abductees in 2004, came in for bitter scorn.[9] Since no one wanted another Korean War, the American opposition lacked alternative options to the Clinton plans. Furthermore, few observers gave the North Korean regime much chance of an extended longevity. Since the entire Soviet edifice had imploded a few years earlier, it was not unreasonable to see a similar outcome for the DPRK just over the horizon. Agreeing to multiyear LWR construction was not unlike being the beneficiary of a life insurance policy on a very ill person. As it turned out, the patient had much more resiliency than predicted.

Negotiations resumed between American and North Korean diplomats (the United States excluded the South Koreans) in Geneva. Amid the talks, Kim Il Sung died reportedly of a heart attack on July 8, 1994. Little disruption took place in the deliberations, and the Great Leader's dynastic heir, Kim Jong Il, stepped into his father's shoes. The younger Kim was decidedly different from his near-mythic father, who projected a revolutionary aura among North Koreans. His son's extravagant life—a love for fast cars, fast women, American films, and Scotch liquor—hardly fit with the DPRK's militarized austerity and tiresomely regimented conformity. Perhaps to atone for past indulgences, Kim habitually donned khaki jumpsuits, which cast him as a bland figure. Notwithstanding his playboy persona, Kim the younger was ruthless. He is widely thought to have masterminded the deadly terrorist blast that killed many officials in the South Korean delegation of Prime Minister Chun Doo Hwan visiting Rangoon in 1983. Rising to the top of the greasy pole, even from a privileged start, no doubt necessitated cunning in what became the communist world's only monarchial-type succession. The Supreme People's Assembly soon rubberstamped Kim Jong Il to the chairmanship of the National Defense Commission, the highest administrative authority. Dear Leader, as he became known to his repressed subjects, soon enough let the Geneva talks culminate in an agreement. Washington believed an agreement would bring nuclear containment, disarmament, and eventually reconciliation to the divided peninsula. These hopes proved far too optimistic.

Washington and Pyongyang signed the Agreed Framework in Geneva on October 21, 1994. It called for the resolution of nuclear crisis in three stages. Most significantly, it pledged the North Koreans to freeze their refueling of the aged graphite reactor at Yongbyon that had been emptied of spent plutonium fuel rods. This provision, in effect, shut down the reactor that produced little electricity but enough plutonium for several bombs. The 8,000 spent rods were to be stored in a cooling pond under IAEA surveillance. The agreement also obligated the North Koreans to suspend construction of two larger graphite reactors. Additionally, Pyongyang reaffirmed its commitment to the Nuclear Nonproliferation Treaty, which meant refraining from pursuing nuclear arms, a commitment it later broke with abandon.

Dear Leader Kim went along with the concessions because he required foreign assistance to hold his ramshackle country together without undergoing the same type of economic reforms begun by Deng Xiaoping in China. From the late 1970s, Deng moved the PRC away from rigid economic policies that paralyzed growth and innovation. While the Chinese Communist Party retained political power, it partially opened its economy to the global market and embraced what it termed as a socialist-market economy, which raised the living standard for hundreds of millions of people.[10] But North Korea's Chairman Kim and his entourage feared similar wide-ranging economic transformations might endanger their hold on power. Instead, they looked to South Korean, Western European, and American bailouts to preserve the dilapidated communist relic.

In compensation to Pyongyang for signing the Agreed Framework, the United States committed to an aid package. It pledged to organize an international consortium to construct first one and then another proliferation-resistant light-water reactor capable of generating 2,000 megawatts each. The reactors were modeled on the South Korean plants and cost some $4.6 billion, of which Seoul and Tokyo would provide the lion's share of the funding. Construction began at Kumho on the central east coast of North Korea but was finally abandoned in 2005 when the deal collapsed; at that time, the project was about one-third completed. A few years later, Seoul newspapers reported that the trucks, cranes, and other heavy equipment were looted from the site.[11]

Since the North needed electrical output before the first new reactor's completion, the Clinton government agreed to ship heavy oil to run its energy-producing generators. Washington sent 50,000 metric tons the first year of this underutilized byproduct of refined petroleum, starting in October 1996. Then it agreed to step up the annual supply to 500,000 metric tons in subsequent years. Washington estimated the total costs at $500 million until 2003, when the first reactor was set to come online.

The US-DPRK accord contained sequencing stipulations as well as promises by both sides. The North agreed to abide by the NPT, which it had threatened to leave. Thus, the IAEA regained entrée into North Korea's nuclear waste sites soon after the signing to determine the volume of plutonium reprocessed by DPRK technicians. By this measurement, the IAEA could gauge the nuclear weapons capability of its hosts. The United States then moved forward on fuel shipments and set up the construction consortium. Once full compliance with IAEA demands was met, then the international consortium must hand over key components for the functioning of the first LWR. When the third and final phase of the agreement took effect at Yongbyon, Pyongyang was obligated to dismantle its out-of-date nuclear installations.[12]

To implement the accord, the United States prevailed on an irked South Korea to lead the international consortium, dubbed the Korean Energy Development Organization (KEDO), along with Japan. During the lengthy negotiations running up to the US-DPRK agreement, Washington sidelined the Seoul government of Kim Young Sam, bypassing complications from the South and protests from the North. For its part, the ROK swallowed its pride after denouncing the United States for shoring up the faltering DPRK with the framework accord. Next, Seoul established KEDO, pumped in lots of its funding, and extended most of the technical assistance. ROK's President Kim valued his country's relationship with Washington more than its temporary humiliation from exclusion at the Geneva talks. KEDO, in fact, was a face-saving edifice anyway. It allowed the envious, prideful, and bitter North Koreans to fool themselves that they worked with an international entity, not their more successful brethren across the DMZ.[13]

The Agreed Framework had a salutary impact on North-South relations. Overall, it tamped down the hair-trigger atmosphere on the Korean Peninsula as the war talk subsided. Concretely, it permitted ROK president Kim and his successors to drop restrictions on cooperation with the North. South Korean businesses made investments in light-manufacturing plants across the DMZ, taking advantage of the cheaper labor costs and docile workforce. Crossborder visits and tourism sprouted. The next ROK government of President Kim Dae Jung expanded the South's engagement in what he called the "sunshine policy," which won him a desperately pursued Nobel Laureate for Peace.

The thaw continued despite periodic icy blasts from the irascible state north of the DMZ. By mid-2007, enough of a détente had been established that two rail lines punctured the heavily fortified DMZ. Yet the broader interconnection between the divided nations proceeded jaggedly rather than linearly, with two steps forward and one backward. Pyongyang thrived on adversarial relations with South Korea and the United States. As with other rogue regimes, the Kim dictatorship employed a provocative foreign policy to gird its internal legitimacy as the nation's defenders. This posture also entailed privileged treatment and massive outlays for the North Korean military. Meanwhile, the country suffered from biblical floods, droughts, and famines during the 1990s in which some two million people died from starvation, disease, and callous neglect by their government.

The Clinton presidency knew the pitfalls of agreements with the North. But American governments are wont to "manage" a crisis to put the danger behind them, leave the problem to the next incumbent, and nullify criticism from the media or the opposition party.[14] Whatever political party held the White House, Democratic or Republican, it encountered ridicule and scorn from its opposition in Congress and among independent policy analysts for treating with Pyongyang. Bill Clinton first faced doubting Thomases, and later George W. Bush ran into similar skepticism. Clinton's Agreed Framework struck critics as a form of appeasement and blind faith in Pyongyang's trustworthiness without independent verification until years afterward. But the lack of realistic options to counter the North's nuclearization left debunkers without a viable alternative short of a possible unwanted conflict. Backers and detractors of the Agreed Framework took comfort in the belief that the Kim regime was destined for near-term doom. Many thought that it would disintegrate before light-water reactors were due for delivery in 2003. It was just one in a series of wrong predictions about the imminent demise of the totalitarian regime.[15]

Notwithstanding the doomsday forecasts, the peninsula calmed down for a few years in a fleeting détente. But tranquility from the North Korean regime was evanescent behavior. In 1998, it test-fired a long-range, multistage missile, the Taepodong, whose flight path traversed over Japanese territory. The rocket launch, once again, riveted world attention on the closed society. Apprehension spiked in South Korea before it dissipated. Japan evinced a much more sustained defensive posture toward the missile threat than Seoul governments, which over time softened their approach. Tokyo did purchase advanced US interceptor missiles designed to hit incoming projectiles from North Korea.

Even in an America preoccupied with the Clinton sex scandal in the White House and ethnic cleansing in Kosovo, the Taepodong incident still captured attention. This latest crisis prompted Washington to broker another arms control agreement with the reclusive regime. It made two high-level efforts in pursuit of a missile accord. The White House appointed former secretary of defense William Perry as a special envoy to North Korea. Then, Secretary of State Madeleine Albright traveled to the rogue communist state to meet with Chairman Kim. To stop the testing and the export of missiles to Libya, Syria, and Iran, the West Wing even considered a presidential visit. The Kim regime was eager to host Bill Clinton, whose officials hinted at more US aid for a missile agreement.[16] As time ran out on his second term, Clinton was preoccupied with unsuccessful attempts to reach a peace settlement between the Israelis and the Palestinians. Then, late in the Clinton presidency, disturbing intelligence surfaced that North Korea was embarking on uranium processing for nuclear arms. This disquieting information disrupted Washington-Pyongyang relations in the next presidential administration.[17] The Taepodong test and the uranium disclosure issues went unresolved as Clinton left office in early 2001.

George W. Bush and Old Wine in New Bottles

Soon after George Walker Bush moved into the White House, the United States fell victim to the 9/11 terrorist attack on the emblematic landmarks of American economic and military power in downtown Manhattan and suburban Washington. These al-Qaeda terrorist assaults temporarily diverted attention from North Korea and placed it squarely on Afghanistan and then Iraq. The DPRK was not left out of the Bush administration's speeches, however. In his 2002 State of the Union address, President Bush identified North Korea as part of the "axis of evil" along with Iraq and Iran. The US attack on Afghanistan and its war preparations against Iraq preoccupied Bush officials at first.

Two crucial factors snapped official thinking back to North Korea: first, the heightened fear of another foreign attack; and second, revelations of secret uranium enrichment in the DPRK. In Bush's still-young presidency, intelligence came to light that Pyongyang had cheated on the Agreed Framework and the NPT by enriching uranium for possible nuclear arms. Producing highly enriched uranium (HEU) emits particulates that scientific instruments can detect and identify. Confirmation of satellite detections derived from two unlikely sources. The first vindication seemingly came from the North Koreans themselves. At an October 4, 2002, meeting in Pyongyang between the US assistant secretary of state for East Asian and Pacific affairs, James A. Kelly, and the DPRK's Deputy Foreign Minister Kang Seok-Ju, the North Koreans acknowledged the US allegations of uranium enriching. Later, the North Korean delegation retracted the admission, arguing that a mistranslation of their comments caused a misunderstanding.

The second affirmation of the American suspicions derived from the bombshell revelations about the surreptitious "nuclear supermarket" of Abdul Qadeer Khan. The Pakistani scientist dealt in a nuclear black market for profit but with approval of his government. Known as the father of Pakistan's bomb, Khan peddled nuclear technology to Iran and Libya as well as North Korea from the late 1990s. North Korea and Iran also collaborated in missile development. Pyongyang provided Scud components to Tehran, which tested North Korean knock-off missiles, thereby giving the Kim regime valuable flight data. Khan's sales fed into this rogue cooperative network. He made over a dozen visits to Pyongyang and sold centrifuges used in uranium enrichment (too few to carry on a full-blown enriching program but adequate to lay a research foundation), together with blueprints and designs. In 2002, a shipment was uncovered of enough aluminum tubing for 4,000 centrifuges bound for North Korea aboard a French cargo vessel. This incident and intelligence findings motivated the United States to air publicly its concerns. In trades for Khan's know-how and equipment, the DPRK transported planeload after planeload of missile components to Pakistan, as it also did to Iran, Syria, and Libya.[18]

Later, Khan released information that North Korea began its uranium enrichment during the late 1990s. He said it possessed "maybe 3,000 or even more" centrifuges by 2002. In any event, Pyongyang claimed to be in the final stages of acquiring sufficient uranium for a nonplutonium weapon in September 2009.[19] In early 2010, South Korea's foreign minister, Yu Myung-hwan, claimed that the DPRK "started its uranium enrichment program at least in 1996," which confirmed Khan's assertion. That date was more than a decade before Pyongyang officially owned up to its uranium program.[20]

Yet the US intelligence estimates of the DPRK's uranium progress were sadly wrong. A top US intelligence officer from the staff of the director of national intelligence told Congress in 2007 that its assessments downgraded North Korean uranium production to just "mid-confidence" from "high confidence." Pyongyang, according to this report, probably acquired some equipment for a uranium effort, but it was less likely to have a "production-scale" uranium program in operation, according to the revised estimate.[21] The 2007 assessment, like others, generated controversy about what was the real status of Pyongyang's uranium effort. It was rejected by Bush officials.[22] The Bush administration stated that North Korean nuclear activity included both uranium and plutonium production.[23] The marked failure of intelligence reporting prior to the Iraq invasion clouded all appraisals—a judgment that persists to this day. Whereas the intelligence on Iraq was dead wrong about the presence of nuclear capabilities, it was equally wrong on North Korea in finding little or no uranium reprocessing for atomic weaponry.

American fears as a result of the October 2003 Kelly-Kang meeting precipitated a punitive reaction. The Bush administration canceled the fuel oil transfers that Clinton officials negotiated under the Agreed Framework with Pyongyang. Not long after that, the US-funded Radio Free Asia began broadcasting antiregime messages for over three hours daily into North Korea. The DPRK reacted by revoking its participation in all its nuclear-freeze accords. Thus, it became more reliant on China's supplies of fuel and food shipments. The North Korean regime hurled vitriolic accusations at the United States and its South Korean "puppet." Seoul held steady in its engagement of its northern neighbor during the first part of the twenty-first century. In fact, business and tourist exchanges generally hummed along because the new accommodating government of President Roh Moo-hyun in Seoul prized stability and development more than confrontation.

By late 2002, America's focus was almost exclusively on Iraq, even after the Hermit Kingdom's uranium-processing declarations in October to the US envoy. Another incident during this period, nevertheless, deepened anxieties about North Korean intentions. In December, a Spanish warship seized an unflagged merchantman in the Arabian Sea bound for Yemen carrying 15 Scud missiles with conventional warheads in its hold. Despite Madrid's protests, Washington allowed the ship to reach its destination because Yemen was cooperating against al-Qaeda terrorists.[24] Given its provocative behavior and its colorful sword-rattling broadcasts, the DPRK grabbed some of the almost exclusive attention devoted to Iraq. In the end, Bush zeroed in on the approaching war against the Gulf state, putting North Korean policy onto the back burner.

Another Korean War versus the Iraq War

In some ways, the Iraq and Korean crises mutually reinforced each other, aggravating the threats and dilemma they posed to a perplexed United States. Bush, as it turned out, espoused polar opposite policies toward the two members of the "axis of evil." Toward Saddam Hussein's Iraq, the White House readied for war and invasion. Senior officials, including its president, came into office predisposed to regime change in Iraq.[25] They justified a military solution against Iraq on the grounds of not only its perfecting WMD (which turned out be nonexistent) but also on its supporting terrorism, menacing neighboring states, and possibly disrupting the flow of Persian Gulf oil. Hussein had an even greater penchant for unpredictability than that of Kim Jong Il. The Iraqi despot unsettled a region much more unstable than Northeast Asia.

Political opponents and Beltway pundits raised an evident contradiction. Why war against Iraq and not North Korea? The DPRK posed an immediate threat with its confirmation of nuclear activities. Yet President Bush pointed his lance at Iraq, not at the DPRK. North Korea's known nuclear program in the early Bush presidency played a paradoxical role in catapulting the United States into hostilities against Iraq. Since the DPRK already possessed some nuclear-arms capacity, the risks of fighting it stood much higher than Iraq, which was merely suspected of pursuing an atomic option. Pyongyang's formidable conventional forces along the DMZ also made it a more muscular adversary than an Iraq weakened from the Persian Gulf War. In short, being a full-fledged member or even a candidate member of the nuclear club brought a measure of protection. Little wonder that

Iran and North Korea have aggressively strained to acquire nuclear weaponry. They saw Iraq's sad fate for pretending to have nuclear arms. Jumping ahead, when Libya came under NATO attack in early 2011, Pyongyang issued a statement pointing out that the Libyans' nuclear disarmament years before the NATO bombing had rendered the North African country vulnerable to military intervention.[26] In short, nuclear arms brought it safety.

George Bush turned back to North Korea briefly in 2003 and tried to deter it from nuclear activity. The president delivered a veiled threat that "all options are on the table" while he focused on Iraq. In May, Bush in joint statement with the visiting ROK president Roh Moo Hyun laid down a stern warning: "We will not tolerate nuclear weapons in North Korea."[27] It was an empty threat. Washington's faint red line never even slowed down Pyongyang's drive for fissile material. It could do so safely thanks to a widening anticoalition insurgency spilling across Iraq. Washington had become bogged down in a fierce land conflict in the Middle East, limiting its actions by mid-2003.

The United States relied on containment and deterrence of North Korea, somewhat as it had against a nuclear-armed Soviet Union. It deployed a squadron of supersonic bombers across the Pacific to Guam Island so as to counter and contain Pyongyang. The onset of the Iraq War, in fact, did drain away high-level diplomatic interest from North Korea, except for the White House's attention to human rights. Soon after passage of the North Korean Human Rights Act in 2004, President Bush appointed as special envoy for North Korean human rights Jay Lefkowitz, who labored to spotlight the appalling abuses above the DMZ among the estimated 200,000 prisoners in Soviet-like gulags.[28]

The United States also took comfort in the de-escalation of intrapeninsula tensions and in its warming relations with the People's Republic of China. The PRC had long since replaced Moscow as the DPRK's main patron. American diplomats hoped that Beijing would rein in its obstreperous charge. Events on the Korean Peninsula were indeed more reassuring than the chronically combustible Middle East. The ROK president Roh Moo-hyun built on his predecessor's (Kim Dae Jung's) "sunshine policy" for greater reconciliation and economic ties with the North. South Koreans invested in factories and funded the Kaesong Industrial Complex, some six miles north of the DMZ. Southern companies in Kaesong employed local workers. Pyongyang required wages to be funneled through the North's bureaucracy, a sore point among the companies and the Seoul government. They knew that the laborers got just a fraction of the salaries. Yet the ROK accepted the DPRK's conditions on the "special economic zones," reasoning that some economic development and exposure to market practices was better than nothing.

South Korean leaders argued for nearly two decades that gradual economic growth in the paranoid DPRK would facilitate liberalization within the North and eventually its "soft landing" when finally the regime fell. Seoul feared a sudden shakeout in the North that would disgorge millions of destitute Northerners onto the South, overwhelming public services and jeopardizing political stability. As a result, South Korean governments generally went along with business ties to the North, even though ROK political figures threw verbal brickbats at their northern neighbor from time to time. Harangues aside, Seoul reached out to its Northern cousins. Not only did it transport rice, fertilizer, and construction materials across the border, it reduced the barriers themselves. It opened railway lines and roads through the DMZ to connect the two countries. Pyongyang taunted the South and greeted its goodwill gestures as supplications.

Eased tensions on the peninsula paired with mounting US priorities in the Middle East convinced the Pentagon to scale back its military forces in South Korea. By the end of 2007, it had reduced its "footprint" to 28,500 from 37,000 troops. Other changes were implemented in the command structure for US and ROK forces. Previously, in the early 1990s, the South Korean military assumed peacetime control of its 600,000-strong military from the Americans. Bush's Defense Department next agreed to turn over wartime operational control to the South Koreans by the end of 2009 (because of peninsular tensions, the Obama administration rescinded this directive at the request of the South Korean army). Additionally, Bush's Pentagon agreed to redeploy its forces and bases back from the DMZ and south of Seoul. For protection from an atomic-arming DPRK, South Korea still sheltered under America's considerable nuclear umbrella.

America's Return to Diplomacy and the Six-Party Talks

The United States decided to cast the October 2002 revelations of uranium enrichment as a multinational problem. Colin Powell, the US secretary of state, favored a multilateral over a bilateral approach. Washington first engaged China, as the North's primary food and fuel supplier, along with Pyongyang in a meeting held in Beijing in April 2003. It served as a progenitor for the expanded membership of Seoul, Tokyo, and Moscow. In August, the Six-Party Talks convened in Beijing for several rounds to curtail the DPRK's nuclear program. After the 9/11 terrorist attacks, the prospect of even low-yield nuclear material falling into jihadi hands haunted American policy makers. Deterrence and containment measures might suffice to bottle up an overt North Korean nuclear threat. Only by ridding the cash-starved country of plutonium could Washington halt a potential sale to a terrorist network. Ultimately, it failed to strip the DPRK of its nuclear material.

After two years of stop-and-go negotiations and four sets of talks, the Six-Party diplomats forged a Joint Statement of Principles on September 19, 2005. The North Koreans agreed to "abandon all nuclear weapons and existing nuclear programs," to rejoin the Nuclear Nonproliferation Treaty, and to readmit IAEA inspectors to their nuclear facilities. In exchange, Pyongyang would get food, fuel oil, and other aid from the Six-Party members. The accord recorded long-held North Korean demands for respect of its national sovereignty. Washington was disappointed when the Joint Statement failed to lead to a resolution of such long-standing issues as securing a peace treaty to replace the armistice dating from the Korean War, a nonaggression pact, and a restoration of diplomatic ties between the two countries.[29] Implementing the Joint Statement waited 18 months because of US reactions to a spate of North Korean illegal activities.

Counterfeit, Illicit, and Desperate

Things rarely ran on rails for long with the DPRK. In this instance, Pyongyang's criminal dealings triggered a sharp US rebuke just after the signing of the Joint Statement. Responding to North Korea's money laundering from drug sales and counterfeiting American currency, Washington took action. The US Treasury's Operation Smoking Dragon imposed financial sanctions on Banco Delta Asia (BDA) in Macau in late September 2005. The Treasury's investigation had gone on for years, but the timing of its action nearly coincided with signing of the Joint Statement, which it disrupted. The Treasury Department's investigation encompassed a range of North Korean criminality. For many years, DPRK "minted" bogus $100 bills and laundered them through BDA as well as passed them to unwitting sellers of commodities destined for North Korea.[30]

Over the years, North Korea's counterfeiting techniques improved so much that it printed $100 bill "supernotes" of exceedingly high quality. A US interagency task force estimated that by 2006 the North Koreans circulated about $45–60 million worth in counterfeit bills. It even manufactured fake cigarettes for export sales. Using provisions from the Patriot Act (passed in the wake of the 9/11 attacks to eliminate fund transfers for terrorists and rogue states), the Treasury banned American banks from doing business with BDA. Foreign financial institutions fell in line with their American counterparts, fearing exclusion from dealings within the US financial system. The Treasury Department's actions proved to be one of the most effective sanctions launched against North Korea.[31] BDA had served as the rogue nation's principal conduit for legal and illicit business. The bank scandal, therefore, became a stumbling block for the deal with the DPRK over its nuclear activity.

North Koreans were nothing if not ingenious in finding wily stratagems for nabbing hard currency. Starting at least as early as 1998, they scammed tens of millions of dollars and euros from United Nations Development Program (UNDP) in North Korea. Their methods were as simple as they were unprincipled. They demanded cash payments for humanitarian assistance, public health, and agricultural projects carried out in the Hermit Kingdom. Yet no UNDP officials were permitted to enter and inspect the agency's funded programs.[32] All the local staff and vendors for supplies were selected and paid by the DPRK government instead of the international organization itself—in violation of the UNDP's own procedures. Handpicked officials by the DPRK administered the record keeping, such as it was, in what amounted to a giant ATM for the Kim Jong Il regime. The Korean dictator used the proceeds to buy the loyalty of the country's political and military elite through cash payments in hard currencies or gifts of luxury goods.

It became a matter of speculation whether millions of dollars from the "cash-for-Kim" scheme were also diverted to the regime's nuclear program. The guessing added to the United Nations' plight. This swindle resembled the dollars-for-dictators scandal engulfing the United Nations over the oil-for-food program within Saddam Hussein's Iraq during the late 1990s. After the Bush administration uncovered and exposed to public scrutiny the UNDP's slipshod and sloppy practices, the agency pulled out of North Korea a few months later in March 2007.[33]

Unwilling and unable to develop its economy for legitimate exports, Pyongyang turned to other novel ways to gain hard currencies. By strong-arming North Korean migrants living in Japan, it garnered annually an estimated $1 billion in remittances from an exiled population too fearful for the well-being of relatives living in the homeland to withhold cash from Pyongyang. Other monies originated from North Korean–run "packinko" gambling parlors in Japan. Like the remittances from expatriate workers, the gambling profits were smuggled out on vessels bound for the DPRK. North Korea also manufactured, shipped, and sold narcotics (sometimes through their embassies and counselor offices) since at least 1976, when one of their diplomats was arrested in Egypt with 880 pounds of hashish in his possession. Over the next quarter of a century, some 50 arrests took place in 20 different countries involving North Korean agents. They were taken into custody for drug trafficking in methamphetamine and heroin.[34]

The North Koreans transferred Soviet-era military equipment to several nations, some of which were even aligned with the United States. Spare parts went to Ethiopia as late as 2007 for its T-55 tanks that came from the Soviet Union during the Cold War. At the time, Ethiopia was helping the United States in confronting Islamist insurgents in Somalia.[35] In addition to its chief customers, such as Iran and Syria, North Korean firms hawked weaponry to Libya, Pakistan, and Yemen.[36] Muammar al-Qaddafi's Libya stocked scores of North Korean Scud-C missiles in its arsenal.[37] A report surfaced during the Hezbollah-Israel War in summer 2006 that the North Koreans had even sold their tunnel-building skills to the Iranian-backed Hezbollah operating in southern Lebanon. Iranian diplomats in the Levantine country smuggled in the Korean advisers "in the guise of [domestic] servants," where they helped build tunnel infrastructure.[38]

In late 2009, a planeload of DPRK conventional arms were impounded in the Bangkok airport by Thailand's government. Owned by a company in the United Arab Emirates and registered in the Republic of Georgia, the Russian-manufactured airplane touched down in the Thai capital to refuel before heading toward Iran. Neither the Georgian government nor the UAE-based firm took responsibility for the illicit use of the aircraft. The intended usages of the military cargo by Iran or by its surrogate movements, Hezbollah and Hamas, remained unknown. The Thai episode demonstrated anew that interrogue exchanges of contraband persisted despite UN sanctions and international policing.[39]

Back to the Future

Pyongyang retaliated against US financial sanctions over the BDA scandal with its reversion to brinkmanship. It fired off a long-range missile and conducted a nuclear test in 2006, both of which violated international agreements. The year after the Taepodong hurtled over Japan in 1998, the DPRK entered into a moratorium. It stipulated North Korea would refrain from lofting any more ICBM-type missiles into the atmosphere while Pyongyang-Washington talks were ongoing. Now seven years later, Pyongyang appeared ready to ignore that pledge and its DPRK-Japan Declaration of 2002, which also called for a launch moratorium and suspension of its nuclear program.

Every nearby capital, plus Washington and Moscow, urged North Korea to forestall its high-altitude missile test. The one plea that counted most came from Beijing, for it provided Pyongyang annually with an estimated $2 billion assistance package. Without the PRC's food, fuel, fertilizer, and other goods, the destitute country to its south would starve and freeze. On the eve of the missile test, the Chinese premier Wen Jiabao stated, "We hope that various parties will proceed for the greater interest of maintaining stability on the Korean Peninsula and refrain from taking measures that will worsen the situation."[40] Polite and circumspect, Wen's meaning could not have been clearer.

Ignoring the pleas, Pyongyang fired six short-range rockets and one long-range, three-stage missile designed to orbit a satellite or lift a warhead. With maximum ranges of between 375 and 995 miles, the six short-range Scud-C and Rodong A rockets landed as expected into the Sea of Japan (East Sea). But unexpectedly, the Taepodong 2, with an estimated range from 3,500 to perhaps even 9,000 miles, crashed off the Korean coast 42 seconds into its flight, a momentous failure for the July 4, 2006 test. In the realm of big rocketry, North Korea appeared a toothless tiger.

Condemnations from abroad came swift and furious but no more so than from Japan. Japanese politicians sounded off about the threat faced from a hostile Pyongyang. Some parliamentarians demanded stepped-up defense expenditures. Tokyo did buy US Patriot 3 missiles for its antimissile defense. But Japan was blocked from lining up tough-minded sanctions on the North Koreans in the United Nations because of Chinese and South Korean opposition. Instead, Beijing, backed by Moscow, offered a nonbinding and hollow draft to the Security Council that "deplores" and expressed "grave concern" for the tests. Washington rejected China's statement as too mild; it was, however, a surprisingly sharp rebuke from DPRK's fraternal communist backer. The PRC took the unusual step of briefly slowing down the flow of its aid, but it did not halt deliveries.[41]

The most ominous repercussion stemming from the flopped ICMB firing was Pyongyang's second act. It announced its plans to detonate a nuclear explosion. Outside observers of the hermetic regime speculated that by testing a nuclear device North Korea could redeem itself after the failed three-stage missile firing. The United States issued categorical objections to a nuclear detonation. The assistant secretary of state for East Asian affairs, Christopher Hill, even declared, "We are not going to live with a nuclear North Korea; we are not going to accept it."[42] Chairman Kim just crossed the US red line with impunity. Aside from loud protests, the United States did nothing when the DPRK's nuclear moment arrived. It was self-defeating diplomacy to threaten and then to yield.

Pyongyang tested an underground nuclear device in the country's northeast corner on October 9, 2006. Prior to detonation, it informed Beijing that it would conduct a test in the range of 4 kilotons (a 4,000-ton TNT equivalent). Sensors recorded a yield of less than 1 kiloton, or below a 1,000-ton

TNT magnitude. By comparison, the United State dropped a plutonium bomb on Nagasaki in August 1945 with a yield of about 20 kilotons to end World War II. Regardless of the small seismic tremor at the site, DPRK officials expressed pride in the blast, for it strengthened their case for blackmail.[43]

Speculation soon arose on the possibility that the North Korean underground test actually fizzled out rather than reaching the announced 4-kiloton level. A low-yield blast alone provided little comfort to some observers. It suggested that the North Korean scientists were not aiming to replicate the Nagasaki design. Since the Nagasaki bomb weighed about four tons, its bulk was far greater than could be lifted on the DPRK missiles. Rather, North Korea may have proceeded directly to a warhead in the range of the 500- to 1,000-kilogram class that could be rocketed to South Korea on a Scud or to Japan on a Nodong-class missile. Such a limited-range weapon could also be directed at the continental United States from an offshore vessel. This analysis proved unsettling in spite of the low-yield and only partial detonation of a plutonium-fueled device.[44]

The United States lost little time in condemning the subpar nuclear experiment. President Bush labeled it a "provocative act." He added that any transfer of nuclear material to "any state or non-state actor" (a reference to terrorist networks) would "be considered a grave threat to the United States."[45] This warning signaled an expansion of America's long-standing deterrence policies. It extended the threat of retaliation for the transfer of nuclear weapons material to terrorists for "dirty" bombs, not just an actual nuclear attack on American soil. The "dirty" weapon used conventional explosives to scatter radioactive material to kill and contaminate by contact without a nuclear blast. Such a device is much easier to construct and use than a complex atom bomb.

Despite all its tough talk before and after the test, Washington undertook no military action. The protracted wars in Afghanistan and Iraq taxed the US military and drained away the White House's penchant for preventive conflict. The Bush doctrine of striking at dangers before they gathered had become a dead letter. The costs in lives and dollars were too prohibitive to adopt a similar course against North Korea. In the final analysis, the North Korean regime was willing to be coaxed, negotiate, and even strike agreements in spite of its overly overwrought histrionics, belligerent posturing, and sulking just beyond the conference table. Both Washington and Pyongyang really had few options other than diplomacy, although for different reasons.

Bush came under fierce congressional and media criticism for his government's handling of the North Korean imbroglio. Democratic members in the House and Senate upbraided the president for allowing the lapse of the Agreed Framework agreement in the wake of the uranium crisis in 2002. They criticized him for his priorities of placing North Korea and Iran behind Iraq on the nuclear-fear scale. "What it [the North Korean nuclear test] tells you is that we started at the wrong end of the 'axis of evil,'" said Sam Nunn, former Democratic senator from Georgia.[46] The chastisers pointed to the loss of IAEA access to the plutonium storage sites when the United States, in their view, overreacted to the intelligence report of the North's secret uranium-enrichment efforts.

The criticisms stung the administration but not as much as the realization that Pyongyang was proceeding full-speed ahead toward an atomic capability. Washington swung into action at the United Nations. After laborious negotiations, it prevailed on the reluctant Chinese, Russians, and South Koreans (the Japanese wanted gloves-off action all along) to impose more sanctions on the DPRK. Of these hesitant states, China was the key power, for it ran political interference for the North along with bestowing material help, including an estimated 80 to 90 percent of its fuel imports. In the end, Beijing accepted a softer embargo policy than the original US draft. China's signature on the resolution signaled indignation at its fraternal ally for carrying out the test. After the detonation, the Chinese government charged, "The DPRK ignored universal opposition of the international community and flagrantly conducted the nuclear test."[47] Afterward, the PRC's indignation soon lapsed; it remained the North's best friend.

Security Council Resolution 1718 demanded that "the DPRK not conduct any further nuclear tests or ballistic missile firings."[48] It barred the transfer of material useful for nuclear, biological, and chemical weapons, and ballistic missiles. It prohibited the travel and froze overseas assets of persons connected to the country's weapons programs. Additionally, it authorized all countries to inspect cargo entering or leaving the North to detect illicit arms. The embargo extended to luxury goods, such as Rolex watches, Mercedes-Benz cars, Harley-Davidson motorcycles, cognac, and perfumes, which Dear Leader used to buy loyalty from the party and military elite. Even though the DPRK cultivated a spartan image, the privileged set wanted to live first-class within the communist classless society. To gain approval for sanctions, the US representative to the United Nations, John R. Bolton, was forced to scrub authority to use military force to stop ships in international waters, thanks to the opposition of Beijing, Moscow, and Seoul.[49]

Nor could Washington count on China to enforce the sanctions it signed, to inspect rigorously trucks entering and leaving the DPRK, or to clamp down on Chinese banks doing cash business with North Koreans. The PRC shares a 870-mile frontier with North Korea and is its critical economic link to the outside world. Beijing indicated that business relations with the pariah nation would be largely unaffected regardless of the Security Council vote.[50] Beijing's assistance extended to setting up joint special economic zones (SEZ) with Pyongyang. The SEZ nurtured entrepreneurship and development in China starting in the 1980s to bypass the then-strict communist orthodoxy. The PRC sought a similar role for SEZ in North Korea to boost its economy and to promote stability in its difficult charge. China's motives entailed a healthy dose of self-interest. Chinese enterprises acquired large mining stakes in North Korean anthracite coal, zinc, copper, iron ore, and molybdenum deposits.[51] China was the DPRK's mainstay. Its trade, investment, and economic assistance amounted to over $3 billion annually.

The world knew of China's complicity in the DPRK's arms export. Even the United Nations issued a report in May 2011 faulting Beijing's enforcement of the international body's sanctions against North Korea. It noted China's failures to halt the shipment of ballistic-missile components on the North's cargo aircraft that touched down on Chinese territory en route to Iran. China's clout in the Security Council was strong enough to wrest changes before the release of the report; rather than naming China, it just identified a "neighboring third country" being at fault.[52]

China's policies also drew censure from a US congressional-formed body, the US-China Economic Commission. It reported in late 2006 that Chinese government-run companies "contributed at least indirectly to North Korea's nuclear program." By covertly helping Pakistan develop its nuclear weapon, China opened the way for its technology and components to flow through A. Q. Kahn's back channels to the DPRK. In addition, North Korean front companies operated freely in China, where they dealt in missile and nuclear equipment.[53] Strategically, Beijing benefited as well from its North Korean dependent. Its ships gained access to North Korean waters, which allowed the Peoples' Liberation Army (PLA) Navy to expand its sphere southward. Some Chinese generals in the PLA enjoyed tweaking the US eagle's feathers by maintaining close ties to their counterparts within the North Korean armed forces. For them, the North was a convenient card to play when Washington backed Taiwan diplomatically or sold arms to what Beijing viewed as its breakaway province. US diplomats realized that China could not be bullied publicly into pressuring North Korea. Moreover, the Sino-US economic relationship loomed larger as China financed the ballooning American federal deficit by buying US Treasury bonds.

Although Seoul voted for the watered-down resolution, the accommodationist ROK government of Roh Moo-hyun balked at suspending trade and investment with its quarrelsome neighbor. Its foreign minister, Ban

Ki-moon, explained to America's top diplomat, Condoleezza Rice, the positive side of its industrial park at Kaesong and its tourism to Mount Kumgang, a Buddhist holy mountain and hot springs. To Ban, who later became the UN secretary general, these endeavors fostered reconciliation between the two Koreas. For her part, Secretary of State Rice urged the return of all countries to the Six-Party Talks as she visited Asia in late 2006 to request full enforcement of the recent UN resolution against Pyongyang.[54] Her conciliatory statements reflected a significant American departure from the first Bush administration's unilateralism, preventive warfare, and regime change. The toll of the Iraq and Afghanistan conflicts dampened the White House's appetite for more hostilities. It now favored multilateral diplomacy.

President Bush's tough counterproliferation actions, moreover, appeared checkmated by the brazenness of the low-yield detonation. Slapping on sanctions and ladling out threats failed to halt the North's nuclear dreams. Eager to avoid a diplomatic setback, the White House embraced a brokered settlement with the North. Meeting on the sidelines of the Asia Pacific Economic Cooperation (APEC) summit in Hanoi in mid-November 2006 with the leaders of the four countries surrounding North Korea, Bush and his aides signaled a willingness to dangle incentives toward the new, uninvited member of the nuclear club. They wanted Pyongyang to resign that membership. Washington offered a peace treaty to replace the armistice signed in 1953 and a lifting of the financial restrictions on Banco Delta Asia. Rice even proposed clearing the way for Pyongyang to join APEC at a future date.[55] To reap rewards, Pyongyang decided to reengage in multilateral negotiations.

Ten days later in a meeting convened in Beijing, Washington's point man, Christopher Hill, presented the North Korean vice minister of foreign ministry, Kim Kye-gwan, a package of incentives and demands in three-way talks with Chinese officials. As a means to lure Pyongyang back to the Six-Party Talks after its 13-month boycott in the wake of the US crackdown on the BDA, the US diplomat listed the types of aid the DPRK could expect for dismantling its plutonium plant at Yongbyon and for an inventory of other nuclear sites. These incentives reflected the split within the Bush government over the handling of the rogue regime. On the one hand, Vice President Dick Cheney espoused a hawkish approach so as not to reward the North for its bad behavior, long-range missile firings, and nuclear test. State Department officials, on the other hand, argued that sanctions and isolation since the uranium enrichment revelation in 2002 failed to stop the DPRK from amassing enough reprocessed plutonium for a possible six or eight atomic bombs. Therefore, a different course of action was required— the one President Bush adopted.[56]

The United States offered enough enticements to woo the North Koreans into Six-Party Talks again in Beijing during late December 2006. The American delegates proposed removing the DPRK from the US State Department's terrorist-state listing if the communist regime dismantled its atomic-weapons program. This proposal met some resistance from South Koreans, who suffered the most at the hands of Pyongyang's terrorism over the years. Delisting was just one of many "carrots" dangled before the North Korean delegation. Secretary Rice, nonetheless, warned Pyongyang that another nuclear test "would deepen its isolation." But it was hard to envision such a possibility. China remained committed to the political survival of its North Korean dependent.[57]

As so often happened, this round of Six-Party Talks also ended inconclusively. The DPRK's negotiators demanded an end to the blacklisting of BDA to gain access to its $12 million balance in the Macao-based bank before discussing denuclearization. As grand masters of procrastination and subterfuge, DPRK envoys broached a complaint about blacklisting on one day. On another, it was American–South Korean military exercises. And yet another time, it was imagined US invasion plans. Or, as US diplomat Hill recounted, "It's something we said about them that hurt their feelings."[58] There seemed no end to the obstacles in the way of resolving the standoff at the close of 2006.

The February 13 Agreement

The New Year opened inauspiciously for the Six-Party Talks. In January 2007, the Bush White House imposed its own economic sanctions on a North Korean firm (along with Chinese and Russian companies) for transferring military-related equipment to Iran and Syria. US officials stated that the Korean Mining and Industrial Development Corporation, which previously shipped missiles to Iran, was a "serial proliferator." The US sanctions came under the Iran and Syria Nonproliferation Act passed by Congress in 2005, which brought to over 40 the number of "economic bans employed by the Bush government since 2001, as it tried to come to grips with arms shipments circulating among rogue states."[59]

At yet another round of the talks, the United States and its partners finally hammered out an agreement with North Korea. The Six-Party negotiators contended that this accord, in fact, was the initial implementing measure for the Joint Statement signed in September 2005. The February 13 agreement offered $400 million in heavy fuel oil (suitable for heating, not for use in vehicles or planes), plus humanitarian and economic assistance to the DPRK, in exchange for a start on dismantling its nuclear facilities within

60 days and for the reentry of international inspection teams. The United States, South Korea, and China agreed to supply the oil; Japan declined to furnish any fuel until the issue of its abducted citizens was resolved with the North.[60] Momentously, the Bush Oval Office pledged to remove North Korea from its terrorist list.[61] The State Department had listed the DPRK as a state sponsor of terror since the 1970s. Proposing to delist Pyongyang caused a furor in Washington circles. Hawks felt it sent a wrong message to a repressive regime. Doves believed that Pyongyang was on a pacific path. They were gravely mistaken, since it subsequently killed more South Koreans in crossborder bombardments.

Additional "working groups" intended to pursue a host of outstanding issues to include the normalization of diplomatic relations, a peace treaty formally ending the Korean War, the lifting of economic sanctions, and an unfreezing of the remaining DPRK assets at the BDA. The agreement left plenty of imponderable questions for resolution. How many nuclear weapons did the Kim regime truly possess? It was generally acknowledged that it had the capacity for six to eight plutonium bombs from the reprocessed spent reactor rods. What happened to the uranium enrichment capability that sparked the United States in 2002 to break off the original fuel shipments under the 1994 Agreed Framework agreement? And the biggest question: would Pyongyang genuinely turn over all its nuclear arms? If it did, it would no longer have any bargaining chips with Washington. Why would the outside world care about a nonnuclear economic basket case?

Compared to President Clinton's Agreed Framework, the February 13 accord surpassed its predecessor in firmness toward the Kim regime. The Bush deal did not promise two light-water rectors in exchange for scraping the old graphite one and ending construction of two additional graphite reactors. Bush's accord brought in China as well as three other neighboring powers—South Korea, Japan, and Russia—instead of being just a US bilateral deal with the North. China might be a dubious partner for the United States; but without its participation, no brokered package with the DPRK could succeed at all. At least China was indirectly on the spot for its North Korean dependency.

The ink had hardly dried on the February 13 agreement before critics assailed it. They charged that the United States had succumbed to the threats, extortion, and blackmail from the cash-strapped Kim regime four months after it detonated a nuclear explosion. Hard-liners argued that President Bush should reject the negotiated pact because it repudiated his legacy of firmness toward renegade regimes. They argued that continued pressure would shorten the political lifespan of the criminal and morally abhorrent Kim dictatorship. The former US representative to the United Nations,

John Bolton, who left his post just two months beforehand, denounced the February 13 agreement. Bolton argued that the agreement "undercuts" the sanction resolution he pushed through the Security Council the previous October.[62] He and other detractors fought an intraparty struggle within Republican ranks. Democrats in the US Congress approved of the administration's agreement but accused it of being so tardy as to have enabled the DPRK to amass enough plutonium for six or more bombs beyond the tested device.[63]

No nuclear disarmament resulted from the February 13 agreement anyway. Instead, the North Koreans refused to comply with their pledge to shut down the reprocessing center at Yongbyon. Chairman Kim's delegates insisted first on the release of the frozen financial assets in the BDA. Finally, Bush officials gave into North Korean demands. It let the Macau Monetary Authority (which had frozen the funds because of the US pressure) release the remaining $12 million.[64] The concluding episode of the BDA saga was a setback for the United States. It reversed its policy as outlined by President Bush in January 2007, when he rejected compromises to bring the DPRK back to the negotiating table.[65] The State Department tried to keep the negotiations running smoothly with a regime that was a connoisseur of derailing the best-laid plans. Once again, the American "Kiminologists" were outguessed and outmaneuvered in the convoluted dealings, which had characterized Washington-Pyongyang relations for two decades.

The United States watched as the 60-day deadline for North Korea to dismantle its Yongbyon facility came and went. The Kim regime let the deadline pass without complying with the agreement. Instead, it fired several short-range missiles into the Sea of Japan. The missed deadline and the missile tests frustrated Washington. In sharp departure from the previous five years, the Bush White House dispatched its key negotiator for direct one-on-one talks with Kim's aides. Christopher Hill flew to Pyongyang in June 2007 without representatives from the other four members of the Six-Party group. There, Hill obtained fresh assurances of the impending shutdown of the plutonium reactor and disablement of the Yongbyon plant.[66] The next month, an international inspection team confirmed that the North Koreans had shuttered their nuclear reactors.

At this time, another event halfway around the globe held profound consequences for US–North Korean relations. On September 6, 2007, Israeli warplanes destroyed a secret nuclear installation in northeastern Syria. Later, evidence filtered out from both Israeli sources and US satellite images that pointed to North Korean cooperation with Syria in constructing a nuclear facility at Al Kibar. Pyongyang and Damascus denied the charges, although they had long collaborated on Scud D missiles. North Korean technicians had operated in the Levantine country over the years, but few outsiders suspected nuclear collaboration. The DPRK had never been caught in nuclear exchanges despite its brisk missile business to other outlaw states. The air bombardment took place several days after a North Korean ship unloaded an undisclosed cargo that was transported to the bombed site.[67] Mohamed ElBaradei, the IAEA's director-general, discounted the nuclearization of the Syrian site on the basis of his interpretation of the satellite images. Subsequent disclosures, however, disproved ElBaradei's conclusion.[68]

In April 2008, the United States went public with intelligence to prove that North Korea assisted Syria in building a nuclear plant. Intelligence officials released photographic images of the site before the Israeli bombing. These images showed a boxlike buildings and nuclear equipment, such as the North Korean reactor. It matched the layout of facilities at Yongbyon. The intelligence documents stated that only North Korea had built a similar reactor in the past 35 years. A senior Bush administration official divulged that the timing of this disclosure was driven by the necessity to pressure the DPRK to come clean on its own atomic arsenal and its proliferation activities.[69]

The October 3 Agreement

The diplomatic fallout from the revelations about the Syrian nuclear plant rattled official Washington as it struggled to keep its North Korean nuclear agreement on track. Despite internal divisions over how to respond to Pyongyang's nuclear proliferation, the Bush government went ahead with its plans to supply fuel oil and food to its mercurial negotiating partner in exchange for its adhering to the Six-Party accord. China and South Korea had already delivered heavy oil to the Kim regime to maintain the momentum of the Six-Party agreement.

In early October 2007, the North's delegation signed off on an agreement to disable their five-megawatt reactor, reprocessing plant, and fuel rod facility at Yongbyon by the end of the year. In this October 3 agreement, the DPRK "reaffirmed its commitment not to transfer nuclear materials, technology or know-how" to other nations or groups. Since the 9/11 terrorist attacks, the United States regarded the nontransference of nuclear capabilities as vital to its national security. In exchange for the DPRK pledge, the US interlocutors reaffirmed the parallel process of removing the country from the US terrorism listing and normalizing diplomatic relations between the two states. No mention was made of Pyongyang's estimated plutonium stockpile (capable of six to eight bombs), from which the 2006 low-yield test presumably derived its fissile material. Likewise, the Kim regime's shadowy uranium capability slipped from censure. Nor did the North's appalling human rights abuses make the Six-Party agenda.[70]

The end-of-the year deadline, just like the others to which Pyongyang consented, came and passed without action on its signed promises. At the start of 2008, the last year of George Bush's presidency, Washington anticipated the consummation of its diplomatic victory brought about by the February 13 deal. But Washington had to contend with Pyongyang's typical foot-dragging on turning over the full declaration of all its nuclear activities and disabling its nuclear facilities. Within the Bush presidency, the familiar hawk-dove cleavage deepened as a consequence of the delays. Per contra, Pyongyang officials asserted they had already made the declaration with their announcement in October of 37 kilograms of plutonium in the country's nuclear inventories. Most experts held the actual amount was closer to 65 kilograms, and they wanted a full declaration.

Meanwhile, the heavy fuel oil continued to flow into the communist state, but not at the rate it believed to be adequate. By early 2008, DPRK officials complained that their country was due 500,000 tons of oil instead of the just 200,000 that had been received. They also argued the Six-Party countries failed to ship the promised equipment and parts for their dying electrical grid. All the while, the Kim regime spewed blistering propaganda against the Untied States. The *Rodong Sinmum*, the official Workers' Party organ, thundered, "Our republic will continue to harden its war deterrent further in response to the U.S. stepping up its nuclear war moves."[71] Amid all the uncertainty and truculence, the New York Philharmonic traveled to Pyongyang and played a historic concert in February inside the drab Stalinist capital, whose parks and boulevards are lined with larger-than-life bronze statues representing revolutionary fighters, peasants, and factory workers in the socialist realism style of the former Soviet Union. The orchestra's musical visit left no discernable influence on the country's Orwellian culture.

To confront Pyongyang's dithering, the Bush administration released satellite images showing North Korean complicity in building a knock-off of their Yongbyon reactor in Syria, as noted earlier. It also relaxed its demands for full DPRK disclosure of its uranium activity. This combination did the trick in a limited way. Two weeks later in May, Chairman Kim's representatives turned over some 18,000 pages of documents relating to their plutonium program at Yongbyon but not other nuclear endeavors.[72] In June, IAEA inspectors confirmed the shutdown of North Korea's only working nuclear reactor and two related facilities at Yongbyon. Pyongyang as well shuttered a pair of dormant construction sites for new reactors. Next, Pyongyang invited international television crews to record the demolition of the Yongbyon cooling tower. The televised coverage of the concrete tower's destruction cost the United States a $2.5 million payment to North Korea to shoot images of the explosion. No humiliation was too small for the DPRK.

None of these actions from the cloistered and xenophobic nation accounted for its suspected uranium processing or its discrepancy between the declared 37 kilograms of plutonium and the estimated amount of around 65 kilograms. One informed expert accused the Bush government of passing off a "sort of Potemkin village of U.S. policy in which there's a great deal of difference between these bold pledges [by American officials] and then subsequent reality."[73] In fact, the gaps and discrepancies haunted future American–North Korean relations. Another wrinkle stemmed from credible sources that Kim Jong Il had suffered a stroke and remained hospitalized for weeks. His absence from North Korea's 60th-anniversary parade in early September 2008 lent credence to the intelligence reports. Finally, North Korean watchers cast a nervous eye at intelligence findings that Pyongyang was completing a new missile test facility in Musudan-ni on the west coast of the communist nation.

American officials publicly fretted about the Six-Party process staying mired in "inertia" through the end of George W. Bush's tenure in January 2009. The DPRK's Foreign Ministry played on Washington's anxiety by announcing steps to reactivate its nuclear program, by threatening to bar IAEA inspectors from Yongbyon, by signaling plans for rocket launches, and by resuming verbal blasts toward the United States after a hiatus.

Since Christopher Hill, the US envoy to Pyongyang, did not have a signed agreement with his DPRK counterparts for a "comprehensive and rigorous" verification protocol, the Bush administration was sorely divided on whether to strike North Korea from the state sponsors of terrorism list compiled by the US Department of State. Secretary of State Rice advocated delisting the DPRK, and Vice President Cheney staunchly opposed it.[74] To end the dispute, Bush struck North Korea from the listing of state sponsors of terrorism on October 11, 2008. This action gained access for US inspectors, not just IAEA technicians, to the main nuclear compound at Yongbyon. Additional sites could only be entered "based on mutual consent," which was tantamount to exclusion because Pyongyang would never allow Americans free rein to travel about the land. By the time Bush left the White House, his administration could justifiably claim some progress with North Korea. But it was a long way from being atomically defanged.

The Bush agreements left unaddressed the status of uranium enrichment, the stockpiles of reprocessed plutonium, the access to possible nuclear sites beyond Yongbyon, and a clear account of Pyongyang's nuclear assistance to Syria. The many economic sanctions stayed in place, however. Critics charged that President Bush merely desired a foreign policy victory in the waning months of his term. John Bolton, by now the chief skeptic, noted that "the negative consequences are not confined to Northeast Asia" but include "Tehran and the capitals of other terrorist states" as "they are considering ways to apply the North Korean model to their own situations."[75] The State Department replied that the deal was the best possible at the time.[76] Yet Bush did not succeed in rectifying two main criticisms of the Clinton-era Agreed Framework. Washington did not gain the removal of nuclear material from North Korea, and it accepted the limitation of international inspectors to just Yongbyon. The issue of uranium enrichment also was left unresolved. Detractors and defenders agreed on one thing—hard diplomatic negotiations lay ahead with the secretive and intractable state.

Obama's Extended Hand and Kim's Fist

President Barack Obama swept into office with an expansive engagement philosophy far different than his predecessor's. In his Inaugural Address, the former US senator from Illinois made no direct reference to North Korea or even to rogue regimes. He clearly had them in mind when he spoke of engaging leaders "who cling to power through corruption and deceit and the silencing of dissent." To them, the new president offered to "extend a hand if you are willing to unclench your fist."[77] Kim Jong Il's response was not long in coming; it differed not at all from his previous reactions to American policy—missile firings, war cries, and even a second nuclear detonation.

Even before Obama strode into the White House, Kim flung down a mailed gauntlet to the president-elect. Days after Obama's election win in November 2008, the DPRK erected hurdles to inspections at the Yongbyon nuclear complex. It disallowed inspectors from taking soil and nuclear waste samples, essential verification measurements. Soon after, it stepped up threats to "wipe out" the Seoul government. It threatened to halt crossborder traffic, scrap accords with the South, and close down the joint Kaesong industrial complex located on the North's territory but financed entirely by the South. DPRK officials announced that they had "weaponized" 30 kilograms of plutonium, although they did not clarify what weaponized meant. The brand-new administration interpreted the sword waving as a perverse call for attention from the US government.[78]

Worse yet, Pyongyang had started down the warpath with South Korea before Obama was sworn in as commander-in-chief. Its military declared "an all-out confrontational posture" against the ROK. The DPRK was stung by Seoul's policy reversals under its new government. Lee Myung-bak took up the South Korean presidency in late February 2008. He reversed the too-generous initiatives of his predecessor, who provided the North with abundant aid without requirements to mend its menacing ways. President Lee chastised the North Korean leadership for pursuing nuclear weapons, violating human rights, and breaching agreements with the South. Adding salt to this reopened wound, Lee defrosted relations of his predecessor with Washington and warmed up to the Bush administration during its last year in office. Pyongyang hated Seoul's reversal.

The Kim regime perceived the South's reshuffled approach imperiling its own rule. In the eyes of its own people and the rank and file of the Korean Workers' Party, Dear Leader was not as feared and respected as they had been repeatedly told by the communist propaganda organs. The ROK challenge represented not a military threat to the DPRK but a political danger to the bona fides of the regime itself. The missile firings and second nuclear test that took place during the first half of 2009 constituted an effort by the Kim regime to retain the loyal support of the military and party faithful. Failure to hang tough might result in a "mass legitimation crisis if it [the regime] is seen as failing on its own ideological terms," as one clear-eyed observer wrote.[79] North Korea's leadership interpreted offers of aid and diplomatic recognition as signs of US abject surrender, which strengthened its hold on power with the military and party elite.

The fledgling Obama presidency touted that its policy of deliberately ignoring North Korea constituted the best policy for managing its dark theatrics. In reality, the new Washington government's initiatives actually tracked those of the two previous administrations. The newly confirmed secretary of state Hillary Rodham Clinton talked softly and eschewed sticks. She set forth an agenda of "great openness" to the DPRK, if only it gave up its nuclear ambitions. Presidents Bill Clinton and George W. Bush made repeated promises of food, fuel, and economic and energy assistance as incentives for nuclear disarmament.[80] In replying, the reclusive nation put the Obama government on notice that it intended to retain and build a nuclear *deterrent*—as it usually termed its nuclear arms. Pyongyang thereby garnered bargaining chips to be exchanged for future economic benefits upon toning down its ominous histrionics.

Commensurate card players, the Kim regime upped the ante by announcing a planned launch of a missile into space to hoist a satellite into orbit. Its neighbors rallied against the firing. Security Council Resolution 1718, adopted after the 2006 nuclear test, held that Pyongyang "shall suspend all activities related to its ballistic missile program."[81] All bark and no real bite, the Kwangmyongsong-2 ballistic missile failed. Indeed, only the first stage ignited; the second and third stages together with the payload crashed into the Pacific.[82] Its trajectory did pose a danger to Japan, which enacted another set of its own economic sanctions against the Kim regime. As for the United States, Obama stated, "We made very clear to the North Koreans that their missile launch is provocative." Obama's special envoy to Pyongyang, Stephen W. Bosworth, uttered an even softer critique of the April launch than the president: "We must deal with North Korea as we find it, not as we would like it to be."[83] Washington did go to the UN for more sanctions.

After two weeks of failed haggling at the United Nations to bring China and Russia around to the American position, the United States settled for a sleight-of-hand Security Council vote. The measure simply called upon members to enforce sanctions already leveled against DPRK enterprises but foolishly suspended earlier to woo Pyongyang back to the negotiating table.[84] Washington adopted a face-saving stratagem because Beijing and Moscow refused to countenance new biting sanctions or even censorious language against the international scofflaw. Instead, the Security Council issued a "presidential statement" agreed to by all 15 members. Unlike the "Chapter VII resolutions," it carried no "legally binding" requirement on UN members to honor the sanctions. Issued by the rotating president of the Security Council, the "presidential statement" just *called on* member states "to comply fully" with their obligations under Resolution 1718. This legerdemain papered over political divisions, allowed the Obama White House to claim a spurious diplomatic coup, and went unexplained by the media.[85]

Pyongyang reacted fiercely to the UN action. It ejected the IAEA inspectors together with four US experts. Next, at the end of April 2009, it made a dubious claim to have harvested plutonium from spent fuel rods located in its nearly dismantled plant. Experts doubted the feasibility so soon; it would take months to restart plutonium processing. What did grab attention was Pyongyang's threat to enrich uranium. It confirmed charges by Bush officials in 2002 that the North indeed had such a program.[86] The DPRK also denounced the United Nations Security Council as "a tool for the U.S. highhanded and arbitrary practices."[87] It next abandoned the Six-Party Talks—a decision that brought negotiations to a standstill for over two years.

Reports circulated among South Korean observers by early 2009 that a slow-moving transition was afoot to replace the stroke-stricken Kim with one of his sons.[88] Nearly a year later, the regime held events to celebrate the 28th birthday of Dear Leader's youngest son, Kim Jung-un. Experienced DPRK watchers construed the celebration as further evidence that the youngest Kim was being groomed to assume the place of his father.[89] Succession problems for Chairman Kim, it was speculated, figured in his decision to test another nuclear weapon. An explosion in the face of US opposition would demonstrate Kim Jong-Il's mastery over the craven Americans to the top military and party officials who were crucial for plans to anoint his chosen successor. As so often was the case, internal political considerations dictated rogue international actions.

On May 25, 2009, Pyongyang announced its second nuclear detonation to a disapproving world. The underground blast went off at Kilju in the country's northeast quadrant. It set off a 4.5-magnitude earthquake. The explosive yield barely registered in the 2- to 4-kiloton range, which exceeded the 2006 test by two to five times. Outside experts judged this test more successful than the earlier semifailure but still a rudimentary effort. These less-than-stellar results were hardly reassuring to other powers. President Obama stated, "North Korea is directly and recklessly challenging the international community." Speaking in the Rose Garden, he vowed to "take action" against what he characterized as "a blatant violation of international law."[90] He convened meetings. World leaders joined in the chorus condemning the nuclear explosion. But after all was said and done, nothing substantial was done to address the North Koreans' alarming conduct. More and more, Pyongyang regarded America's bark as much worse than its bite.

Again weeks of spirited debate took place in the Security Council, where the United States pushed China and Russia to vote for harsh sanctions but settled for less stringent punishments. Resolution 1874 requested (rather than required) UN member states to search for nuclear weapons or technology on North Korean ships. But this applied only to vessels registered by the inspecting power and only in harbors, not in international waters. China opposed forced, high-seas searches as too confrontational. If a ship, suspected of carrying nuclear-arms components, refused to be inspected in a nearby port, the United States or another member country possessed no UN authority to enforce an inspection. A North Korean captain thus could just sail on to his destination.[91]

True to form, the Kim Jong Il regime declared that it intended to confront UN measures with "retaliation." It vowed to "weaponize" all of its plutonium extracted from its Yongbyon fuel rods. Then in a one-two punch, it roared out again what it had denied seven years earlier—it had a uranium-enriching program to produce another type of atomic weapon. Foreign scientists, nevertheless, doubted that the North Koreans commanded the thousands of centrifuges needed to process uranium to weapons grade in sufficient quantities for a nuclear arm. Iran's cooperation with the DPRK, they warned, could speed up the North's enrichment efforts in the future years.[92] Still, in all, Pyongyang's threats aroused regional concerns about the desperate regime.

The prospects were nil for sanctions to bring about a change in Pyongyang's behavior. China and Russia protested too much about fears of destabilization in North Korea resulting in swarms of refugees spilling across their frontiers. If asylum-seekers streamed over any border, it would be the DMZ to rejoin their fellow countrymen in the Republic of Korea. To be fair, every regional power—even the United States—worried about political chaos and a power vacuum in the North stemming from the regime's implosion. Such an outcome might lead to a Sino-American collision, even conflict as in the 1950s. China had even more compelling reason for favoring the prevailing status quo.

The DPRK, despite its rusting industrial economy, was honeycombed with enormous mineral wealth. The estimated value of its reserves of iron ore, coal, zinc, molybdenum, natural uranium, and the world's largest known deposit of magnesium (essential for lightweight aluminum alloys for aircraft and electronics) topped $2 trillion, according to the Korean Chamber of Commerce and Industry.[93] Starved for close-by resources, China's northeastern manufacturers hungered for their neighbor's mineral wealth. The Chinese expanded mining rights to as many as 20 sites. Trade between the two communist states escalated to an estimated $4 billion in 2009.[94] The Chinese currency flows strengthened the DPRK hierarchy while benefiting China. Thus, the international sanctions enabled Chinese firms to exercise a monopoly over North Korean resources at bargain prices for valuable minerals. China's economic penetration into the North pointed toward growing clout over its economy with the development of economic zones, bridges over the Yalu River, and ever-closer commercial connections. Chinese economic heft indicates political leverage in the offing.

For its part, North Korea showed no sign of backing down. Quite the reverse, Pyongyang rattled a missile saber at Hawaii. It boasted its credentials as a "proud nuclear power." Its official Korean Central News Agency bellowed on the eve of the 59th anniversary of the start of the Korean War, "If the U.S. imperialists start another war, the army and people of Korea will wipe out the aggressors on the globe once and for all." It threatened a "fire shower of nuclear retaliation" against the United States and South Korea.[95] To coincide with America's Fourth of July festivities in 2009, the DPRK shot off seven medium-range missiles, some of which flew about 300 miles into the Sea of Japan. Less than a week later, swarms of computer attacks hit US and ROK installations to deny service at the targeted websites. Conducted by an army of zombie computers, the "denial of service" operations blocked access to military and commercial sites, overwhelming them and causing them to crash. Several experts attributed this to North Korean hackers.[96]

The DPRK confronted the Obama presidency with other provocative acts. In early 2009, its soldiers took two naive American journalists into custody along their border with China. They were held by Pyongyang until former president Bill Clinton flew to meet with Chairman Kim in August, and the reporters' captivity reinforced Dear Leader's internal standing amid speculation about his health and grasp on power.[97] The Kim regime persisted in seizing South Korean fishing boats, claiming they strayed into its waters. More ominous were reports of its nuclear cooperation with Myanmar's military junta.[98] Its verbal explosions reminded Secretary Clinton of unruly children, "who are demanding attention." The DPRK propaganda organs labeled her "vulgar."[99] Since it walked out the Six-Party Talks a month before its second nuclear detonation in May 2009, diplomatic negotiations stayed frozen amid the puerile name-calling.

The subsequent years witnessed a similar catalog of warlike antics and propaganda blasts by the rogue regime in Pyongyang. Its declarations to enrich uranium, build light-water reactors, and harvest plutonium, plus missile firings—all violated UN resolutions and signed bilateral agreements. It actions demonstrated a contempt for international law and for diplomatic relations with other states, particularly South Korea. In March 2010, North Korea torpedoed the *Cheonan*, a ROK corvette, killing 46 crewmen. In November, it shelled South Korea's Yeonpyong Island, driving the residents to the mainland. It again noted its uranium refinement capacity in late 2010. In response, South Koreans floated information balloons over the DMZ to foment revolution among the Northern population. Nothing could shake Pyongyang tyranny, not even the coldest winter since 1945, which was marked by suffering, starvation, and death for thousands of average citizens.[100] To preserve its criminal despotism, it expanded its mass prison camps to hold an estimated 300,000 political detainees, who suffered torture, harsh privations, and executions that officials required other prisoners observe.[101]

Pyongyang's persistent bellicosity, according to seasoned North Korea watchers, served to strengthen Chairman Kim's hand during his succession stratagems. To keep the military and party in line, the ailing Kim Jong Il orchestrated crises with the ROK and its US ally while he maneuvered his third son to succeed him. Kim first publicly paraded his youngish heir apparent at a rare party congress in September 2010. Then, the heir apparent, Kim Jong-un, was promoted to four-star army general. Finally, the following February, Kim Jr. became de facto no. 2 in the regime by being elevated to vice chairman of the powerful National Defense Commission. This appointment came in front of thousands of officers of the People's Army and the Internal Security Forces assembled in the April 25 Cultural Hall.[102] The rubber-stamp Supreme People's

Assembly ratified the appointment in April and molded a future that resembled the past. This became apparent when the new ruler announced the launch of a satellite into orbit just two weeks after Washington agreed to send 240,00 tons of food to North Korea in return for a suspension of nuclear tests missile firings in early 2012.

What's the Endgame?

North Korea's true nature—opaqueness, despotism, and duplicity—made negotiations well nigh impossible. It mocked American calls for peace talks and its offers of concessions as signs of abject capitulation. Being grand tournament masters of the blackmail chessboard, the DPPK never crossed the red line. Pyongyang stopped just short of it, while Saddam Hussein's Iraq blundered across it, inviting its own destruction. A conflict posed a risk to the Kim dynasty, for it would lose a large-scale war. Even a limited engagement stood a good chance of washing solvents over the regime's calcified tyranny, leading to its undoing. North Korea watchers realized that Pyongyang's demands cloaked its internal weakness and desperate maneuvers to survive amid a failed communist economic system and its destitute populace. The totalitarian regime periodically resurrected a new cycle of provocations so as to justify its continuance and lend heroic meaning to the average person's grinding hardships.[103] This realization prompted a little-announced refocusing of Washington's policy toward North Korea.

Without fanfare, the Obama administration, according to its telling, quietly adopted a classic containment approach. It backed away from the strident confrontation and regime change options entertained by previous administrations. Instead, it pursued sanction-tightening measures to choke off the sale of nuclear know-how to other states. The president, in fact, stated, "We just want to make sure the government of North Korea is operating within the basic rules of the international community."[104] At the end of his first year in office, Barack Obama had arrived at his understanding of the DPRK's soft-hard cycle. When he visited Seoul, the president asserted "the need to break the pattern that existed in the past in which North Korea behaves in a provocative fashion, then is willing to return to talks...then leaves the talks and seeks further concessions."[105] Washington realized that the road to Pyongyang lay through Beijing, for without its concurrence nothing would come of dealings solely with North Korea. His administration professed that it had learned the wisdom of using long spoons when supping with the devil.

Yet the Obama White House, on another level, clung to its predecessors' approach. High officials still made pronouncements that the United States will not "ever accept a North Korea with nuclear weapons," as Secretary of Defense Robert Gates uttered during a visit to Seoul in October 2009.[106] Like preceding administrations, it held out diplomatic recognition, exchange of ambassadors, financial aid, and a genuine peace treaty (to replace the armistice) until the DPRK disarmed its nuclear weapons capacity. It demanded Pyongyang reengage in the Six-Party negotiations as well. It, too, awaited the implosion of the Kim regime through a military coup or societal uprising against the bitter conditions prevalent throughout the land as happened in Romania with the overthrow of the Ceausescu communist and personalistic dictatorship in late 1989.

While waiting around for the Pyongyang regime to fall apart, the Obama administration observed irresolutely the construction of a new nuclear reactor on its watch. The DPRK took advantage of Washington's less confrontational policy to steal a march around its American foe by building a replacement reactor. Along with a related uranium-enrichment plant, it represented the now-deceased Kim Jong Il's plan to revamp the country's nuclear capabilities after the negotiated abandonment with the Bush White House. By late 2010, the adversarial regime had some 2,000 centrifuges for enriching uranium, paving the way for a uranium-armed bomb.

Waiting around for North Korea to collapse à la communist states in Central Europe amounts to a futile and failed course, especially if the DPRK or its military-corporate entities transfers nuclear material to international terrorists.[107] This plausible fear should dominate considerations of North Korean containment; this apprehension constituted a great difference in the United States containing the USSR because few Americans held it likely that Moscow might slip fissile materials to terrorists. Almost no one possesses the same degree of confidence toward the desperate tyranny north of the DMZ. Above all else, the collapse theory is out of date. China will not permit a sanction-induced implosion of the North Korean regime. Its economic and strategic stakes are far too great to allow its near-satellite to fall into South Korean and American hands. Both master and protégé share the same short-term goal—a Korean Peninsula free of the American military footprint, after which their respective interests will surely diverge. Pyongyang wants unification with South Korea on its terms. Beijing dreams of a peninsula absent of US influence and under its suzerainty as in centuries past. In the meantime, China and North Korea are strengthening their military ties. The drawing closer of the once go-it-alone pariah to China in defense matters represents another indication of the worldwide shift of rogues toward a Cold War–type patron-client alignment.

When Chairman Kim died in mid-December 2011, China sped emergency food supplies to its southern dependency to tranquilize potential unrest. Beijing's goal before and after the crowning of Kim Jung-un in his father's place remains to nudge the DPRK along the Chinese-blazed trail of market socialism while retaining a loose overlordship over its militarized vassal. The PRC's steadying hand helped the transfer of power from father Kim to son Kim go seamlessly. The Chinese and North Korean elites bent their knees to the 28-year-old pudgy figure for the same reasons—to preserve their privileged stake in the long-serving political dynasty. The DPRK officials exorcised any specter of collapse with a Stalinist funeral, public wailing, and top military figures photographed alongside their new commander-in-chief despite Plantagenet-type rumors of a scheming uncle and envious siblings. The intermediate worry is that some political circles in Pyongyang, in struggling to resist Beijing's amassing political clout, might inadvertently trigger a political confrontation leading to peninsular war or to the transference of fissile material to a jihadi cell.

Moreover, an American accommodation of a nuclear-armed North Korea—labeled by every US administration since the Berlin Wall fell as "unacceptable"—brought up glaring inconsistencies toward Iran, whose nuclear ambitions convulsed the Middle East with fear and uncertainty. To draw the contrast sharper, Pyongyang made no bones about its dream of a nuclear "deterrent." Tehran, on the other hand, officially stated it pursued uranium enrichment only for peaceful, civilian electrical power generation. If the United States acquiesced to North Korean nuclearization, then did it not likewise have to accept Iran's ostensibly nonmilitary reactors? Contradictions abound. And so does foreboding.

CHAPTER 5

Lesser Rogues and Troublesome States

Our patience will achieve more than our force.

—Edmund Burke

B, directly threatened by A, joins with C, D, and E, potentially threatened by A, to foil A's design.

—Hans Morgenthau, *Politics among Nations*

Make no mistake, the ultimate guarantee against the success of aggressors, dictators, and terrorists in the 21st century, as in the 20th, is hard power—the size, strength and global reach of the United States military.

—Secretary of Defense Robert Gates

When it came to rogue states in the post–Cold War era, US policy mandarins concentrated mainly on North Korea, Iraq, and Iran. The array of threats emanating from Pyongyang, Baghdad, and Tehran far outweighed those coming from the other countries registered on the US Department of State's listing of state sponsors of terrorism. Libya, Cuba, South Yemen, Syria, and the Sudan—the other listed nations—did periodically raise anxieties in Washington. Their dictatorial rule, inflammatory declarations, human rights abuses, terrorist sponsorship, or initiatives to secure WMD constituted the earmarks of rogue-state behavior. Yet for a variety of reasons, none rose to the upper or, better put, the lower tier of adversarial nations endangering the world community and particularly the

United States and its allies as the triad of pariahs—Iraq, Iran, and North Korea—did. These so-called lesser rogue nations, nevertheless, deserve some attention, as do troublesome states, which could evolve into full-fledged rogue actors.

Libya: The Rise of a Rogue Adversary

Decades before Iran, Iraq, and North Korea endangered the peace, Libya menaced the international stage as pariah-in-chief. Following its 1969 military coup that brought Colonel Muammar al-Qaddafi to power, Libya struck out as a self-styled revolutionary power bent on carrying out terrorism against the West before it developed weapons of mass destruction. After years of sanctions and isolation, Qaddafi's Libya made an about-face, dropped its WMD programs, and rejoined the community of nations. The twists and sudden turns of Qaddafian Libya are of a piece with the country's tortuous past. Even so, Libya constitutes the only full-fledged adversarial state to step back from terrorism and to abandon its WMD agenda. It, therefore, is an exemplar of rogue renunciation, conversion, and partial international reacceptance, years before the country was convulsed in the Arab Spring revolts of 2011 that ended Qaddafi's life.

Prior to Qaddafi ousting the Sanusi monarchy, Libya traveled an exceptional odyssey, even by the extraordinary standards of twentieth-century Middle Eastern history. It went from "Ottoman backwater to Italian colony; from conservative monarchy to revolutionary regime; from rags to riches."[1] That an insignificant country (known for its Roman ruins) residing in the Maghreb emerged to threaten the world beyond its shores was due, in part, to the discovery of oil in 1959. Enormous revenues suddenly accrued to the ruler of the poor, parched land bordering the Mediterranean Sea. Oil alone did not suffice for Libyan sponsorship of terrorism. The catalyst was Muammar al-Qaddafi and his anti-Western impulses, which drew upon Libya's colonial past.

Italy's defeat in World War II broke Rome's colonial hold on Libya that had lasted from 1911 to 1943. Thereafter, Britain and France temporarily administered the newly freed nation. In late 1951, Libya attained independence under United Nations supervision. Ruled by King Muhammad Idris al-Mahdi al-Sanusi, the fledgling state shuffled along behind Western governments on which it economically and politically depended. Libya's oil flowed to Western Europe and the United States. Tripoli signed agreements with Washington, London, and Paris that permitted foreign militaries a presence on Libyan sands.

Meanwhile, the Arab Middle East was undergoing historic changes. The early twentieth-century postcard vista of camels, tents, and mounted nomads was no longer an accurate depiction after 1945. Oil wealth, liberation from colonial rule, and "a rising tide of rebellion against this Western paramountcy"—all transformed the lands from Cairo to Casablanca in ways that eventually traumatized the world beyond.[2] The Arab world painfully internalized the humiliations from colonialism and Westernization. It bitterly resented the loss of its centuries-long lead in astronomy, architecture, mathematics, and medicine that it enjoyed before Europe's age of seaborne expansion.[3]

Under the near-hypnotic oratory of Gamal Abdul Nasser, the Egyptian general turned politician, the vast Arab expanse from the Persian Gulf to the Atlantic throbbed with revolt against its former colonial masters, Western values, and, indeed, the very international order, which relegated the Middle East to a lowly status. Once Nasser seized power by ousting the sybaritic King Farouk in 1952, he consolidated his political position in Egypt and the Arab Middle East. His speeches struck a chord in the hearts of those who hungered for redress against the West. President Nasser espoused modernization, socialist reform, and pan-Arab nationalism directed against Western powers and Israel, the West's newest outpost in the Middle East. His pulsating calls for Arab unity captured the thinking of a young officer in the Libyan army.[4]

Colonel Muammar al-Qaddafi imbibed full drafts of Nasser's pan-Arab, anti-American, and anti-Israeli brew during the early 1960s. When Nasser's Egypt, together with Syria and Jordan, lost the 1967 war against Israel, Qaddafi wallowed in regret. He felt Libya betrayed its Arab brothers by not joining the conflict. This verdict precipitated his decision to overthrow the king. After seizing power, Qaddafi embraced a nationalistic agenda. The new Qaddafi regime expelled US and British troops, nationalized foreign banks, confiscated Italian-owned properties, took over international oil companies, and quashed all parties opposed to its own dictatorial rule. It also suppressed labor strikes, instituted state control of the media, and established special committees to institutionalize the Libyan revolution. Over and above these standard authoritarian practices, Qaddafi always saw himself as a visionary leader.

Four years after the military coup, the Libyan revolution struck out with a burlesque theory of state organization. Spelled out in Qaddafi's *Green Book*, the "third universal theory" called for a governmental system neither Marxist nor capitalist. Unrealistically, it prescribed direct citizen participation in governance without parties or bureaucracy in a form of direct democracy known as *jamahiriyya*, which loosely translates as "state of the masses." The Socialist People's Libyan Arab Jamahiriyya enshrined Qaddafi as Brother Leader to guide and mentor the people, not rule them. Yet the system's popular committees were always strictly controlled from the top. Citizen involvement was always excluded from police, army, and intelligence sectors, which functioned on behalf of Qaddafi.[5] Akin to other dictators, he stepped up a propaganda campaign against foreign foes to mobilize the population behind his regime and to fabricate its legitimacy.

Qaddafi tried to fill Nasser's vacant shoes after the Egyptian's death in 1970 even though other Middle East leaders disputed his claim. He adopted a revolutionary brand of Arab nationalism with himself at the forefront. The Libyan strongman also embarked on more wicked ventures. In the late 1970s, he decided to produce nerve agents and blister gas first at facilities in Rabta and then at subterranean factories in Tarhuna. When Libya's military forces tried to conquer neighboring Chad, they used chemical agents against the Chadian army in 1987.[6] The former army colonel also backed such hard-line rejectionist Palestinian movements as the Popular Front for the Liberation of Palestine and the terrorists-for-hire Abu Nidal Organization. These groups directed their violence not only at Israel but also at so-called moderate Arab governments, judged not sufficiently anti-Israeli by the extremists. Qaddafi used Abu Nidal against his exiled opponents, murdering them in European or Middle Eastern streets.[7]

Libya also adopted violence to achieve a number of the pariah country's foreign policy objectives. Qaddafi aspired for influence throughout Africa as well as in the Arab and Muslim worlds. He bolstered several national liberation movements and terrorist organizations in Africa. His goal was to bring to power pro-Libyan dictators throughout the continent. Libyan-backed groups made attempts on the lives of leaders from Egypt to Chad to Zaire. Qaddafi worked to foment political unrest in Algeria, Togo, and Senegal. With the rise of Islamic militancy, he initially lined up behind radicalized Islamist militants, especially in Algeria and Morocco. As the threat of political Islam became apparent within Libya itself during the 1990s, Qaddafi backed off his earlier assistance. He feared that Islamic rulers nearby posed a risk to his corrupt and secular autocratic government. His deadly exploits reached such heinous proportions that the Reagan administration identified Libya "as the center of global terrorism."[8] President Reagan personally referred to him as the "mad dog of the Middle East" prior to ordering an air strike on the Libyan despot.[9]

Qaddafi's abiding enmity toward the United States made his government a natural ally of the Soviet Union (despite his antipathy for communism) during the 1970s and 1980s. Washington reciprocated. When Ronald

Reagan replaced Jimmy Carter in the Oval Office, America perceived Libya not only as "an adversary in itself but also as the spearhead of Soviet expansionism in the Middle East and Africa."[10] Libya's terrorism caused Western democracies considerable problems, which resonated with the Kremlin's purposes. In return, Tripoli benefited from Soviet patronage. Moscow sold warplanes, armored tanks, and surface-to-air missiles to its ally in North Africa. It also dispatched 2,000 military instructors and technicians to train Libyans and service the sophisticated weaponry.[11]

Nor was Qaddafi's regime a poor dependency; it paid for the imported armaments in hard currencies raked in from rising oil revenues after the 1973 Arab boycott boosted crude prices from Western customers. What's more, the Libyan-Soviet alignment shared a common foe in post-Nasser Egypt. Under Egypt's new leader, Anwar Sadat, Cairo moved from the USSR clientage. Both Qaddafi and the Soviet chief, Leonid Brezhnev, hated Sadat, who gravitated toward the pro-American camp in the Middle East and signed a peace accord with Israel. Anti-Egyptian animosity cemented the budding Qaddafi-Brezhnev friendship.

But Tripoli's actions, while often aligned with Moscow, were steered toward Qaddafi's own ends. He was not a stooge for the Kremlin. Moscow took note of Qaddafi's erratic and unpredictable impulses. His terrorism might lead to a trip-wire confrontation with the United States, compelling Moscow to fight an unwanted conflict or to abandon its Middle East allies to avoid a military clash with Washington. In spite of the Kremlin's weariness, the political alliance still afforded Libya some residual protection from its American nemesis. Like Moscow, Washington, too, had to be cautious about an overly aggressive response leading to a dangerous facedown with the Soviet Union, which might escalate into a shooting war or a public relations victory for the USSR.

The US-Libyan Antagonism

Tripoli's metamorphosis into a malevolent force behind international terrorism virtually foreordained that it would cross swords with Washington. Its sponsorship of terrorist gangs furnished Libya (as well as Iran, Iraq, Syria, and others) with a low-cost instrument of foreign policy. Terrorism amounted to a mostly risk-free tool to harm anonymously much more powerful enemies.[12] Libya, thus, could seemingly escape retribution from the United States.[13] The North African country relied on what is now familiarly known as asymmetrical warfare against the United States; it tried to evade America's strengths while exploiting its vulnerabilities. Even if America and its allies suspected the source of terrorism, it was often difficult to establish with certainty the paymasters or instigators of a bombing or shoot-ing. Proving state-sponsored terrorism beyond a shadow of a doubt in a US courtroom is often maddeningly difficult. So perpetrators more often than not escape punishment, unless the attacked party replies in kind, as did the Reagan administration.

Defenses against terrorism consume vast sums of money, time, and energy. Thus, a marginal country such as Libya could exert pressure dispro-portionate to its geopolitical weight. Libya, however, did not always duck direct showdowns with the United States. For example, Qaddafi claimed the Gulf of Sidra as exclusive Libyan territorial waters in 1973. Later, he expanded his extralegal claim another 12 nautical miles. America and other maritime powers contested Libya's redrawing its coastal boundaries as vio-lating freedom of the high seas. In another instance, mobs torched the US embassy in Tripoli in sympathy with protestors who seized the American embassy in Iran in 1979. President Jimmy Carter, nevertheless, weakly kept the American sword sheathed.

When Ronald Reagan ascended to the presidency, he toughened America's posture toward Qaddafi's provocations. After closing the Washington-based Libyan People's Bureau and expelling its "diplomats" for promoting terror-ism, President Reagan took even more decisive action. On August 19, 1981, American fighter planes shot down two of Libya's Soviet-built SU-22 jets over the Gulf of Sidra when they challenged a US naval presence in the contested international waterway. Next, he embargoed imports of Libyan oil and, more costly for the Qaddafi regime, he disallowed the transfer of oil extraction equipment to the Mediterranean state. The White House also froze Libyan financial assets in American banks. Libya retaliated in the way it knew best—via terrorism.

Reagan discerned Tripoli's hand in a string of deadly moves, including mine laying in the Red Sea, attempted assassination of Hosni Mubarak (Egypt's president), and the hijacking of an Egyptian airline that cost the lives of 60 people in November 1985. Libya also played a role in the simul-taneous Palestinian terrorist attacks on the Israeli airline El Al ticket coun-ters in the airports at Rome and Vienna that killed some 20 travelers in December 1985. Reagan officials were initially divided on the proper reac-tion, but under Secretary of State George Shultz's prodding, Washington finally counterattacked.[14] But not before Qaddafi crossed over the line.

Libyan agents (possibly Abu Nidal operatives) planted a bomb inside a West Berlin disco frequented by US military personnel in April 1986. The detonation killed three nightclub-goers, two of whom were American ser-vicemen, and wounded hundreds. Washington accused Libya of being a part of the bombing plot. Tripoli dismissed the allegations and countercharged that the Reagan government was "obsessed" with Qaddafi.[15]

The United States resolved to react forcefully and in concert with its allies. The European Economic Community (now the European Union) employed measures to restrict Libya from carrying out terrorism, such as reducing Tripoli's consulates and curbing the movement of Libyans once inside Western Europe. But America's European partners refused tougher sanctions, leaving Reagan few options other than to carry out a unilateral attack. Code-named Operation El Dorado Canyon, the US bombing took place on April 15, 1986, against Qaddafi's headquarters, residence, and the presumed terrorist-training installation within the military complex at Sidi Bilal. The bombardment missed Qaddafi but allegedly killed his daughter and other Libyan civilians. Even though the aerial strike caused limited damage, it made the Libyans display "much greater caution afterward, whereas earlier they had boasted of being unafraid to tackle a superpower," in the words of one terrorism authority.[16] In fact, Libyan-engineered terrorism dropped off over the next three years. It cannot be proved but is still argued that the boldness of the US counterattack dampened Qaddafi's ardor for life-threatening actions.

Rather than becoming pacific and reconciled to normal diplomatic practices, Qaddafi lay low, biding his time and hatching terrorist plots. His agents struck back at commercial airlines. Libya was implicated in the downing of France's UTA flight 772 over the Sahara in September 1989, killing 177 people en route to Paris from Brazzaville, Congo. It is believed that Qaddafi burned for revenge against France for expelling his military forces from Chad, which he tried to incorporate into Tripoli's political sphere. Libya denied any wrongdoing in the jet's midair explosion, but a decade later, it made modest financial restitution to some families of the dead.[17] This case of airplane terrorism was eclipsed, at least in American minds, by an even more deadly terrorist assault a few months later.

The most spectacular act of Libyan international terrorism took place in the evening sky over Scotland. Pan Am Flight 103 destined for New York City exploded while flying over the Scottish village of Lockerbie on December 21, 1989, killing all 259 persons on board and 11 more on the ground from falling debris. Much speculation centered on the hypothesis that Qaddafi retaliated for the US air bombardment on his compound in 1986. Later, it was determined that Iran and Syria might also have had a hand in the bombing but only enough evidence could be adduced against Libya to warrant an appeal to the United Nations for a resolution. The Security Council passed Resolution 731 requiring the Libyan government to surrender two agents, who stood indicted in American and British courts for their role in the terrorist attack. Libya's initial refusal to comply resulted in a series of UN economic and travel sanctions that greatly harmed the North African country's economy and international standing.[18] Before these setbacks, it had embarked on the quest for chemical and nuclear arms.

Qaddafi's Search for WMD

For the United States and its close allies, Libya's pursuit of WMD stood at the apex of the rogue-threat pyramid. No other endeavor so defines a rogue adversary as its reach for megadeath weapons, especially nuclear armaments, in the teeth of international opposition. Years later, Libya's renunciation of its nuclear ambitions and decision to open its territory for international arms inspections constituted the sine qua non of its rejoining the community of nations. That pacific outcome did not materialize until nearly two decades after Tripoli initiated its WMD goal during the 1980s.

At the end of that decade, Washington accused Libya of manufacturing chemical weapons. Libyan officials protested that its facilities were for the production of pharmaceuticals. Yet Libya's military used chemical agents in Chad during its invasion of the Saharan county in the 1980s. What's more, it developed short-range missiles with the assistance of North Korea, which sold Libya its version of Soviet Scud rockets. Such delivery systems could be used for projecting gas warheads a couple hundred miles. Libyan businessmen and scientists managed to induce a West German firm into constructing what ostensibly was to be a pharmaceutical plant; in reality, it was a front for a chemical weapons factory.[19]

Libya overcame its deficiency in nuclear expertise by relying on A. Q. Khan, the Pakistani scientist who also sold technology and components to North Korea and Iran with his government's concurrence. Khan, the so-called father of Pakistan's nuclear bomb, specialized in selling "starter kits" for uranium enrichment, built around large numbers of centrifuges. By 1997, the "first tranche equipment arrived" in Libya. Instead of setting up their own production line, the Libyans placed a massive order for "ten thousand P-2 centrifuges, enough to produce fissile material for up to ten bombs a year."[20] Unlike North Korea and Iran, which commanded homegrown technical elites, Libya required a "turnkey program" and lots of assistance from Khan's enterprise. By 2002, it had operational a cascade of centrifuges. Next blueprints for a nuclear bomb arrived. By early 2003, a nuclear facility was becoming a reality. Qaddafi paid an estimated $100 million, perhaps $140 million, to Khan for an extensive supply of equipment and expertise, far more than the arms merchant got from other customers.[21]

Qaddafi's persistent denials of his ultradestructive weaponry rang false. After the US-instigated interception and search of the cargo ship BBC *China* in October 2003, Washington and Britain possessed prima facie evidence. In the hold of the German-flagged vessel were centrifuge components manufactured in Malaysia by the Khan network for sale to Libya. Caught red-handed, Qaddafi owned up to his clandestine bomb making and turned over information about Khan's enterprise. He made an even more astounding turnaround. Seven months after the United States invaded Iraq, when the political atmosphere was thick with American talk of preventive war to find WMD, the Libyan ruler confessed to surreptitious nuclear arming. Was he afraid of an American attack?

Some George W. Bush officials speculated that Qaddafi wanted to escape Saddam Hussein's fate by coming clean and opening Libya to arms inspectors.[22] President Bush himself in unaccustomed subtlety postulated the link between the toppling of Iraq's dictator with the Libyan deal: "In words and actions: we have clarified the choices left to potential adversaries."[23] The threat of US intervention also gave Iran momentary pause when it supposedly suspended its nuclear arming in 2003, with the US military on its doorstep, as recounted earlier. Besides, Qaddafi knew firsthand how difficult and perhaps unrealizable the nuclear prize was for his technologically backward land. Why not make a deal while he still had a few cards to play?

Libya's nuclear disclosures led to Khan's exposure worldwide and to awareness of his collaboration with elements within the Pakistani government. The Libyan ruler also decided to shut down his nuclear program and to permit international inspectors access to all WMD laboratories and factories. Libya's decision represented an astounding volte-face. No other post–Cold War rogue regime had—nor has yet—renounced its atom-bomb dreams. Nonrogue governments in Belarus, Kazakhstan, and Ukraine were persuaded by the George H. W. Bush administration to abandon their nuclear arsenals after the USSR's fragmentation, which raised "doubts about the value of nuclear weapons" to these countries.[24] Likewise, postapartheid South Africa relinquished its nuclear ambitions to gain international acceptance. The rest of the rogue regimes, in contrast, perceived abundant utility in A-bombs. Unlike Qaddafi, the leaders in North Korea, Iran, and, yes, Iraq aspired to these doomsday arms for prestige and protection.

Two months after the BBC *China* incident, Tripoli announced the dismantling of its WMD and ballistic missile programs. It opened nuclear installations to IAEA inspectors to test its compliance with the NPT. It acceded to the Chemical Weapons Convention. Also in December 2003, it agreed to abide by the Missile Technology Control Regime and signed the Comprehensive Test Ban Treaty on nuclear detonations. Inspections soon took place under the IAEA and other international monitors.[25] Except for small stocks of chemical arms, Libya was cleansed of WMD.

In from the Cold

Containment, deterrence, and sanctions played a large role in convincing Libya to mend its ways.[26] Libya shrank on the global chessboard from a dangerous rook to a bypassed pawn. This fall in political fortunes figured in the Libyan leader's migrating out of the diplomatic cold. Even before the disintegration of the USSR in late 1991, Qaddafi realized that his Moscow ally had ceased to be a reliable guardian. He interpreted America's lopsided victory over Iraq's army in early 1991 as a sign of Soviet unreliability. Moscow did not come to the defense of the Arab nation. The Libyan autocrat was especially put off because Baghdad and Moscow had signed a Treaty of Friendship and Cooperation 20 years earlier. Qaddafi asserted that the treaty compelled Moscow to come to the aid of Iraq if "aggression is waged against it."[27] When the USSR tumbled into history, Qaddafi saw that the international landscape was utterly transformed, with America the sole standing superpower. Accordingly, he recalibrated his strategic calculations.

The USSR's end meant that Libya no longer benefited from a powerful, if unreliable, patron, which partially shielded Tripoli from America's reach. Moscow's actions in the Middle East had been predicated on the "hopes that it could gradually 'co-opt' the Arab nationalist revolutionaries and sign them up to socialist ideals."[28] When this goal proved impractical given the propensity of the Middle East states to shift toward Arab nationalism, the Soviets looked for ways simply to offset the preponderance of American naval strength in the Mediterranean. Libyan-Soviet cooperation rested on the mutual objective of limiting US political and military interference. The USSR "became Libya's sole foreign support and a counterweight to its enemies in the West."[29] But Libyan-Soviet ties were on the skids even before the Berlin Wall fell. Mikhail Gorbachev's ascendancy as Communist Party general secretary coincided with the USSR's economic death spiral in the mid-1980s. Gorbachev was evidently much more interested in pulling the Red Army out of Afghanistan, implementing perestroika ("restructuring") of the bankrupt economic system, and signing arms control agreements with the United States than being dragged into Libya's quarrels with America in the Middle East. When the USSR crumbled, Qaddafi lost his lone foreign pillar.

As one of the hypotheses of this volume, it has been stated elsewhere that many terrorist states came to depend on a heavyweight protector. In the shadow of the all-powerful United States, Cuba, for example, relied on the

Soviet Union during the Cold War and on Venezuela now for aid. North Korea currently depends on China to supply material aid and to run diplomatic interference against the United States. Even Iran, which has its own revolutionary Khomeinism, a large talented population, and sizeable oil revenues, looks to the Russian Federation and China to moderate American pressure. Thus, Libya keenly felt the loss of its onetime Soviet backstop. It had no other prop on which to lean.

Libya's diminished oil profits can offer an additional explanation for Qaddafi's political conversion. Sanctions curtailed Libya's ability to acquire spare parts and new extraction technologies. As a consequence, it lacked the ability to maintain revenues, let alone boost funds. Oil production slumped as equipment fell into disrepair. By 2003, Libya exported 1.5 million barrels of oil a day, just half of its 1969 output.[30] The dire repercussions stretched beyond simple revenue shortfalls; they endangered the dictatorship itself. Not dissimilar from other despotic rulers, Qaddafi needed ever-growing funds to buy off key tribal leaders, political figures, and military officers along with the complacency of the larger population. Libyans, particularly urban dwellers, relied on government-funded health care, education, and subsidized food. Costs for this government-purchased loyalty mushroomed amid a rocketing population expansion, which more than doubled from 2 million to 5 million in the two decades after the 1969 coup. Thus, Libya's financial pinch coincided with the loss of its Soviet guarantor. The "breakdown of the Soviet Union was crucial to Libya's sea change in foreign policy" but was not the total explanation of Tripoli's about-face.[31]

America's "shock and awe" military attack on Iraq bred fears in Tripoli. The US-led intervention into Iraq in March 2003 to rid it of nuclear arms no doubt added impetus to Qaddafi's denuclearization plans and strategic reversal. The Libyan strongman reasoned that since the French, Germans, and Russians had been unable to prevent President George W. Bush's invasion into the Persian Gulf state, "this meant the unilateral power of the United States was without limit."[32] He was quoted in *Le Figaro* on April 28, 2003: "When Bush has finished with Iraq, he'll turn on us."[33]

Far more elusive were the psychological and symbolic factors that contributed to Colonel Qaddafi's turnabout. Being ostracized to a narrow stretch along the Mediterranean coast did not comport with his titanic ego and outsized desire to lead the African continent from Cairo to Cape Town. He poured money into sub-Saharan states, backed Nelson Mandela's quest for majority rule and a nonapartheid South Africa, and welcomed African workers to Libya, which took jobs from the Libyans. His quest was rewarded when the African Union (AU) elected him chairman in 2009. Once installed, Qaddafi announced a grandiose destiny of political unification for a deeply fractured continent: "I shall continue to insist that our sovereign countries work to achieve the United States of Africa."[34] Heading the AU fulfilled a long-held goal by the North African autocrat, which carried a measure of receptivity by foreign governments after decades of estrangement.

Colonel Qaddafi's only viable course of action was to seek the good graces of the international society that he so menacingly spurned in the past. Almost overnight, the onetime army colonel executed a U-turn in his policies. Abruptly, he renounced terrorism. Regionally, he backed away from political subversion, military intervention, or destabilizing tactics in Chad, Tunisia, Uganda, and Egypt. He helped broker a peace accord in 1990 between Uganda and Congo for which Libya sent peacekeeping troops to Uganda together with other countries to police the settlement.[35]

Washington was initially skeptical of Qaddafi's steps away from the rogue's gallery. His actions, over time, lessened its skepticism. The dictator broke with his terrorist surrogates. He expelled the Abu Nidal Organization (which went to Iraq), closed terrorist training camps, cut ties to Palestinian militants, and turned over terrorist suspects to Egypt and Jordan. After years of painstaking negotiations begun during Bill Clinton's administration, Tripoli turned over two accused Libyan intelligence officers in 1999 for a Scottish-conducted trial in The Hague, Netherlands, for their part in the downing of Pan Am Flight 103. The handover of the suspects triggered an automatic suspension of the UN economic sanctions imposed on Libya in 1993 to induce Libya to surrender them.

The trial attracted world attention, but the verdict proved to be controversial. One suspected was exonerated for lack of conclusive evidence, and the other, Abdel Basset Ali al-Megrahi, was convicted and imprisoned in Scotland in early 2001. Qaddafi and other high Libyan officials escaped justice. Supposedly dying of cancer, Megrahi was set free on compassionate grounds and returned to Libya in 2009. Later British officials came under scrutiny for releasing the convicted terrorist in their presumed "eagerness for oil deals with Libya."[36] Megrahi's death diagnosis proved premature; he lived well beyond the three months estimated by Scottish authorities. At Washington's urging, Qaddafi also paid out over a billion US dollars to the families of Pan Am Flight 103 and other terrorist incidents. This legal settlement provided Libya immunity from other terrorist-related lawsuits.

Libya's abrupt strategic change did little to transfigure Qaddafi's image; he retained his beyond-the-fringe persona stemming from opéra bouffe antics. Often photographed swathed in flamboyant capes and caps or clad in medal-bedecked military uniforms, he cut a near-hilarious figure in the world media. In late 2007, he made his first visit to a Western country in 34 years, arriving in Paris with a 400-person entourage that included a 30-member female bodyguard unit, Bedouin-style tent for his lodging rather than staying at a five-star hotel, and a Saharan camel to greet visitors in the desert tradition.

Beneath the cartoonish antics, Qaddafi's regime carried on close relations with the Central Intelligence Agency against Islamist threats after its WMD disarmament. The Libyan intelligence service shared information with and interrogated suspected for the CIA. The extensive collaboration and Qaddafi's deep fear of jihadists came to light at the tail end of the antiregime rebellion, when intelligence documents were found in the Tripoli office of Libya's spymaster. Some of the information revealed additional details of the Libyan Islamists in fighting alongside the Afghan *mujahideen* to repel the Soviet invasion of the mountainous country during the 1980s. Some of the Libyan veterans of the Afghanistan resistance challenged Qaddafi upon their return home and then again during the 2011 revolt that overthrew the dictator. [37] Qaddafi's fear of jihadi threats led, in part, to the massacre of reportedly 1,200 Islamist inmates at Tripoli's Abu Salim Prison in 1996, an event that shaped the antiregime rebellion 15 years later.

Although Libya largely moved from the dark side of state behavior after 2003, its subsequent actions were not without relapses. It imprisoned Bulgarian nurses, whom it preposterously accused of infecting hundreds of Libyan children with HIV. Ultimately, the Qaddafi regime released the medical personnel but not before torturing and sentencing them to death. Qaddafi, in another example, was accused of plotting the assassination of the Saudi Arabian ruler, Crown Prince Abdullah, by two participants in the alleged scheme, which came to light in mid-2004. According to the pair's statements, Libyan intelligence chiefs ordered the contract killing to destabilize the desert kingdom and to settle a personal score against Abdullah for a sharp exchange of insults with Colonel Qaddafi at the Arab League summit in 2003. The plotters implicated Qaddafi, who denied the entire conspiracy. Libya's murder plans delayed but did not derail the resumption of normal diplomatic relations with the United States. Nor did Saudi Arabia demand the ouster of Qaddafi. In fact, Riyadh cautioned Washington against another regime change in the region in light of the violent chaos that the United States encountered in Iraq after ousting Saddam Hussein.[38] For its part, the Bush Oval Office did not plan an invasion and occupation of Libya.

When Libya entered the second decade of the twenty-first century, it had edged toward international rehabilitation after years of being a terrorist state. Qaddafi had moved from a terrorist enfant terrible to a run-of-the-mill dictator. The leopard may not have changed its spots; but in the Libyan case the animal had become tamer. What handwriting Qaddafi saw on the wall leading him toward reform remains obscure to outsiders. It may have been a mosaic of anxieties—internal Islamist threats, shrinking oil funds to buy off his population, fears of American military intervention, the irreplaceable loss of Soviet patronage, or the dimming of his revolutionary ardor—that convinced him to throw his lot in with the international community rather than persist in the rogue's gallery. Whatever the exact mix of motivation, Libya stands as a case apart from Iraq, Iran, and North Korea—the aces of adversarial states.

As a study in America's deterrence, containment, and eventual disarmament, Libya also stands out as a seductively easy case history. Largely obscured by Washington's repeated missteps toward Iran, Iraq, and North Korea, its Libyan policy achieved a peaceful resolution. The achievement, much like that of the peaceful winding down of the Cold War itself, spanned successive American presidential administrations stretching from Jimmy Carter, Ronald Reagan, George H. W. Bush, and Bill Clinton to finally George W. Bush. A blend of US bilateral and UN multilateral sanctions, limited military action, behind-the-scenes diplomacy, and flexibility—and luck—carried the day. It demanded some compromised principles by the United States, too. Washington went against its code of conduct by accepting a payment from Qaddafi to the Pan Am Flight 103 victims' families. Libya bought impunity by doling out money to the victim's kin. Some objected to the cash transfer; others reluctantly reconciled themselves to it. Not as principled as the removal of Qaddafi from power would have been, the unedifying but practical negotiations served to denuclearize a dangerous state. Once disarmed of its nuclear and much of its chemical arms capacity, Libya met many of the requirements to reenter the global commonwealth of states. Its strategic turnaround quickened hopes that its model could be applied to North Korea and Iran.[39] History did not repeat itself, however.

The Denouement of a Former Rogue

Like a formerly imprisoned felon upon his release, Qaddafi was only partially integrated back into international society before the Arab Spring democracy uprisings. When popular revolts upended the presidents for life in Tunisia, Egypt, and Yemen in 2011, Qaddafi's political tranquility came to an end as well. But unlike his Tunisian and Egyptian counterparts, who were quickly ousted from power, Qaddafi resolved to kill off in large numbers his insurrectionists. The antiregime demonstrations tapped into the widespread discontent among average Libyans. When anti-Qaddafi protestors took to the streets in Benghazi, the country's second-largest city, they ran into fusillades fired by Libyan security forces, which mowed down over 100 in the beginning days of the violent crackdown. For the first time in his 41-year reign, the autocratic leader faced the prospect of losing power. By a mixture of patronage, repression, and astute tribal alliances, the onetime army colonel met the protestors with militias commanded by his sons or whose ranks were filled with African mercenaries, many of whom knew no Arabic.

The Obama White House reacted hesitantly to the soaring protests across the Arab world. Not wanting to march into another Muslim country, Washington stayed clear of the upheavals in Egypt, Tunisia, Yemen, Syria, and Bahrain. But the Libya revolt drew in the United States, European nations, and Middle Eastern capitals. Libya's suppression of its rebellious citizens, unlike the Tunisian and Egyptian governments, ushered in what promised to be horrific violence against large numbers of defenseless civilians. Speaking on a radio call-in program, Qaddafi vowed that his security forces would pursue resisters "house by house." He then added, "We will find you in your closets. We will have no mercy and no pity."[40] Qaddafi's chilling statements and his violence-prone security forces galvanized international counteractions.

Pushed by Secretary of State Clinton and her allies among West Wing staffers, the Obama administration joined with nine other members of the Security Council (Russia, China, Germany, Brazil, and India abstained) to authorize military operations against the Libyan army and to implement a no-fly zone over the country on March 17, 2011, to protect innocent lives.[41] NATO oversaw the anti-Qaddafi campaign. The United States initially played a lead role, which the Obama Oval Office scaled down after a month, leaving Britain and France as the main military protagonists. Washington confined itself to the vital (but unglamorous) role of providing surveillance and logistical support to the NATO forces. Unflatteringly, President Obama was upbraided by his political opposition for "leading from behind." American expenditures were kept at a minimum, however. The Pentagon lost no lives in the NATO campaign, and Washington spent just over $1 billion, a pittance compared to the over $1.5 trillion on the wars in Afghanistan and Iraq. One unsettling fear stemmed from Washington's failure to recover and lock up thousands of portable shoulder-fired rockets loosened from Libyan armories. With no US troops on the ground to hunt down the antiaircraft weapons, they posed a threat to aviation if triggered by terrorists.

Quickly the air strikes switched from defensive missions to offensive bombings on Qaddafi's government in Tripoli. The air war, unexpectedly, dragged on for months as Qaddafi and his family clung to power despite aerial bombardments, frozen assets abroad, and numerous international demands for his exit. The Libyan protests morphed into a civil war between rebel forces based in the eastern section of the country and Qaddafi's army of personally controlled militias and foreign mercenaries occupying western parts near the capital. Gradually, the anti-Qaddafi forces went from the defensive to the offensive, conquering one regime stronghold after another. After the rebels seized Tripoli, they closed in on the remaining loyalist towns. When Surt (Qaddafi's hometown) fell to the rebel forces, the dictator himself died at the hands of a frenzied mob, nine months after the revolt broke out in Libya. After the passage of decades, six million Libyans turned to the painful process of creating a civil society and a representative government, buoyed only by the immense oil wealth beneath their feet.

Syria: A Rogue's Surrogate Rogue

The Syrian Arab Republic enjoyed a different status within the cluster of rogue players. Despite its use of terrorism as a state instrument and its appetite for weapons of mass destruction, Syria never exhibited the same confident aggressiveness of Iraq, Iran, or North Korea since the USSR's expiration. Its odious instincts and malevolent acts were cut from the same cloth as the three main rogue states. But Syrian foreign conduct became more circumscribed than its counterparts. Even while Syria did cozy up to the Soviet Union during the Cold War, it allied itself more closely with neighboring Iran after the withering away of the Soviet Union. Damascus's subservience to Tehran suggested to Washington and European governments that Syria could be pried away from its reliance on Iran with just the right set of inducements. Syria's rapprochement with Turkey, a rival to Iran, during the past decade also encouraged Western powers that Damascus was open to realignment.

Syria's weakness invited Western wooing, Euro-American diplomatic forays, and softer treatment than meted out to major rogue states. Hope seemed to spring eternal that the Levantine country would reform itself and join with the democracies against its own past and then turn on Iran. Syrian rulers kept their options open with the West so as to ease its pressure on the Damascus regime. It was a pragmatic stance, unprincipled and effective. Because of its rickety economy, political brittleness, and tenuous friendships in the Arab world, it needed Iran. Syria's alliance with Tehran was tantamount to its becoming Iran's proxy against the West. In short, a hollowed-out rogue fell into the clientage of another, stronger rogue, not a major-power patron.

Historical Overview

Syria has flitted in and out of Western consciousness since the Crusades a millennium ago. French knights carved out fiefdoms and constructed castles in the eastern Mediterranean land. After a century, the Crusaders' ill-fated venture to protect pilgrims from murder, rape, and abduction for ransom at the hands of Arab brigands while traveling to the Christian shrines in the Holy Land came to a bloody end. With the receding of the European incursion, local memories of the conflicts faded until awakened by Arab nationalists opposed to British and French colonialism.[42]

The expulsion of the crusading Franks dimmed—but did not erase—France's sentimental attachment to what became a province in the Ottoman Empire. World War I placed the restive Ottoman provinces in play as the Turkish imperial edifice crumbled. France and Britain divided the Middle East into colonies at the Versailles peace conference.[43] The League of Nations recognized French dominion over Syria under its mandate system, by which the League transferred territory to the control of European powers. French rule proved to be a turbulent affair. Arab-Syrian resistance greeted French colonialism with political opposition, popular protests, and violence throughout the interwar period.

After fits and starts, Syria received international recognition as a sovereign state under a republican government during the twilight of World War II. The coming to power of the Baath Party (Arab Socialist Party) in Syria as well as Iraq ushered in a protracted dictatorship. In 1970, Hafiz al-Assad, the defense minister in the Baath government, effected a bloodless coup to become president. He presided over Syrian political fortunes for the next 30 years.[44] Following Assad's death, his son, Bashar al-Assad, assumed the presidency in a rigged election in 2000. The House of Assad's rule represented a victory for their Alawite community, which has made alliances with other minorities in the country to consolidate its power.

The Syrian Alawites are a subsect of the Shiite branch of Islam within a country in which over three-quarters of the population belong to the Sunni stream of Islamic faith. The minority Alawites benefited politically and economically from their hands on the power levers. In turn, this 12 percent of the Syrian population buttressed the detested regime from their privileged army and commercial positions. Syria implemented quasi-socialist policies based on the Baath doctrine, but "it was more tolerant of private enterprise than other radical military regimes of the 1960s."[45] Bashar al-Assad opened up the economy more than his father, enabling life to improve for traders and small manufacturers, who backed his rule.

The advent of the Cold War ushered in Soviet-American competition across the Middle East as the two superpowers jockeyed for sway and surrogates. The revolutionary states of Syria, Iraq, and Egypt soon lined up with Moscow against United States and its local ally, Israel. The Soviet Union rewarded Syria with tanks, planes, and much other military equipment. The Damascus-Moscow alliance was mutually beneficial, allowing the Soviets to spread their influence over the eastern Mediterranean and enabling a third-tier country like Syria to posture as a regional power. Syrian defeats at the hands of the Israel Defense Forces (IDF) in three wars sobered its political and military elite about conventional warfare against the Jewish state. During the Six Day War in 1967, Syria lost control over the Golan Heights to Israel, which has held it to this day. The IDF's growing conventional military power after the 1973 war discouraged Syria from attempting to retake the Golan Heights. Instead Damascus demands the return of the strategic rocky plateau as part of a comprehensive Middle East peace settlement. The belief that Syria constituted the key to an Israeli-Palestinian peace agreement led President Bill Clinton to authorize his secretary of state, Warren Christopher, to make over 20 trips to engage Hafiz al-Assad in talks about a settlement. They came to naught.

Terrorism and the Emergence of a Rogue State

The Syrian Arab Republic resorted to terrorism, in part, so as to stay a political player in a region with much stronger powers. It conducted or supported terrorism, mostly aimed at Israel, at Jordan, and within Lebanon. It also turned to proxies to carry out terrorist-style attacks in Western Europe and Turkey. During the 1970s, the Syrian regime opened its territory for safe havens to Palestinian terrorist networks. Later, it allowed Hamas and Islamic Jihad to open offices in Damascus.[46] After the 1973 war, the Kremlin replenished Syrian armories to sustain its standing in the Arab world. Soviet arms enabled the Assad regime to pose a renewed threat to Israel. Its Soviet-sponsored military buildup also worried Turkey, a NATO member, but the Assad regime gazed westward toward Lebanon, not northward toward Turkey and Syria's lost territory.

Near the start of Lebanon's civil war, Damascus marched into the Levantine country in 1976 ostensibly to restore political order on its doorstep. In reality, Syrian rulers had always considered Lebanon little more than a province of Greater Syria. Damascus's irredentist conquest of Lebanon along with its claims on Jordan and Palestine gained the Syrian regime broad internal popularity. The Arab Republic's rule over Lebanon advanced Damascus's regional goals and "provided a secure source of much-needed rents to finance the regime's neo-patrimonial networks and offset pressure for economic reform."[47] For a time, Lebanon served as a quasi-colony in the Greater Syria nation.

Syria's hand in terrorism had been instrumental in pushing American and Israeli forces out of Lebanon. Damascus along with Tehran played a role in the infamous 1983 truck bombing of the US Marine Corps headquarters that killed 241 US servicemen on a UN peacekeeping mission.[48] Terrorist gunmen and Machiavellian alliances completed the Syrian subjugation of the Levantine country during its civil war (1975–1990). Syrian-Iranian cooperation in building the Hezbollah movement turned it into an effective insurgent force against Israel and later a wily political movement in Lebanese politics.[49] Syrian terrorism likewise undermined Israel's peace feelers to the moderate Arab governments. And Syria enhanced its importance and utility to Moscow through the authorship of political murder and mayhem. One regional expert asserted, "Assad made Syria virtually a member of the Soviet bloc."[50] There was no other way to explain Syrian operations to destabilize Turkey by helping Kurdish rebels, which benefited Moscow more than Damascus.

The United States recalled its ambassador in Syria following the Nizar Hindawi terrorist incident in 1986. A Jordanian working with the Damascus government through its embassy in London, Hindawi tried to hide a Semtex bomb on an Israeli commercial jet. The foiled attempt confirmed Washington's earlier wisdom in placing Syria as a charter member on the State Department's list of terrorist-sponsoring states in the late 1970s.The year 1986 also marked a peak in Syrian involvement in terrorist operations that brought its agents to trials in London, Paris, and other European cities. Hereafter, Syria responded by shutting down terrorist training camps used by Abu Nidal and expelling the group to Libya.[51] Damascus tamped down plots in the West and redirected its violent actions to the Middle East. A year later, Washington returned its ambassador to the Arab Republic. However, it did not delist Syria from its terrorism roster. Syria remained on the terrorism list because of its mounting cooperation with Iran, its terrorism facilitation through Lebanon-based Hezbollah, and hosting Hamas and Islamic Jihad offices in Damascus.[52]

Over time, the Baathist platform calling for an Arab renaissance lost its popular appeal when the ruling party applied its version of socialist ideology to ensure its own longevity in office. Some benefits flowed to the citizenry with rural electrification, highways, and land redistribution. But the hand-me-downs that the bulk of the population got were paltry, uneven, and disproportionately small compared to the bonanzas reaped by the political establishment.

Pragmatic and calculating, Assad was determined to stay in power rather than launch bold initiatives. Syria's roguishness stalled over the years. Toward its neighbors—Israel, Jordan, and Lebanon—the Syrian regime undertook deadly activities, but they were not directly aimed at the United States or even Europe. The Arab Republic has repeatedly suppressed and even crushed with heavy local casualties Islamic fundamentalist movements such as the Muslim Brotherhood as a danger to its own rulers. So it has been less forthcoming to these extremists, denying them safe havens even if they posed a threat to the United States.

The ruling elite faced another problem. Made up of the small Alawite minority, it worried about political destabilization. A breakdown in political order from a foreign or internal catastrophe could pave the way for governmental implosion. The disadvantaged Sunni, who made up 75 percent of the population, might seize on instability to turn the tables on their long-entrenched overlords. That is why the Assad regime is wary of radical Islam, lest it fall to frenzied masses à la the Iranian shah.[53] As its rogue-state profile receded, Syria almost fell from the American radar except as one part of the peace puzzle between Israelis and Palestinians. In contrast to Libya's pervasive promotion of terrorism toward America during the 1980s, Syria gradually adopted a lower-grade terrorist strategy against US interests, at least before the Iraq War.

Making Its Way in the Post–Cold War World

The Soviet Union's breakup similarly impacted Syria as it did Moscow's other client regimes in Libya, Cuba, and North Korea. Bereft of its main weapons supplier and diplomatic prop, Syria perceived the new world order of American dominance. It leaned more heavily on Iran. Given its tense relations with Saddam Hussein's Iraq, Damascus surprised few when it joined the American-led UN counterattack to repel the 1990 Iraqi invasion of Kuwait. It deployed 30,000 troops to join in the defense of Saudi Arabia to forestall Baghdad from rolling tanks into the desert kingdom.

On the heels of the Persian Gulf War, Syria patched up relations with Iraq. It allowed the Hussein regime to circumvent UN oil sanctions by letting Iraqis pump crude through a pipeline into Syrian territory. Hussein sold the oil to the Assad regime at the discounted price of $15 a barrel in exchange for payment outside the UN escrow account. Hussein used these funds to buy loyalty of major political and military figures, to purchase arms on the world market, and to sustain his own family's luxurious lifestyle. The Syrian connection afforded the Iraqi dictator a means to evade the international body's restrictions. Those requirements called on Baghdad to use money derived from UN-sanctioned oil sales to purchase food and medicine for the nation's population. Syria exported an equivalent amount, some 150,000 barrels per day from its own meager oilfields, at the prevailing market price. Thus, it reaped a windfall profit from the difference between home-produced oil and Iraqi shipments.[54] Syria also benefited from the overland shipment of military equipment and dual-use goods to Hussein's

Iraq. Violations of UN sanctions elicited a strongly worded protest from Washington at the beginning of George W. Bush's presidency. Secretary of State Colin Powell even flew to Damascus in a failed attempt to persuade the junior Assad to turn off the Iraqi oil flow.

At the start of the Bush administration, the White House focused abroad on abandoning the Anti-Ballistic Missile (ABM) treaty with Russia and applying targeted UN sanctions on Iraq to do less harm to that country's population. Syria slipped from primary US interest except for its role in aiding Iraq as it smuggled oil through the international embargo. Its prominence as a terrorist hub had markedly slipped from its heyday years earlier. By this time, Damascus had its own concerns with the Muslim Brotherhood, which endangered the corrupt, secular House of Assad. Akin to Libya, which also feared Islamist groups, the Syrian Republic looked for ways to survive in the post-Soviet world.

A series of events refocused America's attention on Syria. Following the 9/11 terrorist attack on the United States, Damascus surprisingly entered into an intelligence sharing with the Central Intelligence Agency against al-Qaeda cells in the Middle East and in Arab exile communities in Europe. Anxious about being on the wrong side of Bush's war on terror as the US attacked Afghanistan, Damascus offered to share intelligence with Washington.[55] The last such collaboration had taken place during the Persian Gulf War against Iraq. Syrian intelligence possessed information about al-Qaeda because of its ties with the Syrian branch of the Muslim Brotherhood, radical Islamists who been at war with the House of Assad for two decades. According to some sources, the Syrian information enabled the United States to thwart more than one terrorist plot aimed at Americans. In communications with Bashar al-Assad, President Bush acknowledged Syria's cooperation against al-Qaeda terrorism.[56]

But within the Bush government, divisions arose about possibly incurring indebtedness to the Arab Republic, which might undercut appropriate American responses to state sponsors of terrorism. Damascus, for example, still furnished its own support for Hezbollah and funneled Iranian arms and trainers through its territory to the Lebanese Shiite movement. Additionally, it still allowed anti-Israeli terrorist networks to keep offices in Damascus.[57] Syrian cooperation, however brief, influenced American governments to perceive a possible deal with the Levantine country, placing it in a lesser-rogue category than Iran or North Korea. Over time, Washington came to regard Syria as pliable to American negotiations. This assumption proved wrong but persistent.

The anti-Islamist round of cooperation collapsed with the 2003 US invasion of Iraq. The Syrian regime grew apprehensive about its own fate.

Collaboration with the CIA lapsed. Syria opened its territory to serve as a corridor for jihadis from throughout the Muslim world to enter Iraq's western expanse, where many died killing US and other coalition troops during the Iraq War.[58] Young Muslim men flocked into Syria, where they were secreted across the Iraqi border to fight the US occupation of the Persian Gulf country. The Assad regime sought to back former Iraqi Baathist officials in their bid to stage a comeback in Iraq after the US withdrawal. Its alignment with former Hussein military officers was intended to assert its political leverage in Iraq and to impede democracy spreading from the recently liberated land.[59]

The United States struck back at the Syrian connection that ran foreign fighters, arms, and money across the border into Iraq. In late October 2008, helicopter-borne Special Operations Forces raided a Syrian village six miles from the border and killed the leader of the insurgent base, who was the chief smuggler for the al-Qaeda in Iraq movement's operations in Syria. Washington justified the attack, like those in Pakistan and Somalia, as a self-defense mission to protect American and allied forces fighting in Iraq. It also asserted that it had long complained to Syria over the transit of militants to Iraq.[60] Damascus chose not to retaliate overtly against the US raid. Nor did it immediately turn off the spigot to prospective jihadis.

Earlier, the George W. Bush government enacted a new set of economic sanctions on the Arab Republic in 2004. The United States and France stepped up international pressure on Syria's colonial-type dominance over Lebanon by securing passage of Security Council Resolution 1559, which called for "a free and fair electoral process in Lebanon's upcoming presidential election." The resolution also called for "all remaining foreign [i.e., Syrian] forces to withdraw from Lebanon" in September 2004.[61]

The next year, the Bush government again recalled the US ambassador to Syria for the regime's suspected complicity in the killing of the former Lebanese prime minister Rafik Hariri with a car bomb in early 2005. The widely popular Hariri had become too vocal against Syria's continued military presence in Lebanon. His death was attributed to Syria and its allies by Lebanese and foreign observers. Hezbollah and Damascus denied the assassination charges, but an international tribunal indicted four members of the Shiite movement in July 2011. Not unexpectedly, Hassan Nasrallah, the Hezbollah leader, announced that no Lebanese government will be able to carry out the arrests of the suspects "whether in 30 days, 60 days, 1 year, 2 years, 30 years or even 300 years."[62] Arresting and handing over the four men to the UN Special Tribunal on Lebanon for trial amounted to igniting an ethnic powder keg in the fragmented country.

Following Hariri's murder in 2005, vociferous anti-Syrian demonstrations exploded in Beirut and other Lebanese cities. The Lebanese had long chafed under Damascus's heavy-handed rule until the "Cedar Revolution," when large, raucous street protests, French-led international condemnation, and American diplomatic exertions forced the Syrian army to withdraw. The Arab Republic, nonetheless, remains intimately involved in Lebanese affairs via Hezbollah, secret agents, and large bribes to political movements within the country.[63] Syria took some comfort in the ascension to the Lebanese leadership of Nasrallah's man, Prime Minister Najib Mikati, in early 2011. Hezbollah had come a long way from its insurgent roots in the early 1980s.

Chemical and Nuclear Concerns

Above all, Syria's clandestine chemical and nuclear programs ensured the Arab Republic a place on America's most-watched list. According to one expert, the "heart of Syria's WMD posture is its indigenous chemical warfare (CW) program."[64] The WMD seed may have been the transference of mustard agent from Egypt before the 1973 conflict. Although Syria did not resort to gas weapons during the Yom Kippur War, it started soon afterward to produce its own stocks of chemical arms. Damascus might have stepped up its indigenous CW production to offset its vulnerability to conventional Israeli capabilities, as demonstrated again in another Syrian defeat when Israel intervened militarily into Lebanon in 1982. Assistance came from North Korea and especially Iran to overcome Syria's low level of industrial capacity.[65]

Chemical plants were built near Al-Safira, Hama, and Homs. During the following two decades, Syrian technicians learned to produce their own mustard, sarin, and nerve gases. They also learned to encapsulate these deadly agents in warheads on Scud-type missiles, airplane-delivered bombs, and long-range artillery shells. Neither would Syria renounce its right to possess chemical weapons, nor would it sign the Chemical Weapons Convention. Nongovernment reports state that Syria has improved its CW capabilities since 2005 in cooperation with Iran.[66] Chemical agents just whetted its appetite for nuclear weapons.

American unease about Syria's nuclear-arming intentions existed for years. Damascus did sign and ratify the Nonproliferation Treaty in 1969. But Syria's dangerous profile—dictatorship and terrorism—raised anxieties in Washington and other capitals about its clandestine WMD exertions. Damascus pursued nuclear capabilities since the 1980s with several countries. Its lack of industrial and financial resources discouraged foreign firms from constructing nuclear power plants. China built a nuclear research reactor that went online in 1996, but international experts estimated its capacity too small to pose a proliferation danger. Before the Chinese-built reactor became operational, Damascus concluded a Comprehensive Safeguards Agreement with the IAEA. The Sino-Syrian cooperation caused American and Israeli headaches about Syria's nuclear intentions during the 1990s.[67]

When the United States failed to turn up nuclear weapons in Iraq after its 2003 invasion, speculation swirled that a desperate Hussein transported his nuclear equipment into Syria to avoid American detection. That conjecture still persists in some circles.[68] The prevailing view, nonetheless, is that Hussein's Iraq possessed no nuclear arms after the Gulf war. Rather, it was engaged in a colossal bluffing game with Iran. Other assessments concluded that Syria had contacts about nuclear issues with Iran and the A. Q. Khan network.[69] North Korea also played a role. After all, the DPRK regime had long sold missile technology to Syria as well as to other Middle Eastern states. North Korean cargo vessels had been spotted in Syrian ports. What's more, it is highly likely that Pakistani nuclear components wound up in Syrian hands after being sold to them by North Korea.[70]

Syria's suspected atomic-arms agenda was exposed by the sudden attack of September 6, 2007, in which Israeli warplanes bombed an installation near the town of al-Kibar in the country's northeastern quadrant.[71] After the military operation, it was also reported that a number of North Korean personnel lost their lives at the blasted nuclear compound.[72] The similarity of North Korean nuclear installations and the one bombed in Syria pointed to Pyongyang-Damascus collaboration. Syria protested the military strike, blamed Israel for the assault, and denied any atom-bomb facilities on its territory, an assertion made more untenable with the release of satellite imagery.[73] The Israeli government generally stayed mum on the bombardment. Even without Israel's official confirmation, there was little doubt about the origin of the raid or its success.

Ex post facto analyses zeroed in on North Korean assistance in building the bombed nuclear project. The Syrian facility appeared to be modeled on the North Korean main plant in Yongbyon, known well to IAEA inspectors. Doubters of Pyongyang's hand in Syrian nuclear efforts noted that the regime, while it sold missile components and expertise to many nations, never before transferred nuclear technology to another country. The DPRK's desperate search for saleable exports emasculated that argument, especially after the rollup of the Khan network.[74] The emergence of the Syrian nuclear project, undetected by the IAEA, was tantamount to another failure for the UN nuclear watchdog organization. Satellite images taken before and just after the Israeli aerial bombardment corroborated intelligence estimates of Syrian nuclear advances.

The United States shared in the Israeli evidence during the months leading up to the bombing. It was reported that the George W. Bush government
demanded proof of the Syrian nuclear activities before giving its blessing to
the preemptive strike. Accordingly, nuclear material, taken by Israeli com-
mandos operating on the ground, was turned over to Washington.[75] Finally,
the IAEA concluded in a 2011 report that the bombed site was "very likely
a covert reactor," which Syria should have declared under the Safeguards
Agreement.[76] In the raid's aftermath, fresh evidence surfaced of other Syrian
exertions to generate alternative WMD. Intelligence reports cited a mysterious explosion at a secret Syrian base, when a Scud-C missile was being
loaded with a mustard-gas warhead in late July 2007. The blast reportedly
killed several Syrian and Iranian engineers near the northern town of Aleppo
on the Turkish border.[77]

An Unholy Marriage

The Syrian-Iranian axis took hold in the wake of Iran's antishah revolution.
Both states stood to benefit from an alliance that aimed at Israel. Damascus
keenly felt what it perceived as a betrayal by Egypt for entering into a peace
agreement with the Jewish state in the Camp David accords. To Syria, this
loss of Egyptian partnership against Israel could be offset by cooperation
with the new Islamic Republic. The Syrian-Iranian modus operandi also
strengthened the Arab camp with the addition of a non-Arab state. Syria's
alliance also did much to promote Shiite Iran's cause in the Sunni Arab
world. The Syrian Arab Republic did, in fact, try to assuage anti-Iranian
sentiments among its fellow Arab states, many of which remained deeply
anti-Persian.[78] The Syrian-Iranian axis also reinforced the opposition to US
influence in the region. Washington was unable to split them apart or to disable one of the partners. As one authority wrote in 2009, "It is noteworthy
that the USA has very little leverage over them [Syria and Iran] today."[79]
Both countries have fended off isolation that so plagued North Korea (except
for China) since the Cold War ended by the alliance and the circle of foreign
contacts it entailed.

The Syrian-Iranian marriage of convenience is not free of tensions and
ambiguities, however. They compete for influence in Lebanon while cooperating there. Syria harbors strong irredentist claims on Lebanon, which
it wants returned to the semicolonial status prior to its 2005 pullout. Iran
has a different agenda. Access and maneuverability within Lebanon affords
Iran a virtual border with Israel for mischief-making activities. It supports
Hezbollah as a standby weapon against the Israelis. If the IDF or the US
Air Force bombed Iranian nuclear facilities, Tehran would almost assuredly

unleash Hezbollah to attack Israel in retaliation. Furthermore, Iran through Hezbollah has a gateway to the Mediterranean, giving Tehran an outpost on a sea long regarded as a mare nostrum by the West. Syria's dependency is so great on Iran that any distinction in its aims does not create a difference with Tehran.

The Syrian-Iranian meddling in Lebanon leaves that small Middle Eastern country politically unsettled. It has also left Lebanon as an epicenter of the larger Arab-Persian conflict. Saudi Arabia had given political latitude to Syria's revanchist designs on Lebanon in exchange for limiting Iran's reach in the fractured country. Damascus and Riyadh, thus, enjoyed an uneasy interaction, which neither wanted to fail despite the personal animosity between the rulers. When Syria was rocked by offshoots of the Arab Spring rebellions in early 2011, initially Riyadh rhetorically stood behind the Assad regime out of fear that its overthrow would further destabilize the Middle East.[80] Later, it withdrew its ambassador to protest Assad's brutal clampdown on the demonstrators. Kuwait and Bahrain also recalled their envoys, leaving Syria even more isolated. A onetime friend of Assad, Turkey also backed away from the murderous dictator as his tanks and snipers mowed down antiregime crowds. The Turks presented a counterweight to Iran's Syrian patronage. The Turkish-Iranian rivalry dates to the Ottoman-Safavid times, although it diminished over the years. When antiregime protesters took to Syrian streets, tension again flared between Ankara and Tehran. The Turks criticized Syria and aided the anti-Assad demonstrators by sheltering them on their territory. This galled the Iranians, who aided the regime with advisers and equipment to interrupt the rioters' electronic communications via the social media. The Turkish-Iranian competition over Syria rekindled their jockeying for regionwide political standing and diplomatic influence.[81]

The escalating street protests and diplomatic isolation drove Syria deeper into the Iranian embrace. Well before momentous revolts in the Middle East, Iran's leverage over and assistance to Syria reached a level not totally dissimilar to a patronage-and-proxy relationship between a regional patron and its smaller, debilitated rogue partner. It is almost as if the rogue Iranian master, like China or Soviet Union, had its own renegade client. Syria's alliance with Tehran came to "resemble a patron-client relationship," as characterized by a former Israeli negotiator to Syria in 2008.[82] Whereas Iran depended on Russia for advanced defensive missiles, Syria, in turn, relied on Iran to supply it with sophisticated radar and other arms. Tehran transferred a radar system that upgraded Syrian detection and defensive capabilities vis-à-vis Israel's warplanes.

Iran also benefits from the earlier warning of Syrian radar if the Israelis launch an air operation against Tehran's nuclear sites.[83] Iran's transfer of the radar violated a 2007 United Nations sanction that banned Tehran from selling or transferring arms. The Iranian clerics simply ignored the international body, and no one raised a finger to stop them. The hard-pressed House of Assad relied all the more on its Iranian overlord as Damascus faced mounting international exclusion. Yet the Islamic Republic's dependence lessened a bit on Syria for ground passage to its Hezbollah proxy. With Hezbollah in the Lebanese political driver's seat since early 2011, the Beirut government can open airports and harbors to direct Iranian transit, obviating Iran's reliance on the Syrians.

Actions and Counteractions

Iran's stalwart backing of Syria undercut the Obama administration's diplomatic initiative to alter the Syrian president Bashar Assad's alliance with Tehran. Soon after arriving at the White House, Barack Obama undertook a rapprochement with the Arab Republic so as to woo it away from Iran's clientage. The United States sent a high-level trade delegation to meet with the Assad regime in June 2010. The Syrian-Iranian partnership remained intact despite America's wheedling. Washington misunderstood the codependency of Syria and Iran. They need each other far more than American trade, investment, or diplomatic normalization. The survival of both regimes rode on anti-American actions and propaganda.

Hostility to the United States expediently served as a distraction from internal oppression. In the Syrian case, the regime's anti-Americanism rested on its popular policy to eliminate Israel from the Middle East map. The majority Sunni population shared their governments' goal; it gave them something in common with the despised Alawite ruling establishment. As scholar Barry Rubin wrote, "Militancy is the glue that holds Syria together and keeps Bashar [Assad] stuck to the throne."[84] Damascus, the weaker partner in the Syrian-Iranian alliance, was buttressed by the Islamic Republic during the widespread, bloody protests against the Assad regime beginning in 2011. Iran feared the loss of its satellite in the eye-for-an-eye struggle with the United States. Hezbollah fighters and Iranian cadre aided in the grim killing of Syrian protesters. Tehran dispatched its Quds Force, the covert-action arm of the Islamic Revolutionary Guards Corps, to Syria to provide instructions on repressing large street demonstrations. The Quds Force gained much thuggish experience in savagely suppressing Iranian demonstrators in 2009 after its fraudulent presidential elections. Both security forces shared a hunt-them-down-and-kill-them mentality toward antigovernment rebels.

Syria's other foreign protector, the Russian Federation, blocked UN sanctions against the beleaguered Assad regime in early 2012. Russia's veto and other anti-American measures torpedoed the White House's "reset" policy to return Russo-American relations to the rapprochement of the 1990s. In the Syrian case, Moscow together with Beijing bristled at outside interference within states, apprehensive about international condemnation for the suppression of their own populations in the Caucasus and Tibet, respectively. Russia took the lead in heading off Washington's push for Security Council resolutions, loudly proclaiming it had been duped into the UN resolution that opened the way for NATO-led military attacks on Libya and the ouster of Qaddafi. Reminiscent of its former Soviet Empire, the Kremlin prized Syria as a customer for its arms industry and as a host to its reopened naval base in Tartus. The PRC joined the Russian Federation in vetoing an Arab League peace plan calling for a transition from Assad to his vice president and a unity government to pave the way for democratic elections. As for Damascus, it welcomed the return of Moscow's diplomatic shield and arms sales. Like North Korea's shift into China's orbit, the Syrian regime gravitated back into a Russian guardianship while staying bound to Iran.

Syria's crushing of initially peaceful protests knocked Obama's outreach gambit into a cocked hat. Washington changed course and imposed sanctions on Bashar al-Assad and six other Syrian officials for their crackdown on political uprisings across the country that resulted in the death of several thousand antiregime rebels. The sanctions froze any assets that the Syrian leaders had in American financial institutions.[85] Next, it pressed the IAEA to hold a vote within its 35-member governing body to find Syria in violation of the UN Nuclear Nonproliferation Treaty. Passage of such a finding would pave the way for a Security Council resolution against the Assad regime.[86] The antinuclear response coincided with American efforts to press the Security Council to condemn the savage Syrian repression of antiregime demonstrators. The US Department of State gathered evidence of the Assad dictatorship's human rights abuse for possible referral through the Security Council (if it could get Russian and Chinese votes) to the International Criminal Court in The Hague for prosecution. President Obama belatedly joined other world leaders in calling for the resignation of the 45-year-old ruler. Months later in October 2011, Washington recalled its ambassador to Damascus out of fear for his personal safety in the tumultuous country. Washington generally took counsel of its fears that Assad's fall from power might fuel regionwide ethnic and sectarian violence among Alawites, Sunni, Shiites, and Kurds.[87]

Make no mistake: Syria is not a pacifist state willing to live in harmony within its neighborhood. It shoots and tortures its citizens with abandon. It indirectly sponsors terrorism through Hezbollah, which has carried out attacks against Westerners and Israelis. The Syrian Arab Republic has served as a conduit for Iranian arms, as a training base, and in terrorist mentorship to Hezbollah. More than any Sunni-headed Arab state, Syria has relished its hostility to Israel. Yet next to Iran, Syria is much less a renegade player. Nor is it a freelance rogue on its own independent powerbase. In fact, without Iranian backing, Syria might be little more than a fiercely repressive dictatorship struggling poorly to contain a restless population. Battered by drought and insurrection, the regime staggered as the economy and its support eroded among minority groups, business elite, and the middle class as the revolts blazed across the country.[88]

Even the typically standoffish Arab League brokered a plan to halt the violence and convene talks between the Assad regime and its opposition. Its gambit into the Syrian bloodbath stemmed not from tenderhearted humanitarianism but from the calculus of turning back Iranian penetration into what in reality is a mostly Sunni-populated country. As with Turkey, the League members aspired to return Syria to the Sunni fold and erase Shiite Iran's proxy, which lent the dreaded Persians a corridor into Lebanon and across to the Mediterranean, their first outpost on that sea in over 2,300 years. Deprived of Syrian support and Iranian matériel, Hezbollah would also be dealt a blow in Lebanon, where Sunni and Christian populations suffered at the hands of the Shiite militia. Before the ink could dry, the agreement passed into irrelevancy because of the deadly struggle between the two protagonists on Syrian streets. Syria's agony persisted, leaving the outside observers to conclude that the Levantine country's fate would never be the same as before the revolt.

Troublesome States: Sudan, Cuba, and Venezuela

With nearly any classification, there are cases that exhibit some—but not all—of the characteristics. This is true of rogue states, too. Not to mention that the marginal cases create doubt about their exclusion. Therefore, a brief discussion of Cuba, Venezuela, Sudan, and South Yemen is in order. With the exception of Venezuela, the other three countries have long been designated as terrorist-sponsoring nations on the State Department's list. South Yemen, as noted in chapter 1, enjoyed a different fate as time passed. It came off the terrorist registry because it ceased to be a separate country after its negotiated merger with North Yemen in 1990. Cuba and Sudan remain on the list, along with Iran and Syria.[89] None of the marginal rogue states acted with anything near the pugnacity of North Korea, Iraq, or Iran after the Soviet Union fell apart. They are more troublesome countries rather than genuine rogues. Troublesome nations, however, do generate anxiety in foreign chancelleries for their worrisome behavior, albeit at a lower threshold than full-fledged rogue players.

Sudan's antecedents reach back nearly 3,000 years to the Kingdom of Kush. But its modern-day sovereignty began with the withdrawal of British rule in 1956. Being the biggest country in Africa geographically (before the separation of the Republic of South Sudan in mid-2011) bestowed neither enduring peace nor just governance on the impoverished country. Coups and military rule gave promise of a fresh start to the Sudanese. But mainly, the rulers squandered opportunities and disappointed their countrymen. The 1989 coup looked to repeat history. It saw, rather, the rise of the Islamists, who soon dominated the executive, the military, and the judiciary. They imposed *shari'a* laws on society, indoctrinated the armed forces in Islamist practices, hosted Afghan-Arab *mujahideen* on Sudanese soil, and established contacts with terrorists.[90]

For four decades, the Republic of the Sudan has sheltered violent international extremists. The Palestinians' Black September movement, indeed, murdered the US ambassador Cleo A. Noel and the deputy chief of mission Curtis G. Moore in Khartoum on March 1, 1973. During the 1980s, Libyan terrorists resided in Sudan. Abu Nidal, Osama bin Laden, Carlos the Jackal, and other hitmen also found sanctuary in Sudan. The *mujahideen* victory in Afghanistan over the Red Army coincided with the Islamization of Sudanese society. Aroused by a passion for the restoration of an Islamic caliphate, Khartoum welcomed jihadis from Afghanistan and promoted jihads in Algeria, Bosnia, and Yemen in the early 1990s.

Sudan's links to international terrorist networks prompted the United States to designate the country as a state sponsor of terrorism in 1993. Over the years, Washington has pulled its ambassadors from Sudan and then returned them. Likewise, it supplied and suspended development and military assistance to Khartoum governments. The George W. Bush government imposed sanctions on Sudanese citizens implicated in genocidal violence within the Darfur province in 2007. In addition, Islamist terrorist movements operated from Sudan, while carrying out attacks in neighboring Somalia, Ethiopia, and Eritrea.[91]

For all the ups and downs in Sudanese-American relations, the northeast African country never evolved into a front-rank rogue state. Why? In brief, Sudan lacked the military and economic wherewithal to confront the United States in the way Iran, Iraq, and North Korea did. Sudan, in many respects, resembled a failed state rather than a small-bore powerhouse, even in its region. With puny armaments, a backward economy, and no major patron, the Republic of the Sudan lacked the means to mount a direct threat. More than that, Sudan retreated from being terrorist central to the world's dagger men when it came to light that it had aided in the failed assassination of Egypt's President Hosni Mubarak by the Egyptian Islamic Jihad. That complicity triggered an international revulsion against the Khartoum government. The Sudanese leadership, in reaction, inaugurated steps "to end the isolation of Sudan as a pariah state."[92] It turned Carlos the Jackal over to the French, expelled other terrorists, and asked Osama bin Laden to leave. Another reason Sudan escaped top billing as a rogue nation came from the fact that it did not develop nuclear arms. The country may have flirted with acquiring chemical weapons, however.

A suspected Sudanese sarin-manufacturing site became a retaliatory target for the United States. After the al-Qaeda bombing of the two US embassies in East Africa, the Clinton White House decided to strike back at a suspected nerve-gas plant in Sudan as well as Osama bin Laden's training camps in Afghanistan. Soil samples taken from outside the al-Shifa pharmaceutical facility near Khartoum reportedly indicated the residue of O-ethyl methylphosphonothioic acid, best known as EMPTA, which is produced as VX nerve agent is synthesized. On August 20, 1998, US cruise missiles slammed into the al-Shifa plant.

This air strike was an earlier and smaller version of George W. Bush's preventive-strike strategy. No one suspected that the plant was involved in the embassy bombings. So the decision to bomb it was purely preventive in nature. The outcome also resembled the larger Bush action against Iraq because after the missile strike, the evidence justifying the bombardment looked dubious.[93] The dispute over the legitimacy of the Clinton decision is still unsettled. Aside from the attack on the al-Shifa factory, Sudanese-American relations never degenerated to the level of Washington's confrontations with the three major rogue states.

International concerns about Sudan more recently centered on that country's role in harboring terrorists and playing into the general instability of the Horn of Africa. Sudan, Somalia, Eritrea, and Yemen (across the Gulf of Aden) form a patchwork of failing states that are either unwilling or unable to police lawless areas within their boundaries. Al-Qaeda or its clones can take shelter, train, and direct terrorism to the world beyond these ungovernable spaces. Of these, Yemen is currently the main threat, as it is home to al-Qaeda of the Arabian Peninsula, which was behind the attempted downing of a Detroit-bound commercial jet in December 2009. The Sudan itself is in a strife-filled process of fragmenting along ethnic and sectarian fault lines. Non-Arab peoples in the center as well as the south and west demand reform and autonomy from a domineering central government. The Khartoum regime is made up of a comparatively small group of Arabs. It is led by President Omar Hassan al-Bashir, an indicted war crimes suspect by the International Criminal Court. Fighting and bloodshed are common in many parts of the country as of this writing. It is for these reasons that Washington kept Sudan on its terrorism list.[94]

Cuba: A Rogue Faded into History

After seizing power in a rural revolution, Fidel Castro turned Cuba into a pillar of the communist bloc during the Cold War. The Cuban armed forces, as touched on in chapter 1, served as legionnaires for the Kremlin's overt and covert interventions in Africa and Latin America. Soon after installing a Marxist regime in Havana's presidential palace in 1959, Castro was "sponsoring expeditions to overthrow governments in the Dominican Republic, Nicaragua, Haiti, and Panama."[95] Castro's Cuba proceeded to recruit, train, and arm young men to wage guerrilla wars against governments in Argentina, Colombia, Peru, and Venezuela. Ernesto "Che" Guevara, Castro's comrade-in-arms, headed a small insurgent cell to establish a revolutionary regime in Bolivia before his death there in 1967.

Communist Cuba shifted in the 1970s to cultivating so-called revolutionary regimes in Latin America, which in reality were military dictatorships or authoritarian rulers cloaked in socialist slogans; they included Peru, Chile, and Panama. It deployed troops and intelligence operatives to Africa, particularly in the Congo, Angola, Ethiopia, and Somalia. It intervened in Nicaragua to assist the Sandinistas during the 1980s, with Moscow's backing.[96] The Soviet Union's demise hit its Cuban proxy with a body blow. Cuba lost its ideological raison d'état as Communism's spear point. Only with Moscow's generous assistance could Havana hold out against US sanctions and marginalization policies.

Without Soviet subsidies, Cuban military forces declined precipitously. Ten years after the Berlin Wall crumbled, the Revolutionary Armed Forces (FAR) fell 50 percent in size and budget. A Pentagon report concluded over a decade ago that FAR posed just a "negligible conventional threat to the United States." The same assessment noted Cuba's "biotechnology industry is one of the most advanced in emerging countries and would be capable of producing BW [biological weapons] agents."[97] Despite some fleeting concern over Cuba's BW capability, Washington proved much more critical of Havana's human rights abuses and suppression of political dissidents. Washington's biting embargo policy toward Cuba has come under regular criticism from Western European capitals since the USSR's breakup. The

Cuban immigrant lobby, which is mainly centered in Miami, kept much of the economic quarantine in place until recently by basing its endorsement in US elections on the sanctions.

The Cuban economy also sank without Soviet largess. Two years after the Soviet Union disappeared, Cuba had suffered "a total economic implosion of between 40 and 50 percent from the 1989 level."[98] Cuba's communist system was ill-suited to generate prosperity. The island had been the playground of North American tourists before Castro's takeover. Since his dictatorship, the once-thriving tourist industry shriveled. People lost their jobs, the military grew its own food, the lights went out, and factories stood idle. Its sugar-cane exports were too meager to salvage the country. Boycotted and marginalized by Washington and the Organization of the American States (OAS), Cuba staggered before Castro compromised his revolutionary principles. He reached out to Canada, Western Europe, and English-speaking Caribbean countries. He flung open the doors to European tourists who spent hard currency for the Caribbean sun. He reversed the ban on average citizens holding dollars that came from remittances sent by family members in the United States.

Despite its threadbare condition, Cuba was still hailed for its socialist revolution by Venezuela's President Hugo Chavez, who saw Castroism as a model for his own country. But in point of fact, Chavez threw the beleaguered Cuban economy a lifeline to stave off its collapse by deferring, forgiving, or subsidizing Cuba's payments for Venezuelan oil or other exports since the early twenty-first century. He funneled some $5 billion annually to the island. Inside Cuba, the government witnessed a transfer of power from the ailing Fidel Castro to his slightly younger brother Raul, whose transition was accompanied by limited steps toward a market economy.[99]

More and more, China also strengthened diplomatic ties with Havana and donated funds for hurricane relief and other projects when the Chinese president Hu Jintao visited the island in late 2008.[100] China developed into Cuba's "second largest trading partner, exporting electronics, buses, trains, light manufactured goods, and now tourists."[101] Joint Cuban-Chinese ventures mined nickel and explored for offshore oil. Culturally, nonetheless, it is the Cuban-Venezuelan ties that really bind. Cuba reciprocated its benefactor's generosity by dispatching nurses, doctors, and teachers to Venezuela. Cuba also sent military officers and security experts to train Chavez's armed forces in regime-protection skills.[102]

Of late, Washington slightly eased its isolation and sanctioning of the Castro regime. The OAS revoked its 47-year suspension of Cuba from the 34-member group in mid-2009 for its subversive operations during the Cold War. The unanimous vote, backed by Washington, cleared the way for Havana to rejoin the OAS.[103] President Obama eased travel restrictions to Cuba to expand contacts between the two countries.[104] Younger Cuban Americans in Miami are less interested in the Cold War animosities than their parents. Both countries seem headed toward a slow-moving dismantling of the barriers that divided them for the past half century.

The Castro regime gradually implemented reforms away from its centralized, Soviet-style economy. Ex-president Fidel Castro himself voiced doubts about the communist system when he said, "The Cuban model doesn't even work for us anymore."[105] The Communist Party went along with opening nearly 200 professions to private enterprise. Later, at the end of 2011, Havana proclaimed a new property law that promised to permit Cubans to purchase and sell real estate. It also permitted cell phones and computers, plus the freedom to sell private automobiles. As a major break from socialist housing, it still set restrictions aimed at controlling financial speculation and limiting ownership to two homes. Yet the communist government had to contend with grassroots laissez-faire practices such as a vibrant black market dealing in construction materials stolen from state distributors. What breathed new life into the moribund Cuban economy came from overseas cash remittances. The Obama administration relaxed restrictions on Cuban Americans sending money to the island. Everyone inside Cuba and elsewhere, nevertheless, awaits even greater changes once Fidel and Raul Castro pass from the scene and new rulers take the helm of a wheezing economy. Until then, Cuba is headed toward a final reckoning as "the last Utopia."[106]

The passing of the Cuban revolutionary generation may well lead to the Caribbean nation's reintegration into the Western Hemisphere along with the country's elimination from the US terrorist listing. Its rogue-nation agenda has already lapsed and its pariah listing is anachronistic, except for its persistent dictatorship and dearth of civil liberties. No one should minimize the barbarities of Cuba's ongoing human rights abuses, encompassing harsh treatment of political prisoners and harassment of their families. However, Castroism's threat to the region, aside from Havana's training missions for Hugo Chavez's security forces, has diminished from its communist heyday when it was the region's purveyor of subversion and insurgency. Cuba made tactical changes and hunkered down to be spared a tropical version of the velvet revolutions that swept communist regimes from power in Central Europe in the wake of the Soviet Union's implosion. A defunct economy, an incoherent politico-economic system, and a cornered pawn on a kingless chessboard, Cuba has the look and feel of a museum piece in the globalizing twenty-first century, when many governments developed resources, educated their populations, and searched for comparative advantages in the world market. Cuba's vanguard role in yesteryear's Soviet imperialism leaves it a rogue dinosaur.

Although blunt and time-consuming instruments, Washington's policy of sanctions, exclusion, and marginalization worked against Cuba. Containment and deterrence were preferable to another intervention into the island, as in the 1961 Bay of Pigs fiasco, when the United States half-heartedly backed anti-Castro forces in a failed invasion. A direct military attack, as in Panama to displace the Noriega regime, would have inflamed anti-US sentiments in the Western Hemisphere. The only realistic option against Castro's troublemaking lay with a protracted squeeze of economic punishment and political isolation. By getting OAS cooperation in its policy, the United States scored a major victory among states wary of the Colossus of the North. It demonstrated anew that a nonmilitary posture can gain converts even from lukewarm partners. Washington's anaconda squeeze relentlessly undermined a revolutionary state because it was vigorously applied over many years and backed by hard power.

Contemporary Cuba constitutes another case study of declining rogue seeking shelter from a richer patron—one of this work's themes. Insular, spartan, authoritarian polities find it hard to survive except in clientage with a stronger overlord. For three decades, Cuba leaned on the Soviet Union. Since its demise, the Castro regime nestled closer to Venezuela. That South American country, in turn, subsidizes Havana's failing system amid its slogans exhorting "socialism or death." In return, the Castro brothers manufactured, advised, and labored for Hugo Chavez's revolutionary legitimacy in Latin America. Thus, the Cuban Athens goes to the Venezuelan Rome, not with classical cultural and wisdom but with socialist credentials and fading revolutionary glory. Havana also went hat in hand to Caracas for financial bailouts. That postrevolutionary Cuba had to lean on capitalist, class-ridden, and electorally consensual Venezuela is ironic; but then again, history has been the seat of even greater ironies.

Venezuela: A Rogue in the Making?

Under the leadership of its most famous son, Simon Bolivar, Venezuela was the cradle for all of South America's independence from Spain's colonial rule in the first quarter of the nineteenth century. Even so, dictatorial rule, political instability, and revolutionary turbulence characterized long periods of Venezuelan history. At mid-twentieth century, the military stood aside from direct political involvement, opening the way for a stretch of democratically elected governments. Elections proved to be no guarantee of political tranquility, however. Attempted military coups during the 1990s signaled dissatisfaction with traditional political parties' inability to solve structural poverty and income inequalities.

In 1998, Hugo Chavez, a military officer who had played a role in the failed coups, won election to the presidency on a reform platform. He and his ruling United Socialist Party of Venezuela still command the loyalty of about half their countrymen. Many of the poor hold an emotional tie with him akin to a televangelist. Through constitutional changes, fraudulent election practices, and manipulation of government functions, Chavez retained power. His Latin American brand of popular authoritarianism portends an entrenched despotism and economic ruin.

By harnessing the country's large petroleum revenues, the aspiring caudillo sought to institutionalize his "Bolivarian Revolution," entailing a pro-Chavez mass movement, equitable revenue distribution, and corruption-less government. His domestic reforms faltered, in part, because of falling oil profits. Oil production slumped from 3.2 million barrels a day in 1998 to 2.4 barrels in 2009 thanks to governmental failures.[107] About half of the output is sold to friendly countries, including Cuba, at discounted prices from the current market rate, with the rest of the cost to be paid over 25 years. Subsidized oil is delivered to some 30 Latin American countries along with other financial assistance to buy friendship and to forge an anti-US bloc.[108] High oil prices on the world market have not been enough to keep the country solvent. It is chronically short of cash and is running a debt in excess of $12 billion. Its growing authoritarianism and sputtering economy are one thing; the country's international policy is quite another.

It is the anti-US aspects of *chavismo* that worried Washington most. Hugo Chavez, a self-declared US enemy, took pains to taunt and test American patience. President Chavez availed himself of many opportunities to lambast the United States or its leaders. One particular scathing and memorable episode took place at speech before the UN General Assembly in 2006, when Chavez called President George W. Bush "the devil" and spoke about the smell of "sulfur of Satan" still lingering around the podium where the American leader had previously delivered remarks.[109] Venezuela also indulged in actions, not just words.

The Chavez regime funneled some $300 million to the Colombian-based terrorist movement widely known by its acronym, FARC (Fuerzas Armadas Revolucionario de Colombia or Revolutionary Armed Forces of Colombia). FARC's coca production and drug-fueled violence led to a profusion of allied narcotics cartels, drug kingpins, and political instability. For Chavez, it was sufficient that FARC was the enemy of Colombia, which was a friend of the United States.[110] FARC's drug trafficking and terrorism nearly turned

Colombia into a failed state as the Marxist-insurgent group violently seized nearly one-third of the countryside. This insurgent narcostate-within-the-state threatened to destabilize the entire country with its bloodshed. FARC evolved from an unreconstructed Castro-Guevara ideology to a vastly profitable criminal enterprise. Its leftist propaganda appealed to Chavez's personal infatuation with Cuban-inspired movements and to his ideological pretensions.

The United States has aided the Bogotá government's Plan Colombia with some $7 billion since 1999 in military and civil assistance to combat the FARC guerrillas. The largely unheralded Colombian-US success against the FARC menace stands as a testament to what competent political leadership in Bogotá and skilled American special operations forces can accomplish in reducing cocaine output, although some of the cultivation and processing was simply pushed into neighboring Peru.[111] Almost alone in Latin America, Chavez considered Washington's assistance as Yankee imperialism in the region.

The Chavez regime looked to Russia for the purchase of conventional arms, such as shoulder-fired missiles and AK-47 rifles, along with expertise to build nuclear plants. The arms deal stirred momentary anxiety in Colombia and the United States about Venezuelan intentions—something Chavez relished.[112] The nuclear talk, however, prompted wider concern as the Venezuelan-Russian relationship deepened. Chavez traveled repeatedly to Moscow to boost his prestige as the new Castro. In 2010, he signed an agreement with President Dmitry Medvedev for a Russian-built nuclear facility ostensibly to reduce Venezuela's reliance on oil-produced electricity. Since the agreement was nothing more than a "declaration of intention" and Venezuela lacks the funds to pay for construction, it reflected "anti-Western moods" in Caracas and Moscow more than a substantive contract.[113] But Chavez's nuclear intentions were clear.

The Venezuelan-Iranian relationship particularly heightened Washington's apprehensions. Chavez and Iran's President Ahmadinejad share similarities in coming to power; both galvanized their respective underclass's rage as an election vehicle. They both revile the United States and seek to rally their neighbors against America. Chavez, a self-promoted US enemy, traveled eight times to Tehran, which he called a "strategic ally." Iran reciprocated. It dispatched members of its elite and shadowy Quds Force to receptive governments below the Rio Grande, with an "increased presence" in Venezuela, according to the Pentagon in 2010.[114] Reports of Iranian agents helping train Venezuelan security forces came on the heels of Venezuelan announcements thanking Tehran for its assistance in developing the South American country's future nuclear program.

After wresting control of the country's judiciary and national election council, Chavez will no doubt prevail in the 2012 elections, if he survives his cancer bout. This very triumph, however, will also no doubt place him at growing odds with his freely and fairly democratically elected counterparts in Latin America, where he will stand out as the sore thumb of the continent. His leftist dictatorial allies in Bolivia, Ecuador, and Nicaragua are all under political pressure for faltering economies and internal opposition. The Caracas caudillo remains undeterred and outspoken. His volubility contributed to the frustration of King Juan Carlos I of Spain, who uttered the YouTube video sensation "Por qué no te callas?" (Why don't you [just] shut up?) at the voluble Venezuelan president during the 2007 Ibero-American Summit in Santiago, Chile.

For all Chavez's vitriolic fulminations, bluster, and grandstanding with such US enemies as Ahmadinejad, Venezuela does not stand today as a front-rank rogue adversary. It is important to draw a distinction between troublesome states and rogue adversaries. Venezuela is neither Iran nor North Korea. Nor does its difficult behavior accord with that of Saddam Hussein's Iraq or of Libya at the height of its terrorist sponsorship. Chavez grabbed Castro's falling mantel as head of the Western Hemisphere's anti-US club. The antigringo rhetoric still resonates in some Latin American quarters, but the overall appeal has become dated as the Cold War recedes in memory and the continent's economic growth takes off, in part, through trade links with Asia.[115] Cuban-style revolutions are out of fashion in much of Latin America, and so are their imitators.

Venezuela's internal problems serve to check any big rogue-nation aspirations. The Chavez regime is hampered by a sluggish economy, erratic electrical power deliveries, sky-high crime with a murder rate greater than Mexico, and among the world's highest inflation.[116] Unlike North Korea or Hussein's Iraq, Hugo Chavez faces strong domestic resistance, albeit from weakened opposition parties. His recurring cancer might also curtail his ambition, despite his protestations that he is cured. Unlike Iran, Venezuela lacks Tehran's effectiveness in expanding its influence via organizations such as Hezbollah and Hamas. Nor does it possess the revolutionary fervor of Islamist Iran coupled with Tehran's desires to restore its Persian imperial presence in the Gulf region. As for North Korea, its ruthless and efficient totalitarian system places it in a league of its own. Iran's nuclear program is on the verge of producing atom bombs, and North Korea's nuclear bomb dreams are partially realized. Venezuela's nuclear ambitions are still just dreams.

Nothing written here prohibits Venezuela from attaining "roguedom" at some undetermined point along with, say, Myanmar. That Southeast Asian state, formerly known as Burma, was ruled by a bare-knuckled military junta until it stepped aside for a nominal civilian government following the 2010 election. Critics dismissed the makeover because the new regime is led by retired military officers and the military retains dominance under the constitution. Myanmar has served as a transshipment point for North Korean armaments to Iran and Syria. Like North Korea, it is closely aligned with China. Myanmar is also suspected of clandestine nuclear activities in collaboration with Pyongyang.[117] Optimists about the apparent political reform under way since the start of 2011 remain cautious about the Burma Spring.[118] But if its economic and political restructuring takes root, moving the country from authoritarianism and isolation, then even this protorogue state is in fidelity with the theme of this volume—rogue states as solitary and insular polities are transient. They die alone or cohabit with patrons.

Venezuela's Chavez, unlike Myanmar military rulers, is loquacious and fiery in his anti-Americanism. Obviously, Chavez's actions might worsen. It happened to Saddam Hussein, who ran heedlessly into the abyss, with his alarming nuclear feints. Venezuela's nuclear enterprises (assisted by the Russian Federation) warrant close monitoring. If Venezuela evolves into a genuine rogue nation—with WMD, exported terrorism to the greater region, and systematic, large-scale human rights violations—it will demonstrate that the rogue malady persisted and leapt from former Soviet clients to another generation of dictatorships—a growth phenomenon entirely in line with history. Rogue entities, as earlier noted, have long been a part of international politics, even though their existence is historically short.

Afghanistan: The Nonrogue Failed State

Pre-9/11 Afghanistan under the Taliban rule represented a distinct case of bad political behavior, closer to a failed state than rogue nation. Afghanistan did draw American and international censure and sanctions for granting sanctuary to Osama bin Laden in 1996, when he and his inner circle left Sudan. The Arab foreigners planned and carried out terrorism from their new home in south central Asia. But the Kabul government itself did not pursue hostile activities toward the United States. Nor did it amass nuclear, chemical, or biological weapons. Its economic and technological backwardness ruled out the manufacture of WMD. Neither did it import or seek such arms from rogue regimes or independent purveyors such as A. Q. Khan in Pakistan.

Afghanistan was implicated in the 9/11 terrorism attacks by its association with al-Qaeda, but it was not directly responsible. The United States and its NATO allies intervened into Afghanistan when the Mullah Mohammed

Omar government refused to hand over bin Laden to be prosecuted in the West for committing the September 11 terrorist attack. The Afghan leader professed to be bound by the *Pashtunwali* obligation of hospitality. This tribal code dictated that hosts must protect their guests. Thus, the Omar government underestimated the costs of granting protection to bin Laden and his coterie.[119]

Prior to what al-Qaeda operatives termed "the planes operation," Clinton's State Department kept Afghanistan off the terrorist listing, despite serious provocations emanating from the mountainous country. Bin Laden unfurled his famous 1998 fatwa against the United States and the West from Afghanistan. He instigated the diabolical terrorist attacks from his Afghan camps.[120] Clinton officials, however, held that it is too arduous politically to delist a country. They believed that designating a state as a terrorist exporter limited their flexibility to mix carrots with sticks to induce a change in its political actions.[121]

Instead, Washington resorted first to an executive-order, unilateral sanctions and then to UN Security Council boycotts against commercial exchanges with the Taliban regime. It demanded the surrender of bin Laden for his role in the 1998 terrorism against US embassies in Tanzania and Kenya and later the attack on the USS *Cole* in Aden in 2000. Despite a series of economic penalties, the Taliban leaders refused to show bin Laden the exit door.[122] Their recalcitrance persisted until the US-led invasion in fall 2001, which toppled Mullah Omar and chased most al-Qaeda members from Afghanistan. The US-led NATO invasion and occupation began a decade-long insurgency against a resurgent Taliban and other militant movements that persists to this day.

The Afghanistan case brings up a critical distinction between rogue states and failed nations. Rogues engage in crossborder terrorism. They seek WMD, something Afghanistan never did. Rogue regimes control their own sovereign territory. They tightly govern their populations. Tellingly, these regimes design and execute aggressive actions against neighbors and region. In contrast, failed—or failing—states such as Yemen, Somalia, or even Pakistan lack governance over wide swaths of their own soil. The ungoverned lands fall prey to terrorist movements, from which substate actors can execute international terrorist plots. The governments themselves are not rogue-like. Quite the contrary, Yemen, Somalia, and the Philippines as well as other lands *in extremis* want for adequate political and military power to enforce their writ in inaccessible wildernesses where terrorists take root and thrive. Moreover, Sana, Mogadishu, and Manila look to the United States for martial and economic assistance to combat their local insurgency-based terrorists. These and other defective states seek

America's assistance and largess. Not so for North Korea, Iraq, Iran, and even some lesser bad actors—they pursued their own independent courses. Genuine rogue regimes, even the bit players, most often face off against Washington, if only with bluster.

A Few Concluding Observations

Throughout the ages, freestanding, warlike polities have for brief periods threatened the international order while existing outside the orbit of great powers. The last quarter of a century witnessed another of these episodes. The immediate years after the USSR fell apart witnessed a sudden profusion of rogue states, for which the world was ill-prepared after four decades of reasonably predictive actions from the two superpowers and their allies. Rogue entities in earlier historical periods possessed similar traits. The post–Cold War adversarial states fought, subverted, and confronted other countries for their own nefarious ends. They differed from their historical predecessors by going after WMD, which exponentially heightens their destructive power and their danger to other countries.

Now, as in the past, heavyweights conspire against small, aggressive, free-lance states bent on upsetting political order. Taking on all comers alone is a dangerous game for a pariah, no matter how much a garrison state it is. Cuba, Libya (before its revolution), and Sudan passed from rogue status to nations less threatening to global peace. At this juncture, Syria's Assad barely clings to power amid a popular revolt. Self-preservation traditionally dictates that outgunned rogues align with stronger protectors. Sometimes renegade regimes are useful to a major state, as when the Soviet Union employed them in its chess match with the United States. Today, China seems to be in the same business. As the world relapses back to great power politics, modern-day Machiavellians will look for their "prince" and find him in personages such as Kim Jong Il or Bashar al-Assad. Be this as it may, lone-wolf states have traditionally succumbed or aligned themselves with a more powerful patron. Much the same state of affairs is occurring in our period. Syria hunkered behind a resurgent Russia opposed to the West, North Korea moved under the wing of an ascending China, and an isolated Iran took advantage of the Sino-Russo pushback against America—all very reminiscent of the Cold War competion among great powers and their satellites. Some adversarial nations—Sudan, Libya, and Cuba—slipped from the adversarial column. But as some rogues disappear, others will, no doubt, emerge. It is still too early to know whether Venezuela is a rogue-in-the-making or merely another Latin American authoritarian state. At the very least, it has a dangerous linkage to Iran.

Current rogue behavior sets them against the prevailing international society in the early twenty-first century. Their reliance on dictatorship, repression, and brutal security forces makes their rule hard but brittle. As with all tyrannies, they live and die by the sword. They are inherently unstable like most police states. Rogue regimes fear internal change. Externally, they pursue risky approaches at times, in part, to consolidate their rule or exert their regional presence. The historical trajectory of rogues has pointed toward an axis or at least connections with a potential guardian power. Present-day adversarial states also are maneuvering from isolation to the protective eaves of a powerful patron, as Syria fell in with Iran, North Korea draws closer to China, Iran seeks an anti-Western security bloc with China and Russia, and Cuba is on Venezuelan life support.

Without foreign buttressing, the stand-alone rogues must curtail their regional threats, as did Libya in 2003 and Cuba after the Soviet Union split apart. Or they can suffer the fate of Iraq, which the United States militarily crushed, although it paid a high price to quell an antiforeign insurgency and furious sectarian violence in the aftermath of its invasion. History's muse is too scornful and unpredictable to hazard a confident prophesy, but the historical record augurs against longevity for rogue regimes. Today's world of instant communication via the Internet, YouTube, Twitter, and Facebook along with the allure of the youth culture act as powerful solvents eating away at closed, repressive regimes premised on threats to neighbors in the name of ideological abstractions.

Until rogues succumb or fall under the sway of a restraining power, the United States and allied nations must tackle the challenges they present. Direct conflict, as in the Iraq War, against another rogue nation is far too expensive in economic and human costs for serial application. Proceeding to invasion, regime change, and occupation is an option but an unlikely one, especially since the United States amassed staggering debts with a more than $1 trillion price tag for the Iraq and Afghan wars. The human toll likewise was steep with over 6,000 US military deaths, tens of thousands seriously wounded, and hundreds of thousands of inhabitants killed in the two theaters. America's dark economic picture is crimping its international endeavors. Intervention-cum-nation-building remedies for derelict countries are almost beyond consideration, given America's struggling economic recovery, cash-strapped federal budget, and blooming entitlement debt.

The only viable approach is one embodying containment and deterrence to confront the threats emanating from rogue states. This approach requires the hard power of military forces to give it credibility. Armed might, in part, persuaded Libya and perhaps Iran to halt their drive for WMD, as noted earlier. Libya's Qaddafi believed President Bush planned to invade his country once the Iraq campaign ended. The Libyan strongman decided to renounce his nuclear program and open his country to international arms inspectors. Iran also appears to have suspended the development of weapons in its nuclear-energy effort at the time of the US invasion into Iraq. Earlier, the North Korean regime seemed awed by America's application of electronic, push-button military technology during the Persian Gulf War, the first time that "smart" weapons had been deployed with devastating effectiveness. The threat of military action, therefore, can serve as a powerful inducement to some outlaw states to disarm. A "carrots"-laden approach (without any sticks) comes off as bribery from a weak hand, as North Korea so often surmised about the American "nice" approach.

Hard power also reinforces antirogue alliances and international sanctions to contain and deter rogue-state aggression. Containment and deterrence need not be totally pacific. The containment-plus approach against Saddam Hussein following the Persian Gulf War encompassed air strikes, no-fly zones, and even on-the-ground assistance to Iraqi Kurds for a decade. The US-led NATO military siege against Slobodan Milošević was accompanied by political campaigning training and funds for antiregime dissidents in nearby countries, who went on to organize demonstrations that toppled the Serbian dictator. Even before the Arab Spring uprisings engulfed Syria, the United States had secretly financed the political opposition. The US Department of State funded a satellite television channel that beamed in anti-Assad programming beginning in April 2009.[123] South Korean democracy activists have floated balloons into the DPRK laden with antiregime messages calling for protests among the Northern population to no avail. This angers Pyongyang but so far has been ineffective. Computer viruses and cyber warfare offer more subtle—and deniable—sabotage instruments than aerial bombardments to undermine rogue threats.

Taking advantage of emerging technologies and software, the United States has opened a new front in the cause to nurture democracy in closed societies. Authoritarian countries such as Iran, North Korea, Syria, Myanmar, and China shut down their citizens' access to the Internet and cell phone networks in order to eliminate their means to communicate with each other and the outside world. Disabling telecommunications systems hampers the dissidents' ability to stage protests and to escape from security forces. It also curtails the rebels' ability to transmit text and photos to the global media to rally international support.

Washington now minimally funds the development of independent cell phone networks and wireless communications that can be linked directly to the global Internet. It needs to do more. These alternative pathways can sidestep an autocrat's censorship by harnessing the innovations of the so-called liberation-technology movement sweeping the planet.[124] The promising techniques launched a new weapon in the information wars against rogue states. Low-budget and easily accessible, "shadow" cell phone systems and stealth Internet networks offer antidictatorship capabilities that enhance deterrence and containment. Antiregime messages hit rogue regimes where they are most vulnerable—their own populations. Rogue regimes are synonymous with autocratic rule. Policies and techniques to undermine autocracies complement sanctions and containment. The single best antidote to rogue regimes is democracy.[125]

Notes

1 The Rogue Phenomenon

1. Michael R. Gordon and General Bernard E. Trainor, *Cobra II: The Inside Story of the Invasion and Occupation of Iraq* (New York: Pantheon, 2006), 390–433.
2. For an article critical of the media's handling of the statue's collapse, see Peer Maass, "The Toppling," *New Yorker*, January 10, 2011, pp. 25–31 and 54.
3. Thucydides, *History of the Peloponnesian War*, trans. Rex Warner (London: Penguin Books, 1972), 408.
4. Ernst Badian, *Foreign Clientelae, 264–70 B.C.* (Oxford: Clarendon Press, 1958), 281.
5. Richard B. Barker, *Uncle Sam in Barbary: A Diplomatic History* (Gainesville: University of Florida Press, 2004), 145–47; and Joseph Wheelan, *Jefferson's War: America's First War on Terror, 1801–1805* (New York: Carroll and Graf Publishers, 2003), 350–66.
6. Piracy Reporting Centre of the International Maritime Bureau, http://www.icc-ccs.org/piracy-reporting-centre; accessed October 21, 2011.
7. Jim Michaels, "Pirates' New Tactics Make Navies' Job Harder," *USA Today*, January 7, 2011, p. 6.
8. Adrian Tinniswood, *Pirates of Barbary: Corsairs, Conquests, and Captivity in the Seventeenth-Century Mediterranean* (New York: Riverhead Books, 2010), 210–27 and 233–43.
9. E. G. Chapulina, "The Barbary Corsairs," *Blackwood's* 328, no. 1982 (December 1980): 483–89.
10. Simon Smith, "Piracy in Early British America," *History Today* 46, no. 5 (May 1996): 30–33.
11. For greater treatment of early rogues, see Thomas H. Henriksen, "The Rise and Decline of Rogue States," *Journal of International Affairs* 54, no. 2 (Spring 2004): 349–73.
12. Avner Cohen, *Israel and the Bomb* (New York: Columbia University Press, 1998), 277.

13. Thomas Erdbrink and Joby Warrick, "Iran Derides Sanctions, Talks of Reducing Cooperation with Inspectors," *Washington Post*, June 11, 2010, A8.

14. James Adams, *The Unnatural Alliance: Israel and South Africa* (London: Quartet Books, 1984), 187–96; and Seymour Hersh, *The Samson Option: Israel's Nuclear Arsenal and American Foreign Policy* (New York: Random House, 1991), 271.

15. Mitchell Reiss, *Bridled Ambition: Why Countries Constrain Their Nuclear Capabilities* (Washington, DC: Woodrow Wilson Center Press, 1995), 32.

16. Ibid., 10–11.

17. Yevgeny Primakov, *Russia and the Arabs: Behind the Scenes in the Middle East from the Cold War to the Present* (New York: Basic Books, 2009), 57–72.

18. For a defense of backing strongmen, see Jeane J. Kirpatrick's well-known article, "Dictatorships & Double Standards," *Commentary*, November 1977, 12–30.

19. Thomas H. Henriksen, *American Power after the Berlin Wall* (New York: Palgrave Macmillan, 2007), 210–12.

20. John Marcum, *The Angolan Revolution: Volume II, Exile Politics and Guerrilla Warfare, 1962–1976* (Cambridge, MA: MIT Press, 1978), 275.

21. Sheldon M. Stern, *Averting "The Final Failure"* (Stanford, CA: Stanford University Press, 2003), 388.

22. Walter Laqueur, *The New Terrorism: Fanaticism and the Arms of Mass Destruction* (New York: Oxford University Press, 1999), 160.

23. Christopher C. Harmon, *Terrorism Today* (London: Frank Cass, 2000), 13.

24. Louise Richardson, *What Terrorists Want* (New York: Random House, 2006), 23–37.

25. "An Overview of the State Department's State Sponsors of Terrorism," http://terrorism.about.com/od/statesponsors/a/StateSponsors.htm, accessed November 11, 2009.

26. US Department of State, State Sponsors of Terrorism, http://www.state.gov/j/ct/c14151.htm, accessed February 16, 2012.

27. George Bush and Brent Scowcroft, *A World Transformed* (New York: Alfred A. Knopf, 1998), 320.

28. The sheriff analogy is that of Richard N. Haass, *The Reluctant Sheriff: The United States after the Cold War* (New York: Council of Foreign Relations, 1997), 6.

29. For an excellent study of movements of rage, see Ken Jowitt, *New World Disorder: The Leninist Extinction* (Berkeley: University of California Press, 1992), 275–77.

30. Thomas L. Friedman, "Clinton's Security Aide Gives a Vision for Foreign Policy," *New York Times*, September 22, 1993, A18.

31. Bill Clinton, "Remarks to Future Leaders of Europe in Brussels, January 9, 1994," in *Public Papers of Presidents, William J. Clinton, Volume I* (Washington, DC: Government Printing Office, 1994), 11.

32. Christopher Marquis, "U.S. Declares 'Rogue Nations' Are Now 'States of Concern,'" *New York Times*, June 20, 2000, A1.

33. Anthony Lake, "Confronting Backlash States," *Foreign Affairs* 73, no. 2 (March/April 1994): 45–46.

34. The National Security Strategy, September 2002, http://georgewbush-white-house.archives.gov/nsc/nss/2002/print/nss5.html, accessed August 5, 2011.

35. For more on this view, see James Mann, "N. Korean Missiles Have Russian Roots, Explosive Theory Suggests," *Los Angeles Times*, September 6, 2000, A1.

36. David Albright, *Peddling Peril: How the Secret Nuclear Trade Arms America's Enemies* (New York: Free Press, 2010), 15–26.

37. Bill Gertz, "Chinese Companies Sent Missile Parts to N. Korea," *Washington Times*, July 20, 1999, A1.

38. "Center for Nonproliferation Studies at the Monterey Institute for International Studies," cited in Barbara Slavin, "Missile Program Holds Key to N. Korea's Foreign Relations," *USA Today*, November 6, 2000, p. 1.

39. Joby Warrick, "Iran Close to Nuclear Capability, IAEA Says," *Washington Post*, November 7, 2011, A1.

40. Many front-rank theorists slight the role of rogue players in international affairs. See John J. Mearsheimer, *The Tragedy of Great Powers Politics* (New York: W. W. Norton, 2001); Hans Morgenthau, *Politics among Nations: The Struggle for Power and Peace*, 5th ed. (New York: Knopf, 1973); Kenneth Waltz, *Theory of International Politics* (Reading, MA: Addison-Wesley Company, 1979); and Robert J. Art and Kenneth N. Waltz, *The Use of Force: Military Power and International Politics*, 7th ed. (Lanham, MD: Rowman and Littlefield, 2009).

41. For a description of this argument, see Robert S. Litwak, *Rogue States and U.S. Foreign Policy: Containment after the Cold War* (Washington, DC: Woodrow Wilson Center Press, 2000), xiv.

2   Iraq: Quintessential Rogue State

1. Abraham D. Sofaer, *The Best Defense? Legitimacy & Preventive Force* (Stanford, CA: Hoover Institution Press, 2010), 56–57 and 107–16.

2. Galia Golan, *Soviet Policies in the Middle East: From World War II to Gorbachev* (New York: Cambridge University Press, 1990), 157.

3. Barry Rubin, "The Gulf States and the Iran-Iraq War," in *The Iran-Iraq War: Impact and Implications*, ed. Efraim Karsh (London: Macmillan, 1989), 121–25.

4. Robin Wright, "Chemical Arms' Effects Linger Long after War," *Los Angeles Times*, November 19, 2002, A1.

5. Saïd K. Aburish, *Saddam Hussein: The Politics of Revenge* (London: Bloomsbury, 2000), 257.

6. George Bush and Brent Scowcroft, *A World Transformed* (New York: Alfred A. Knopf, 1998), 360.

7. Lee Allen Zatarain, *The Tanker War: America's First Conflict with Iran, 1987–1988* (Philadelphia: Casemate, 2008), 7–25.

8. James A. Baker III, *The Politics of Diplomacy: Revolution, War and Peace, 1989–1992* (New York: G. P. Putnam's Sons, 1995), 263.
9. Hamdi A. Hassan, *The Iraqi Invasion of Kuwait: Religion, Identity and Otherness in the Analysis of War and Conflict* (London: Pluto Press, 1999), 36–39.
10. Quoted in Micah L. Sifry and Christopher Cerf, eds., *The Gulf War Reader: History, Documents, Opinion* (New York: Random House, 1991), 100.
11. Joel Brinkley, "Israel Puts a Satellite in Orbit a Day after Threats by Iraqis," *New York Times*, April 4, 1990, A3.
12. Amatzia Baram, "The Iraqi Invasion of Kuwait: Decision-Making in Baghdad," in *Iraq's Road to War*, ed. Amatzia Baram and Barry Rubin (New York: St. Martin's Press, 1993), 12.
13. Sifry and Cerf, *Gulf War Reader*, 102.
14. Bush and Scowcroft, *World Transformed*, 306–7.
15. Baker, *Politics of Diplomacy*, 263.
16. Charles Tripp, *A History of Iraq* (New York: Cambridge University Press, 2002), 248–50.
17. Dilip Hiro, *Desert Shield to Desert Storm: The Second Gulf War* (New York: Authors Choice Press, 2003), 77–96.
18. Bush and Scowcroft, *World Transformed*, 311.
19. Pamela Fessler, "Glaspie Defends Her Actions, U.S. Policy before Invasion," *Congressional Quarterly Weekly Report*, March 23, 1991, pp. 759–60.
20. For a representative criticism, see "Kuwait: How the West Blundered," *Economist*, September 29, 1990, pp. 22–23; and Michael R. Gordon and Bernard E. Trainor, *The General's War: The Inside Story of the Conflict in the Gulf* (Boston: Little, Brown, and Company, 1995), 14–30.
21. Hiro, *Desert Shield to Desert Storm*, 103–4; and John F. Burns, "A Cadillac and Other Plunder," *New York Times*, December 30, 2002.
22. Bush and Scowcroft, *World Transformed*, 332.
23. Baker, *Politics of Diplomacy*, 276.
24. Bush and Scowcroft, *World Transformed*, 326.
25. Khaled Bin Sultan with Patrick Seale, *Warrior: A Personal View of the Gulf War by the Joint Forces Commander* (New York: HarperCollins, 1995), 193–99.
26. "The President's News Conference on the Persian Gulf Conflict," Washington, DC, March 1, 1991, George H. W. Bush Presidential Library, http://www.presidency.ucsb.edu/ws/index.php?pid=19229#axzz1mR3NJPZx, accessed February 15, 2012; and "Remarks and an Exchange with Reporters Prior to Discussions with Prince Bandar sin Sultan of Saudi Arabia," February 28, 1991, George H. W. Bush Presidential Library, http://bushlibrary.tamu.edu/research/public_papers.php?id=2751&year=&month=, accessed February 15, 2012.
27. Kenneth M. Pollack, *The Threatening Storm: The Case for Invading Iraq* (New York: Random House, 2002), 17 and 369.
28. John F. Burns, "Iraq's Thwarted Ambitions Litter an Old Nuclear Plant," *New York Times*, December 27, 2002, A1.

29. Todd Harrison and Zack Cooper, "Selected Options and Costs for a No-Fly Zone Over Libya," in *Backgrounder* (Washington, DC: Center for Strategic and Budgetary Assessments, March 2011), 2.
30. Robert S. Litwak, *Rogue States and U.S. Foreign Policy: Containment after the Cold War* (Washington, DC: Woodrow Wilson Center Press, 2000), 126.
31. For an insider's account of the failed Iraqi rebellion, see Robert Baer, *See No Evil* (New York: Three Rivers Press, 2002), 177–205.
32. Madeleine Albright, *Madam Secretary* (New York: Miramax Books, 2003), 272.
33. Pollack, *Threatening Storm*, 55–58 and 66.
34. "The Bush Assassination Attempt," Department of Justice/FBI Laboratory Report, http://www.fas.org/irp/agency/doj/oig/fbilab1/05bush2.htm, accessed May 22, 2011.
35. David Von Drehel and R. Jeffrey Smith, "U.S. Strikes Iraq for Plot to Kill Bush," *Washington Post*, June 27, 1993, A1.
36. The Independent Inquiry Committee on the Oil-For-Food Program, http://www.iic-offp.org/story27oct05.htm, accessed June 20, 2011.
37. Richard Butler, *The Greatest Threat: Iraq, Weapons of Mass Destruction, and the Crisis of Global Security* (New York: Public Affairs, 2000), 234–41.
38. "Clinton's Statement: We are Delivering a Powerful Message to Saddam," *New York Times*, December 17, 1998, A16.
39. William J. Clinton, "The President's Radio Address," December 19, 1998, http://www.presidency.ucsb.edu/ws/index.php?pid=55434, accessed May 14, 2011.
40. Rachel Ehrenfeld, *Funding Evil: How Terrorism Is Financed—and How to Stop It* (Chicago: Bonus Books, 2005), 107–8 and 168.
41. Thomas E. Ricks, "Containing Iraq: A Forgotten War," *Washington Post*, October 25, 2000, A1.
42. Colum Lynch, "Russia Threatens Veto of U.N. Iraq Resolution," *Washington Post*, June 26, 2003, A5.
43. Condoleezza Rice, "Promoting the National Interest," *Foreign Affairs* 79, no. 1 (January/February 2000): 61.
44. James Mann, *The Rise of the Vulcans: The History of Bush's War Cabinet* (New York: Viking, 2004), 362–63.
45. David Wurmser, *Tyranny's Ally: America's Failure to Defeat Saddam Hussein* (Washington, DC: American Enterprise Institute, 1999), 137.
46. Douglas J. Feith, *War and Decision: Inside the Pentagon at the Dawn of the War on Terrorism* (New York: Harper, 2008), 203–4; and Bob Woodward, *Plan of Attack* (New York: Simon and Schuster, 2004), 21.
47. Steven Lee Myers and Eric Schmitt, "Iraq Rebuilt Bombed Arms Plant, Officials Say," *New York Times*, January 22, 2001, A1.
48. Ibid.
49. Robert S. Litwak, *Regime Change: U.S. Strategy through the Prism of 9/11* (Washington, DC: Woodrow Wilson Center Press, 2007), 125.

50. Pollack, *Threatening Storm*, 105.

51. George W. Bush, "State of the Union Address," January 29, 2002, http://georgewbush-whitehouse.archives.gov/news/releases/2002/01/20020129-11.html, accessed February 16, 2012.

52. George W. Bush, "Graduation Speech at West Point," June 1, 2002, http://georgewbush-whitehouse.archives.gov/news/releases/2002/06/20020601-3.html, accessed February 15, 2012.

53. Patrick E. Tyler, "Britain's Case: Iraq's Program to Amass Arms Is 'Up and Running,'" *New York Times*, September 25, 2002, A1.

54. Commission on the Intelligence Capabilities of the United States Regarding Weapons of Mass Destruction, Report to the President, March 31, 2005, p. 45; http://govinfo.library.unt.edu/wmd/report/wmd_report.pdf, accessed February 16, 2012.

55. Paul R. Pillar, *Intelligence and U.S. Foreign Policy: Iraq, 9/11, and Misguided Reform* (New York: Columbia University Press, 2011), 350–64.

56. George W. Bush, "President Bush Outlines Iraqi Threat," White House Press Release, October 7, 2002, http://georgewbush-whitehouse.archives.gov/news/releases/2002/10/20021007-8.html, accessed February 16, 2012.

57. Richard Morin and Claudia Deane, "71% of Americans Support War, Poll Shows," *Washington Post*, March 19, 2003, A14.

58. For a more detailed account of the Security Council wrangling before the Iraq War, see Woodward, *Plan of Attack*, 167, 221–26, 174–84; and Thomas H. Henriksen, *American Power after the Berlin Wall* (New York: Palgrave Macmillan, 2007), 175–77.

59. Barry Rubin, *The Truth about Syria* (New York: Palgrave Macmillan, 2007), 192.

60. For a discussion connecting Hussein and Osama bin Laden, see Stephen F. Hayes, *The Connection: How al Qaeda's Collaboration with Saddam Hussein Has Endangered America* (New York: HarperCollins, 2004), 78–93. For a more limited al-Qaeda role in helping set up Iraqi terrorist camps, see Lawrence Wright, *The Looming Tower: Al-Qaeda and the Road to 9/11* (New York: Alfred A. Knopf, 2006), 296.

61. Jim Michaels, *A Chance in Hell: The Men Who Triumphed over Iraq's Deadliest City and Turned the Tide of War* (New York: St. Martin's Press, 2010), 91–94.

62. Kimberly Kagan, *The Surge: A Military History* (New York: Encounter, 2009), 196.

63. Sabrina Tavernise and Andrew W. Lehren, "A Grim Portrait of Civilian Deaths in Iraq," *New York Times*, October 22, 2010, 10A.

64. Robert A. Pape, *Dying to Win: The Strategic Logic of Suicide Terrorism* (New York: Random House, 2005), 239.

65. John Prados, *Presidents' Secret Wars: CIA and Pentagon Covert Operations from World War II through the Persian Gulf* (Chicago: Ivan R. Dee, 1996), 466–67.

66. For a clear statement about a return to a less internationalist posture, see Walter A. McDougall, *Promised Land, Crusader State: The American Encounter with the World since 1776* (Boston: Houghton Mifflin, 1997), 211–22.

3   Iran: Ace of the Axis of Evil

1. Frederic Wehrey, David E. Thaler, and Nora Bensahel, *Dangerous but Not Omnipotent: Exploring the Reach and Limitations of Iranian Power in the Middle East* (Santa Monica, CA: RAND, 2009), 11.
2. Michael Axworthy, *A History of Iran: Empire of the Mind* (New York: Basic Books, 2008), 220.
3. John Prados, *Presidents' Secret Wars: CIA and Pentagon Covert Operations from World War II through the Persian Gulf* (Chicago: Ivan R. Dee, 1996), 97.
4. James A. Bill, *The Eagle and the Lion: The Tragedy of American-Iranian Relations* (New Haven, CT: Yale University Press, 1988), 90.
5. Nikki R. Keddie, *Modern Iran: Roots and Results of Revolution* (New Haven, CT: Yale University Press, 2006), 130.
6. Bill, *Eagle and the Lion*, 86, 94–97; and Abbas Milani, *The Myth of the Great Satan* (Stanford, CA: Hoover Institution Press, 2010), 59–65.
7. Axworthy, *History of Iran*, 237.
8. Cecil V. Crabb, *The Doctrines of American Foreign Policy: Their Meaning, Role, and Future* (Baton Rouge: Louisiana State University Press, 1982), 281.
9. "Policeman of the Persian Gulf," *Time* Magazine, August 6, 1973. Downloaded http://www.time.com/time/magazine/article/0,9171,903988,00.html, accessed April 3, 2009.
10. William L. Cleveland, *A History of the Modern Middle East*, 2nd ed. (Boulder, CO: Westview Press, 2000), 414.
11. Peter G. Bourne, *Jimmy Carter: A Comprehensive Biography from Plains to Postpresidency* (New York: Scribner, 1997), 453–55.
12. Vali Nasr, *The Shia Revival: How Conflicts in Islam Will Shape the Future* (New York: W. W. Norton and Company, 2006), 125–26 and 144–45.
13. Scott Kaufman, *Plans Unraveled: The Foreign Policy of the Carter Administration* (DeKalb: Northern Illinois University Press, 2008), 198.
14. Paul B. Ryan, *The Iranian Rescue Mission: Why It Failed* (Annapolis, MD: Naval Institute Press, 1985), 79–93.
15. Cleveland, *History of the Modern Middle East*, 423.
16. Lee Allen Zatarain, *The Tanker War: America's First Conflict with Iran, 1987–1988* (Philadelphia: Casemate, 2008), 284–89.
17. Axworthy, *History of Iran*, 268.
18. George P. Shultz, *Turmoil and Triumph: My Years as Secretary of State* (New York: Charles Scribner's Sons, 1993), 237.
19. Hala Jaber, *Hezbollah: Born with a Vengeance* (New York: Columbia University Press, 1997), 78–79.

20. August Richard Norton, *Hezbollah: A Short History* (Princeton, NJ: Princeton University Press), 33 and 71.
21. Naim Qassem, *Hizbullah: The Story from Within* (London: SAQI, 2005), 137.
22. Judith P. Harik, *Hezbollah: The Changing Face of Terrorism* (London: I. B. Tauris Company, 2005), 37.
23. Nasr, *Shia Revival*, 143.
24. Shultz, *Turmoil and Triumph*, 804.
25. For more on the Iran-Contra incident, see Martin Anderson, *Revolution: The Reagan Legacy* (New York: Harcourt Brace Jovanovich, 1988), 386–403.
26. Dilip Hiro, *Neighbors, Not Friends: Iraq and Iran after the Gulf Wars* (London: Routledge, 2001), 257.
27. Thomas H. Henriksen, *American Power after the Berlin Wall* (New York: Palgrave Macmillan, 2007), 5–18.
28. Cited in Hiro, *Neighbors, Not Friends*, 31.
29. Kenneth M. Pollack, *The Persian Puzzle: The Conflict between Iran and America* (New York: Random House, 2005), 253–58.
30. Martin Indyk, "The Clinton Administration's Approach to the Middle East," in *Challenges to U.S. Interests in the Middle East: Obstacles and Opportunities* (Washington, DC: Washington Institute, 1993), 4.
31. Ibid.
32. Henriksen, *American Power*, 53–55 and 132–39.
33. Amir Taheri, *The Persian Night: Iran under the Khomeinist Revolution* (New York: Encounter Books, 2009), 12.
34. Ibid.
35. Madeleine Albright, *Madam Secretary* (New York: Miramax Books, 2003), 320–26; and Bill Clinton, *My Life* (New York: Alfred A. Knopf, 2004), 751.
36. James F. Dobbins, *After the Taliban: Nation-Building in Afghanistan* (Washington, DC: Potomac Books, 2008), 83–85 and 88–89.
37. Pollack, *Persian Puzzle*, 329.
38. James Bennet, "Seized Arms Would Have Vastly Extended Arafat Arsenal," *New York Times*, January 12, 2002, A5; and Nicholas Blanford, "Palestinian Ties to Iran, Hezbollah Look Firmer," *Christian Science Monitor*, January 18, 2002, p. 8.
39. Seymour M. Hersh, "The Iran Game: How Will Tehran's Nuclear Ambitions Affect Our Budding Partnership?," *New Yorker*, December 3, 2001, p. 42.
40. George W. Bush, "State of the Union Address," January 29, 2002, http://frwebgate.access.gpo.gov/cgi-bin/getdoc.cgi?dbname=2002_presidential _documents&docid=pd04fe02_txt-11, accessed May 7, 2010.
41. Shaul Shay, *The Axis of Evil: Iran, Hezballah and the Palestinian Terror* (New Brunswick, NJ: Transaction Publishers, 2005), 42–77.
42. Bruce Hoffman, *Inside Terrorism* (New York: Columbia University Press, 1998), 193–97.
43. Barry Rubin, "The Gulf States and the Iran-Iraq War," in *The Iran-Iraq War: Impact and Implications*, ed. Efraim Karsh (London: Macmillan, 1989), 121–23.

44. "Gulf Leaders Back Kuwait in Alleged Iran Spy Case," *Asharq al-Awsat* (English edition), May 12, 2010, http://www.aawsat.com/english/news. asp?section=1&id=20913, accessed May 18, 2010.

45. Agence France-Press, "Iran says it respects Bahrain's sovereignty," February 19, 2009, http://www.google.com/hostednews/afp/article/ALeqM5iJJ6dq6_glysxs 0ublSRZ5bs1ZIA, accessed February 15, 2012.

46. Gilles Kepel, *Jihad: The Trail of Political Islam* (Cambridge, MA: Harvard University Press, 2002), 316–20.

47. Robert F. Worth, "Saudi Arabia Arrests 149 Qaeda Suspects, Many with Ties to Yemen, Over 8 Months," *New York Times*, November 27, 2011, A9.

48. James Wynbrandt, *A Brief History of Saudi Arabia* (New York: Facts on File, 2004), 267.

49. *The 9/11 Commission Report: Final Report of the National Commission on Terrorist Attacks upon the United States* (New York: W. W. Norton, 2004), 60.

50. Madawi Al-Rasheed, *A History of Saudi Arabia* (New York: Cambridge University Press, 2010), 263–67.

51. Michael Slackman, "Arab Unrest Propels Iran as Saudi Influence Declines," *New York Times*, February 23, 2011, A6.

52. Wehrey, Thaler, and Bensahel, *Dangerous but Not Omnipotent*, 12.

53. Harik, *Hezbollah*, 169–70.

54. Jaber, *Hezbollah*, 79.

55. Farnaz Fassihi, "Lebanon Vote Elevates Hezbollah," *Wall Street Journal*, January 26, 2011, A11.

56. Michael R. Gordon and Andrew W. Lehren, "U.S. Strains to Stop Arms Flow," *New York Times*, December 7, 2010, A1.

57. Michael Slackman, "Egypt Accuses Hezbollah of Plotting Attacks and Arms Smuggling to Gaza," *New York Times*, April 14, 2009, A6.

58. Ashraf Khalil and Nada Raad, "Cairo Court Convicts 26 Hezbollah Spies," *Wall Street Journal*, April 29, 2010, A15.

59. Joseph Felter and Brian Fishman, "Iranian Strategy in Iraq: Politics and 'Other Means,'" Occasional Paper of the Combating Terrorism Center, West Point Military Academy, October 13, 2008, pp. 49–66; http://www.ctc .usma.edu/wp-content/uploads/2010/06/Iranian-Strategy-in-Iraq.pdf, accessed February 15, 2012.

60. Youchi J. Dreazen, "Record Number of U.S. Troops Killed by Iranian Weapons," *National Journal*, July 28, 2011, http://www.nationaljournal.com/record -number-of-u-s-troops-killed-by-iranian-weapons-20110728?mrefid=site _search, accessed July 29, 2011.

61. Jay Solomon, "U.S. Sees Iranian, Al Qaeda Alliance," *Wall Street Journal*, July 29, 2011, A1.

62. Associated Press, "Iran Lends Hand to Afghan Neighbor," *Philadelphia Inquirer*, November 30, 2006, A6.

63. Bill Gertz, "Iran's Meddling in Afghanistan 'Not Significant,'" *Washington Times*, May 11, 2010, A9.

64. Hassan M. Fattah, "U.S. Sets Up a Perch in Dubai to Keep an Eye on Iran," *New York Times*, November 20, 2006, A1.

65. Peter Grier, "A Leaner, Looser 'Star Wars' System," *Christian Science Monitor*, June 3, 2007, A1.

66. Demetri Sevastoulo, Guy Dinmore, and Neil Buckley, "Experts Skeptical on Chances for Missile Deal," *Financial Times*, June 21, 2007, A1; and Charles Clover, "Western Bid to Allay Russia's Missile Concerns," *Financial Times*, July 6, 2011, A1.

67. Rich Gladstone, "Turkey to Install U.S.-Designed Rada, in a Move Seen as Blunting Iran's Missiles," *New York Times*, September 3, 2012, A7.

68. Gordon Corera, *Shopping for Bombs: Nuclear Proliferation, Global Insecurity, and the Rise and Fall of the A. Q. Khan Network* (New York: Oxford University Press, 2006), 57–58, 66–70, and 165–66; and Matthew Kroenig, *Exporting the Bomb: Technology Transfer and the Spread of Nuclear Weapons* (Ithaca, NY: Cornell University Press, 2010), 134–42.

69. Joby Warrick and Glenn Kessler, "Iran's Nuclear Program Speeds Ahead," *Washington Post*, March 10, 2003, A1.

70. David E. Sanger, "U.S. Rejected Aid for Israeli Raid on Iranian Nuclear Site," *New York Times*, January 11, 2009, A1.

71. Pollack, *Persian Puzzle*, 368.

72. James A. Baker III and Lee H. Hamilton, co-chairs, *The Iraq Study Group Report* (New York: Filiquarian Publishing, 2007), 64–65.

73. Michael Abramowitz, "Second Life for Study Group," *Washington Post*, May 21, 2007, A1.

74. Joshua Teitelbaum, *What Iranian Leaders Really Say about Doing Away with Israel* (Jerusalem, Israel: Jerusalem Center for Public Affairs, 2008), 7.

75. Jeffrey Goldberg, "Questions about Ahmadinejad's Famous Quote," *Atlantic Monthly*, April 3, 2009, http://jeffreygoldberg.theatlantic.com/archives/2009/04/questions_about_ahmadinejads_f.php, accessed May 18, 2009.

76. Teitelbaum, *What Iranian Leaders Really Say*, 14.

77. National Intelligence Estimate, "Iran: Nuclear Intentions and Capabilities," September 2007, http://www.dni.gov/press_releases/20071203_release.pdf, accessed May 13, 2009.

78. Nick Timiraos, "Behind the Iran-Intelligence Reversal," *Wall Street Journal*, December 8–9, 2007, A9.

79. National Intelligence Estimate, "Iran: Nuclear Intentions and Capabilities," 7.

80. Axworthy, *History of Iran*, 284.

81. Jon Ward, "NIE Authors Accused of Partisan Politics," *Washington Times*, December 7, 2007, A1.

82. David E. Sanger, "U.S. Presses Its Case against Iran Ahead of Sanctions Vote," *New York Times*, June 8, 2010, A1.

83. Adam Entous, "U.S. Spies: Iran Split on Nuclear Program," *Wall Street Journal*, February 17, 2011, A1.

84. Steven R. Weisman, "New Penalties Set as Bush Calls Iran a Threat to Peace," *New York Times*, January 10, 2008, A1.

85. Transcript, "President Obama's Inaugural Address," *New York Times*, January 20, 2009, P2.

86. Thomas Erdbrink, "Iranian Missile Launch Confirmed," *New York Times*, May 21, 2009, A1.

87. Alan Cowell and William J. Broad, "Iran Reports Missile Test, Drawing Rebuke," *New York Times*, July 10, 2008, A1.

88. Barack Obama, "Remarks by the President on a New Beginning," Cairo, Egypt, June 4, 2009, http://www.whitehouse.gov/the-press-office/remarks -president-cairo-university-6-04-09, accessed February 15, 2012.

89. Thomas Erdbrink and William Branigin, "Iran's President Rebukes Obama; Candidates Reject Election Review," *Washington Post*, June 28, 2009, A10.

90. Inter Press Service, Iran, "Poll Finds Public Support for Nuke Power over Weapons," September 22, 2009, http://ipsnews.net/news.asp?idnews=48555, accessed June 21, 2010.

91. Scott Wilson, "Muted Response Reflects U.S. Diplomatic Dilemma," *Washington Post*, June 15, 2009, A1.

92. John F. Burns, "Persian Station in Britain Rattles Officials in Iran," *New York Times*, June 29, 2009, A9.

93. Michael Slackman, "Hints of Iranian Flexibility on Nuclear Issues," *New York Times*, August 21, 2009, A1.

94. For a sample of political commentary against the Obama administration's detached posture toward Iran, see Thomas L. Friedman, "As Ugly as It Gets," *New York Times*, May 26, 2010, A23; and Dan Senor and Christian Whiton, "Five Ways Obama Could Promote Freedom in Iran," *Wall Street Journal*, June 17, 2009, A13.

95. For a brief overview of George W. Bush's pro-freedom policies in the "color revolutions," see Henriksen, *American Power*, 202–5.

96. Jeff Zeleny and Helene Cooper, "Obama Warns against Direct Involvement by U.S. in Iran," *New York Times*, June 17, 2009, A1; and Mark Lander, "Obama Resists Tougher Stand," *New York Times*, June 20, 2009, A1.

97. Con Coughlin, "Iran's Nuclear Subterfuge," *London Daily Telegraph*, June 6, 2010, p. 28.

98. Justin Blum, "Iran Gains U.S. Military Technology through Malaysia Middlemen," Bloomberg.com, http://www.bloomberg.com/apps/news?pid=n ewsarchive&sid=aK4daf8MD.Bw, accessed June 8, 2010.

99. Jo Becker, "Web of Shell Companies Veils Trade by Iran's Ships," *New York Times*, June 8, 2010, A1; and Claudia Rosett, "Iran's Hong Kong Shipping Shell Game," *Wall Street Journal*, August 30, 2011, A17.

100. Janine Zacharia, "Iran Tried to Send Weapons to Gaza Strip, Israel Alleges," *Washington Post*, March 16, 2011, A5.

101. Joe Lauria and Jay Soloman, "U.N. Slaps Iran with New Curbs," *Wall Street Journal*, June 10, 2010, A1.

102. Jay Solomon, "U.S. Sanctions Iran Individuals, Firms," *Wall Street Journal*, June 17, 2010, A10; and Stephen Fidler and Laura Stevens, "EU Targets Iran Despite Members' Trade Ties," *Wall Street Journal*, June 18, 2010, A8.

103. Jeremy Bowen, "Ahmadinejad: New UN Iran Sanctions 'Fit for Dustbin,'" *BBC News*, June 10, 2010, http://news.bbc.co.uk/2/hi/world/middle_east /10280356.stm, accessed June 15, 2010.

104. Jay Solomon, "U.S. Shifts Its Strategy toward Iran's Dissidents," *Wall Street Journal*, June 11, 2010, A10.

105. Jay Solomon, "Senators Press Obama on Iran's Central Bank, *Wall Street Journal*, August 8, 2011, A10.

106. Barbara Opall-Rome, "U.S. Backs Israeli Munitions Upgrades," *Defense News*, May 3, 2010, p. 1.

107. Paul Richter, "Obama Clarifies Remarks by Biden," *Los Angeles Times*, July 8, 2009, A15; and Yaakov Katz, "Israel, US Hold Joint Maneuvers to Simulate Attack against Enemy State," *Jerusalem Post*, June 11, 2010, p. 3.

108. Joe Pappalardo, "How Israel's Biggest Drone Could Take out Iranian Nukes," *Popular Mechanics*, February 23, 2010, p. 15; and Charles Levinson, "Israel Weighs Merits of Solo Attack on Iran," *Wall Street Journal*, April 19, 2010, A13.

109. Uzi Mahnaimi, "Israel Stations Nuclear Missile Subs off Iran," *London Sunday Times*, May 30, 2010, p. 3.

110. Isabel Kershner, "Israel Tests a Long-Range Missile," *New York Times*, November 2, 2011, A6.

111. William J. Broad and David E. Sanger, "Worm Was Perfect for Sabotaging Centrifuges," *New York Times*, November 18, 2010, A1.

112. Christopher Dickey, R. M. Schneiderman, and Babak Dehghanpisheh, "The Shadow War," *Newsweek*, December 20, 2010, p. 28.

113. David E. Sanger, "Iran Moves to Shelter Its Nuclear Fuel Program," *New York Times*, September 1, 2011, A1.

114. Michael Slackman and Ethan Bronner, "Saudis, Fearful of Iran, Send Troops to Bahrain to Quell Protests," *New York Times*, March 15, 2011, A1.

115. David E. Sanger and Eric Schmitt, "U.S.-Saudi Tensions Intensify with Mideast Turmoil," *New York Times*, March 14, 2011, A14.

116. Michael Singh and Jacqueline Newmyer Deal, "China's Iranian Gambit, *Foreign Policy*, October 31, 2011), http://www.foreignpolicy.com/articles/2011/10/31/china_iran_nuclear_relationship, accessed November 3, 2011.

117. Tony Capaccio, "Iran Continues Its 'Drive to Enrich Uranium,' Defense Agency's Chief Says," Bloomberg.com, March 10, 2010, http://www .bloomberg.com/news/2011–03–09/un-sanctions-aren-t-stopping-iran-s -nuclear-enrichment-dia-says.html, accessed March 17, 2011.

118. Jay Solomon, "U.S. Sees Iranian, Al Qaeda Alliance," *Wall Street Journal*, July 29, 2011, A1.

119. Peter Finn, "Iranian Militant Linked to Murder Plot," *Washington Post*, October 15, 2011, A1.

120. Roya Hakakian, *Assassins of the Turquoise Palace* (New York: Grove Press, 2011), 202–11.

121. Director General, "Implementation of the NPT Safeguard Agreement and Relevant Provisions of Security Council Resolutions in the Islamic Report of Iran," IAEA, November 8, 2011, http://graphics8.nytimes.com/packages/pdf /world/2011/IAEA-Nov-2011-Report-Iran.pdf, accessed November 9, 2011.

4 North Korea: Blackmailing Rogue

1. For a clear view of North Korea's food problems, see Nicholas Eberstadt, *The End of North Korea* (Washington, DC: AEI Press, 1999), 61–69; and Chae-Jin Lee, *China and North Korea* (Stanford, CA: Hoover Institution Press, 1996), 9–12.

2. Blaine Haarden, "North Korean Nuclear Test a Growing Possibility," *Washington Post*, March 27, 2009, A1.

3. David F. Sanger, "Cheney, in Korea, Orders Halt to U.S. Pullout," *New York Times*, December 22, 1991, A7.

4. Michael J. Mazarr, *North Korea and the Bomb: A Case Study in Nonproliferation* (New York: St. Martin's Press, 1995), 82–88.

5. A transcript of President Bill Clinton's Inaugural Address, "We Force the Spring," *New York Times*, January 21, 1993, A11.

6. Raymond Tanter, *Rogue Regimes: Terrorism and Proliferation* (New York: St. Martin's Press, 1998), 222–28.

7. Michael R. Gordon, "U.S. Will Urge U.N. to Plan Sanctions for North Korea," *New York Times*, March 20, 1994, A1.

8. Joel S. Wit, Daniel B. Poneman, and Robert L. Gallucci, *Going Critical: The First North Korean Crisis* (Washington, DC: Brookings Institution Press, 2004), 221–38.

9. James Broke, "North Korea and Japan Sign a Deal on Abductions," *New York Times*, May 23, 2004, A6.

10. John Gittings, *The Changing Face of China: From Mao to Markets* (New York: Oxford University Press, 2005), 261–67.

11. Choe Sang-Hun, "North Korea Said to Be Looting Heavy Equipment," *New York Times*, December 31, 2009, A8.

12. Wit, Poneman, and Gallucci, *Going Critical*, 331–36.

13. Mazarr, *North Korea and the Bomb*, 175–80.

14. Wit, Poneman, and Gallucci, *Going Critical*, 333–41.

15. Mark Mazzetti, "In '97, U.S. Panel Predicted a North Korea Collapse in 5 Years," *New York Times*, October 27, 2006, A6.

16. Bill Clinton, *My Life* (New York: Alfred A. Knopf, 2004), 751 and 828.

17. Wit, Poneman, and Gallucci, *Going Critical*, 374–75.

18. Gordon Corera, *Shopping for Bombs: Nuclear Proliferation, Global Insecurity, and the Rise and Fall of the A. Q. Khan Network* (New York: Oxford University Press, 2006), 92–93, 99, 101–2; and Matthew Kroenig, *Exporting the Bomb: Technology Transfer and the Spread of Nuclear Weapons* (Ithaca, NY: Cornell University Press, 2010), 135, 175, and 200.

19. R. Jeffrey Smith and Joby Warrick, "Revisiting N. Korean Nuclear Program," *Washington Post*, December 28, 2009, A2.

20. Choe Sang-Hun, "North Korea Started Uranium Program in 1990s, South Says," *New York Times*, January 7, 2010, A8.

21. Glenn Kessler, "New Doubts on Nuclear Efforts by North Korea," *Washington Post*, March 1, 2007, A1.

22. For a contrary view about a change in the intelligence, see John R. Bolton, "North Korea Climbdown," *Wall Street Journal*, March 2, 2007, A17.

23. Warren Hoge, "U.S. Presses North Korea over Uranium," *New York Times*, March 7, 2007, A13.

24. Michael R. Gordon and Mark Mazzetti, "North Korean Arms Ethiopians as U.S. Assents," *New York Times*, April 8, 2007, A1.

25. There are many sources advancing the notion of the Bush administration's strident anti-Hussein sentiments. For just two books, see Bob Woodward, *Plan of Attack* (New York: Simon and Schuster, 2004), 9–14, and James Mann, *Rise of the Vulcans: The History of Bush's War Cabinet* (New York: Viking, 2004), 187–88 and 332–58.

26. Mark McDonald, "North Korea Suggests Libya Should Have Kept Nuclear Program," *New York Times*, March 25, 2011, A12.

27. Dana Milbank and Karen DeYoung, "President Sees 'Progress' on N. Korea," *Washington Post*, May 15, 2003, A2.

28. For a chilling memoir from one of the former inmates, see Hang Chol-Hwan, *Aquariums of Pyongyang: Ten Years in the North Korean Gulag* (New York: Basic Books, 2000).

29. "Full Text of 6-Party Talks Joint Statement," *China Daily*, September 19, 2005, http://www.chinadaily.com.cn/english/doc/2005–09/19/content_479150.htm, accessed March 13, 2011.

30. Press Room U.S. Department of Treasury, "Treasury Designates Banco Delta Asia as Primary Money Laundering Concern under USA Patriot Act, September 15, 2005, http://www.ustreas.gov/press/releases/js2720.htm, accessed on March 4, 2009.

31. David Lague and David Greenless, "Squeeze on Banco Delta Asia Hit North Korea Where It Hurt," *New York Times*, January 18, 2007, A8.

32. Warren Hoge, "U.N. to Audit Its Activities after Reports on North Korea Program," *New York Times*, January 20, 2007, A3.

33. "Background and Overview of Allegations against UNDP," UNDP and DPR Korea, http://undp.org/dprk/, accessed March 12, 2011.

34. Jasper Becker, *Rogue Regime: Kim Jong Il and the Looming Threat of North Korea* (New York: Oxford University Press, 2005), 162–63.

35. Michael R. Gordon and Mark Mazzetti, "North Korean Arms Ethiopians as U.S. Assents," *New York Times*, April 8, 2007, A1.

36. Katherine Shrader, "North Korean Client List Is Said to Take in Iran, Syria, and 16 Others," *Philadelphia Inquirer*, October 13, 2006, p. 1.

37. Ashish Kumar Sen, "Gaddafi Prepares for Blitz of Scuds," *Washington Times*, August 18, 2011, A1.

38. Briefs, "North Koreans Assisted Hezbollah with Tunnel Construction," *Terrorism Focus* 3, no. 30 (August 1, 2006): 1. This source cites the international Arab newspaper *al-Sharq al-Awsat*, July 29, 2006.

39. Daniel Michaels and Margaret Coker, "Arms Seized by Thailand Were Iran-Bound," *Wall Street Journal*, December 21, 2009, A8.

40. "Chinese Urges N. Korea Not to Test Missile," *China Daily*, June 29, 2006, http://www.chinadaily.com.cn/china/2006-06/29/content_628845.htm, accessed February 15, 2012.

41. Choe Sang-hun, "Japan and South Korea Wrangle over Response to North's Missiles," *New York Times*, July 12, 2006, A8.

42. Dafna Linzer, "Pyongyang Warned on Weapon Test," *Washington Post*, October 5, 2006, A20.

43. Calla Huan Sheng, "Hecker Talks North Korea," *Stanford Daily*, March 6, 2009, p. 1. An interview with the nuclear scientist Siegfried Hecker after his sixth visit to the DPRK.

44. Richard L. Garwin and Frank N. von Hippel, "A Technical Analysis: Deconstructing North Korea's October 9 Nuclear Test," Arms Control Association, November 2006, p. 2, http://www.armscontrol.org/act/2006_11/tech, accessed March 2, 2009.

45. David E. Sanger, "Bush Urges Quick Action on North Korea," *New York Times*, October 9, 2006, A1.

46. David E. Sanger, "For U.S., a Strategic Jolt after North Korea's Test," *New York Times*, October 10, 2006, A1.

47. "China Resolutely Opposes DPRK's Nuclear Test," *Xinhua News Agency*, October 9, 2006, http://news.xinhuanet.com/english/2006-10/09/content_5180203.htm, accessed February 15, 2012.

48. United Nations Security Council, Resolution 1718, October 14, 2006, http://www.un.org/News/Press/docs/2006/sc8853.doc.htm, accessed February 15, 2012.

49. Warren Hoge, "Security Council Supports Sanctions on North Korea," *New York Times*, October 15, 2006, A1.

50. John O'Neil and Norimitsu Onishi, "China Said to Start Enforcing North Korea Sanctions," *New York Times*, October 16, 2006, A1.

51. "China Striving to Secure DPRK Mineral Rights and Natural Resources," Center for International Cooperation for North Korean Development, Report number 07–4-20–1, April 20, 2007, p. 1.

52. Michael Wines, "Secret Bid to Arm Qaddafi Sheds Light on Tensions in China Government," *New York Times*, September 11, 2011, A1.

53. Bill Gertz, "China Cited as N. Korea Supplier," *Washington Times*, October 31, 2006, p. 1.

54. Thom Shanker and Martin Fackler, "South Korea Says It Will Continue Projects in the North," *New York Times*, October 19, 2006, A1.

55. Helene Cooper and David E. Sanger, "U.S. Signals New Incentives for North Korea," *New York Times*, November 19, 2006, A1.

56. Helene Cooper and David E. Sanger, "U.S. Offers North Korea Aid for Dropping Nuclear Plans," *New York Times*, December 6, 2006, A6.

57. AP, "U.S. and Japan Issue Warnings to North Korea on Nuclear Test," *New York Times*, January 5, 2007, A6.

58. Joseph Kahn, "Talks End on North Korea's Nuclear Weapons," *New York Times*, December 23, 2006, A7.

59. Bill Gertz, "Sanctions Imposed on Iran, Syria Arms Suppliers," *Washington Times*, January 5, 2007, A8.

60. U.S. Department of State, "North Korea—Denuclearization Action Plan," February 13, 2007, http://2001-2009.state.gov/r/pa/prs/ps/2007/february/80479.htm, accessed February 15, 2012.

61. Glenn Kessler, "U.S. Flexibility Credited in Nuclear Deal with N. Korea," *Washington Post*, February 14, 2007, A11.

62. Jim Yardley, "North Korea to Close Reactor in Exchange for Raft of Aid," *New York Times*, February 13, 2007, A1.

63. Helen Cooper and Jim Yardley, "Pact with North Korea Draws Fire from a Wide Range of Critics in U.S.," *New York Times*, February 14, 2007, A8.

64. Glenn Kessler, "To Prod N. Korea, U.S. Relents in Counterfeiting Case," *Washington Post*, April 11, 2007, A1.

65. Steven R. Weisman, "How U.S. Turned North Korean Funds into a Bargaining Chip," *New York Times*, April 12, 2007, A8.

66. Choe Sang-Hun, "North Korea 'Prepared' to Shut Down Reactor, U.S. Envoy Says," *New York Times*, June 23, 2009, A5.

67. Glenn Kessler, "N. Korea, Syria May Be at Work on Nuclear Facility," *Washington Post*, September 13, 2007, A12; and Mark Mazzetti and David E. Sanger, "Israel Struck a Nuclear Project Syria, Analysts Say," *New York Times*, October 14, 2007, A1.

68. Paul Richter, "West Says N. Korea, Syria Had Nuclear Link," *Los Angeles Times*, January 17, 2008, A1.

69. David E. Sanger, "Bush Administration Releases Images to Bolster Its Claims about Syrian Reactor," *New York Times*, April 25, 2008, A6.

70. Helen Cooper, "North Koreans Agree to Disable Nuclear Facilities," *New York Times*, October 4, 2007, A1.

71. Times Wire Service, "North Korea Says It Will Boost Its 'War Deterrent,'" *Los Angeles Times*, January 4, 2008, A1.

72. Helene Cooper, "North Korea Gives U.S. Files on Plutonium Efforts," *New York Times*, May 9, 2008, A6.

73. Glenn Kessler, "Message to U.S. Preceded Nuclear Declaration by North Korea," *Washington Post*, July 2, 2008, A7.

74. Dick Cheney with Liz Cheney, *In My Time: A Personal and Political Memoir* (New York: Threshold Editions, 2011), 486–87.

75. John R. Bolton, "Bush's North Korea Surrender Will Have Lasting Consequences," *Wall Street Journal*, October 13, 2008, A10.

76. Helene Cooper, "U.S. Declares North Korea Off Terror List," *New York Times*, October 13, 2008, A1.

77. Transcript of President Barack Hussein Obama, "The Address: 'All This We Will Do,'" *New York Times*, January 21, 2009, P2.

78. Choe Sang-Hun, "North Korea Says It Has 'Weaponized' Plutonium," *New York Times,* January 18, 2009, A8.
79. B. R. Myers, *The Cleanest Race: How North Koreans See Themselves—And Why It Matters* (Brooklyn, NY: Melville House, 2010), 168.
80. Mark Landler, "Clinton Takes Softer Tone on North Korea," *New York Times,* February 16, 2009, A7.
81. United Nations Security Council Resolution 1718, adopted October 14, 2006, http://www.un.org/News/Press/docs/2006/sc8853.doc.htm, accessed February 15, 2012.
82. William J. Broad, "North Korean Missile Launch Was a Failure, Experts Say," *New York Times,* April 6, 2009, A1.
83. Choe Sang-Hun and David E. Sanger, "North Koreans Launch Rocket over the Pacific," *New York Times,* April 5, 2009, A1.
84. John S. Park, "North Korea, Inc.," U.S. Institute of Peace Working Paper (April 22, 2009), 10–13.
85. Neil MacFarquhar, "North Korea: U.N. Council to Tighten Sanctions," *New York Times,* April 14, 2009, A8.
86. Kwang-tae Kim, "Plutonium Harvesting Under Way," *Washington Times,* April 26, 2009, A6.
87. Jae-Soon Chang, "North Korea Threatens Nuclear, Missile Tests," Associated Press, April 29, 2009; and Choe Sang-Hung, "N. Korea Issues Threat on Uranium," *New York Times,* April 30, 2009, A1.
88. Choe Sang-Hun, "North Korean Leader, Thin and Limping, Returns to Assembly and Gains New Term," *New York Times,* April 10, 2009, A6.
89. Jaeyeon Woo, "Pyongyang Honors Son of Leader on Birthday," *Wall Street Journal,* January 9–10, 2010, A8.
90. Choe Sang-Hun, "North Korean Nuclear Claim Draws Global Criticism," *New York Times,* May 26, 2009, A1.
91. David E. Sanger, "U.S. to Confront, Not Board, North Korean Ships," *New York Times,* June 16, 2009, A1.
92. Blaine Harden, "North Korea Says It Will Start Enriching Uranium," *Washington Post,* June 14, 2009, A1.
93. Blaine Harden, "Value of N. Korea Sanctions Disputed," *Washington Post,* June 12, 2009, A8.
94. China Expanding Mining Rights in N. Korea," Korean Chamber of Commerce and Industry, January 15, 2010, http://www.nkeconwatch.com/2010/01/15/china-expanding-mining-rights-in-n-korea, accessed January 15, 2011; and Gordon G. Chang, "Implications of China's Economic Penetration of North Korea," *China Brief* 11, no. 13 (July 15, 2011): 10–13.
95. Choe Sang-Hun, "North Koreans Condemn U.S. and Sanctions at Huge Rally," *New York Times,* June 26, 2009, A8.
96. Ellen Nakashima, Brian Krebs, and Blaine Harden, "U.S., South Korea Targeted in Swarm of Internet Attacks," *Washington Post,* July 9, 2009, A11.
97. Choe Sang-Hun, "In South Korea, Freed U.S. Journalists Come under Harsh Criticism," *New York Times,* August 22, 2009, A4.

98. Simon Roughneen, "Myanmar's Ties to N. Korea Escape Scrutiny," *Washington Times*, August 9, 2009, A1.
99. Glenn Kessler, "N. Korea Escalates War of Words, Calls Clinton Vulgar, Unintelligent," *Washington Post*, July 24, 2009, A14.
100. Chico Harlan, "Hungry North Korea Seeks Food Handouts," *Washington Post*, February 22, 2011, A6.
101. Mark McDonald, "North Korean Prison Camps Massive and Growing," *New York Times*, May 4, 2011, A8.
102. "Kim Jong-Un Gets Promoted," *Chosun Ilbo* (South Korea), February 16, 2011, p. 1.
103. Myers, *Cleanest Race*, 167.
104. David E. Sanger, "Coming to Terms with Containing North Korea," *New York Times*, August 9, 2009, sec. IV, p. 3.
105. Helene Cooper and Martin Fackler, "Obama Takes Stern Tone on North Korea and Iran," *New York Times*, November 19, 2009, A6.
106. Lara Jakes, "Gates Says US Won't Accept Nuclear North Korea," *Washington Post*, October 21, 2009, A10.
107. Gordon G. Chang, *Nuclear Showdown: North Korea Takes on the World* (New York: Random House, 2006), 221–25.

5 Lesser Rogues and Troublesome States

1. Dirk Vandewalle, *A History of Modern Libya* (New York: Cambridge University Press, 2006), 1.
2. The quoted phrase is from Bernard Lewis, "The Roots of Muslim Rage," *Atlantic Monthly*, September 1990, p. 5, http://www.theatlantic.com/magazine/archive/1990/09/the-roots-of-muslim-rage/4643/, accessed June 23, 2010.
3. Fouad Ajami, *The Dream Palace of the Arabs: A Generation's Odyssey* (New York: Pantheon Books, 1998), 111–49; and Jim al-Khalili, *The House of Wisdom: How Arabic Science Saved Ancient Knowledge and Gave Us the Renaissance* (New York: Penguin Press, 2011), 273–79.
4. Yehudit Ronen, *Qaddafi's Libya in World Politics* (Boulder, CO: Lynne Rienner Publishers, 2008), 5.
5. Hanspeter Mattes, "Formal and Informal Authority in Libya since 1969," in *Libya since 1969: Qaddafi's Revolution Revisited*, edited by Dirk Vandewalle (New York: Palgrave Macmillan, 2008), 56–58.
6. Walter Laqueur, *The New Terrorism: Fanaticism and the Arms of Mass Destruction* (New York: Oxford University Press, 1999), 243.
7. Patrick Seale, *Abu Nidal: A Gun for Hire* (New York: Random House, 1992), 136–39.
8. George P. Shultz, *Turmoil and Triumph: My Years as Secretary of State* (New York: Charles Scribner's Sons, 1993), 678–79.

9. Seymour M. Hersh, "Target Qaddafi," *New York Times Magazine*, February 22, 1987, p. 22.

10. Ronen, *Qaddafi's Libya in World Politics*, 21.

11. Harry Gelman, "The Soviet Union in the Less Developed World: A Retrospective Overview and Prognosis," in *The Soviet Union and the Third World: The Last Three Decades*, ed. Andrzej Korbonski and Francis Fukuyama (Ithaca, NY: Cornell University Press, 1987), 294.

12. In the 1979 Export Administration Act, the US Congress mandated that the Department of State list and report on "countries that have repeatedly provided state support for international terrorism." See Office of the Coordinator for Counterterrorism, Patterns of Global Terrorism, 1996, Publication 10433 (Washington, DC: US Department of State, 1997), v.

13. Bruce Hoffman, *Inside Terrorism* (New York: Columbia University Press, 1998), 186.

14. Shultz, *Turmoil and Triumph*, 677–81.

15. John Tagliabue, "2 Killed, 155 Hurt in Bomb Explosion at Club in Berlin," *New York Times*, April 6, 1986, A1.

16. Laqueur, *New Terrorism*, 170.

17. Paul Lewis, "Libya Offers Some Cooperation in Plane Bombings," *New York Times*, February 13, 1992, A8.

18. Ronen, *Qaddafi's Libya in World Politics*, 45–48.

19. Thomas C. Wiegele, *The Clandestine Building of Libya's Chemical Weapons Factory: A Study in International Collusion* (Carbondale: Southern Illinois University Press, 1992), 145–47.

20. Gordon Corera, *Shopping for Bombs: Nuclear Proliferation, Global Insecurity, the Rise and Fall of the A. Q. Khan Network* (New York: Oxford University Press, 2006), 108–9.

21. Ibid., 120.

22. Douglas J. Feith, *War and Decision: Inside the Pentagon at the Dawn of the War on Terrorism* (New York: Harper, 2008), 515; and Donald Rumsfeld, *Known and Unknown: A Memoir* (New York: Sentinel, 2011), 630.

23. David E. Sanger and Judith Miller, "Libya to Give Up Arms Programs, Bush Announces," *New York Times*, December 20, 2003, A1.

24. Mitchell Reiss, *Bridled Ambition: Why Countries Constrain Their Nuclear Capabilities* (Washington, DC: Woodrow Wilson Center Press, 1995), 322.

25. Sharon A. Squassoni and Andrew Feickert, *Disarming Libya: Weapons of Mass Destruction*, a Congressional Research Report (Washington, DC, 2004), http://fpc.state.gov/documents/organization/32007.pdf, accessed June 30, 2011.

26. Thomas E. McNamara, "Survival Instinct: Why Qaddafi Turned His Back on Terror," *New York Times*, May 6, 2004, A19.

27. Quoted in Ronen, *Qaddafi's Libya in World Politics*, 100.

28. Yevgeny Primakov, *Russia and the Arabs: Behind the Scenes in the Middle East from the Cold War to the Present* (New York: Basic Books, 2009), 386.

29. Ronen, *Qaddafi's Libya in World Politics*, 81.
30. Dirk Vandewalle, "Libya in the New Millennium," in Vandewalle, *Libya since 1969*, 215–38.
31. Ibid., 100.
32. Luis Martinez, *The Libyan Paradox* (New York: Columbia University Press, 2007), 45.
33. Ibid.
34. "Gaddafi Vows to Push Africa Unity," London, BBC News, February 2, 2009, http://news.bbc.co.uk/2/hi/africa/7864604.stm, accessed June 20, 2011.
35. Vandewalle, *History of Modern Libya*, 182.
36. John F. Burns, "Senate Hearing on Lockerbie Sets off More Finger-Pointing," *New York Times*, July 26, 2010, A4.
37. Rod Norland, "Files Note Close C.I.A. Ties to Qaddafi Spy Unit," *New York Times*, September 3, 2011, A1; and Thomas Erdbrink and Joby Warrick, "Papers Show Gaddafi Fears of Islamists," *Washington Post*, August 31, 2011, A7.
38. Patrick Tyler, "Two Are Said to Tell of Libyan Plot to Kill Saudi Ruler," *New York Times*, June 10, 2004, p. 1; and Associated Press, "Libya's Role in Alleged Assassination Plot Cited," *Washington Post*, December 23, 2004, A18.
39. For more on this hoped-for application, see Jon B. Alterman, "Postscript: Libya as Harbinger? The U.S.-Libyan Rapprochement," in Vandewalle, *Libya since 1969*, 240.
40. Mark Landler and Dan Bilefsky, "Specter of Rebel Rout Helps Shift U.S. Policy on Libya," *New York Times*, March 17, 2011, A1.
41. Dan Bilefsky and Mark Landler, "U.N. Approves Airstrikes to Halt Attacks by Qaddafi Forces," *New York Times*, March 18, 2011, A1.
42. Rodney Stark, *God's Battalions: The Case for the Crusades* (New York: HarperCollins, 2009), 83–98 and 246–48.
43. David Fromkin, *A Peace to End All Peace: The Fall of the Ottoman Empire and the Creation of the Modern Middle East* (New York: Avon Books, 1989), 94.
44. Dilip Hiro, *The Essential Middle East: A Comprehensive Guide* (New York: Carroll and Graf Publishers, 2003), 506.
45. William L. Cleveland, *A History of the Modern Middle East*, 2nd ed. (Boulder, CO: Westview Press, 2000), 388.
46. Flynt Leverett, *Inheriting Syria: Bashar's Trial by Fire* (Washington, DC: Brookings Institution Press, 2005), 10–13.
47. Bassel F. Salloukh, "Demystifying Syrian Foreign Policy under Bashar al-Asad," in *Demystifying Syria*, ed. Fred H. Lawson (London: London Middle East Institute at SOAS, 2009), 166.
48. Amal Saad-Ghorayeb, *Hizbu'llah: Politics and Religion* (London: Pluto Press, 2002), 51–52.
49. Hala Jaber, *Hezbollah: Born with a Vengeance* (New York: Columbia University Press, 1997), 73–74.

50. Daniel Pipes, "Terrorism: The Syrian Connection," *National Interest* (Spring 1989), http://www.danielpipes.org/1064/terrorism-the-syrian-connection, p. 9, accessed June 6, 2011.
51. Seale, *Abu Nidal*, 225–57.
52. Pipes, "Terrorism: The Syrian Connection," 18.
53. Salwa Ismail, "Changing Social Structure, Shifting Alliances and Authoritarianism in Syria," in Lawson, *Demystifying Syria*, 25.
54. Dilip Hiro, *Neighbors, Not Friends: Iraq and Iran after the Gulf Wars* (London: Routledge, 2001), 301.
55. Clifford Krauss, "U.S. Welcomes Thaw in Relations with 'Pragmatic' Syria," *New York Times*, January 2, 2002, A1.
56. Seymour M. Hersh, "The Syrian Bet," *New Yorker*, July 28, 2003, http://www.newyorker.com/archive/2003/07/28/030728fa_fact, accessed June 20, 2011.
57. Leverett, *Inheriting Syria*, 142–43.
58. Barry Rubin, *The Truth about Syria* (New York: Palgrave Macmillan, 2007), 192.
59. Hugh Naylor, "Syria Is Said to Be Strengthening Ties to Opponents of Iraq's Government," *New York Times*, October 7, 2007, A4.
60. Ann Scott Tyson and Ellen Knickmeyer, "U.S. Calls Raid a Warning to Syria," *Washington Post*, October 28, 2008, A1; and Erich Schmitt and Thom Shanker, "Officials Say U.S. Killed an Iraqi in Raid in Syria," *New York Times*, October 28, 2008, A1.
61. United Nations Security Council Resolution 1559, September 2, 2004, http://www.un.org/News/Press/docs/2004/sc8181.doc.htm, accessed February 16, 2012.
62. Nada Bakri, "Hezbollah Rejects Charges over '05 Killing of Hariri," *New York Times*, July 2, 2011, A6; and Nada Bakri, "Indictment in Harri Assassination Is Published," *New York Times*, August 17, 2011, A8.
63. Salloukh, "Demystifying Syrian Foreign Policy," 172.
64. Leverett, *Inheriting Syria*, 13.
65. Peter Brookes, *A Devil's Triangle: Terrorism, Weapons of Mass Destruction, and Rogue States* (Lanham, MD: Rowland and Littlefield, 2005), 222.
66. Chemical Overview, Syrian Profile, Center for Nonproliferation Studies, Monterey Institute of International Studies, http://nti.org/e_research/profiles/Syria/Chemical/index.html, accessed June 2, 2011.
67. Nuclear Overview, Syria Profile, Center for Nonproliferation Studies, Monterey Institute of International Studies, http://nti.org/e_research/profiles/Syria/Nuclear/index.html, accessed June 2, 2011.
68. Rubin, *Truth about Syria*, 192; and Rowan Scarborough, "Assad's Fall Could Solve Iraqi Weapons Mystery," *Washington Times*, January 23, 2012, A1.
69. Corera, *Shopping for Bombs*, 235.
70. David Albright, *Peddling Peril: How the Secret Nuclear Trade Arms America's Enemies* (New York: Free Press, 2010), 166–68.

71. For analysis of the intelligence relating to the Syrian atomic facility, see "Syria's Nuclear Reactor," *Foreign Policy*, April 25, 2008, http://blog.foreignpolicy.com/posts/2008/04/25/syrias_nuclear_reactor, accessed June 25, 2011.

72. Uzi Manhnaimi and Sarah Baxter, "Israelis Seized Nuclear Material in Syrian Raid," *Times On Line*, September 30, 2007, http://www.freerepublic.com/focus/f-news/1900827/posts, accessed February 16, 2012.

73. David E. Sanger and Mark Mazzetti, "Israel Struck a Nuclear Project in Syria, Analysts Say," *New York Times*, October 14, 2007, A1.

74. Mark Mazzetti and David E. Sanger, "Raid on Syria Fuels Debate on Weapons," *New York Times*, September 22, 2007, A1.

75. Manhnaimi and Baxter, "Israelis Seized Nuclear Material in Syrian Raid," accessed August 12, 2010.

76. Paul Brannan, "ISIS Analysis of the IAEA Report on Syria: IAEA Concludes Syria 'Very Likely' Built a Reactor," Institute for Science and International Security, May 24, 2011, http://isis-online.org/uploads/isis-reports/documents/ISIS_Analysis_IAEA_Report_Syria_24May2011.pdf, accessed June 3, 2011.

77. Matthew Kalman and Bill Hutchinson, "Israel to Syria: Use Chem Weapons and We'll Wipe You off Map," *New York Daily News*, September 20, 2007, p. 3; and "Syrian Site Reportedly Used for Chemical Arms," *Washington Post*, September 20, 2007, A16.

78. Jubin M. Goodarzi, *Syria and Iran: Diplomatic Alliance and Power Politics in the Middle East* (London: I. B. Tauris, 2009), 23.

79. Ibid., 294.

80. Neil MacFarquhar, "Saudis Scramble in Bid to Contain Regional Unrest," *New York Times*, May 28, 2011, A1.

81. Farnaz Fassihi, "Iran Feels Heat over Support for Damascus," *Wall Street Journal*, August 31, 2011, A10.

82. Itamar Rabinovich, *The View from Damascus: State, Political Community and Foreign Relations in Twentieth-Century Syria* (London: Vallentine Mitchell, 2008), 345.

83. Reportage of the Iranian radar transfer took place a year after it occurred. Charles Levinson, "Iran Arms Syria with Radar," *Wall Street Journal*, July 1, 2010, A1.

84. Rubin, *Truth about Syria*, 236.

85. Anthony Shadid, "U.S. Imposes Sanctions on Syrian Leader and 6 Aides," *New York Times*, May 19, 2011, A1.

86. Joby Warrick, "IAEA Connects Syria to Secret Nuclear Program," *Washington Post*, May 11, 2011, A11.

87. Jay Solomon, "U.S. Pushes to Try Syria Regime," *Wall Street Journal*, June 18, 2011, A8.

88. Anthony Shadid, "Syria's Ailing Economy Poses a Threat to Assad," *New York Times*, June 24, 2011, A1.

89. State Sponsors of Terrorism, U.S. Department of State, http://www.state.gov/j/ct/c14151.htm, accessed February 16, 2012.

90. Robert O. Collins, *A History of Modern Sudan* (New York: Cambridge University Press, 2008), 194–95.

91. Combating Terrorism Center, *Al-Qaida's (Mis)Adventures in the Horn Africa* (West Point, NY: Combating Terrorism Center, 2007), 83–84.

92. Collins, *History of Modern Sudan*, 216.

93. For an inside account of the justification of the attack, see Daniel Benjamin and Steven Simon, *The Age of Sacred Terror* (New York: Random House, 2002), 353–64 and 380.

94. Jeffrey Gettleman, "As Secession Nears, Sudan Steps up Drive to Stop Rebels," *New York Times*, June 21, 2011, A8.

95. Mark Falcoff, *Cuba: The Morning After* (Washington, DC: AEI Press, 2003), 97.

96. Rhoda P. Rabkin, *Cuban Politics: The Revolutionary Experiment* (New York: Praeger, 1991), 144–57.

97. US Department of Defense, *The Cuban Threat to U.S. National Security* (Washington, DC, 1998), p. 2, http://www.fas.org/irp/dia/product/980507-dia-cubarpt.htm, accessed July 24, 2011.

98. Brian Latell, *After Fidel: The Inside Story of Castro's Regime and Cuba's Next Leader* (New York: Palgrave Macmillan, 2005), 233.

99. Juan Forero, "Cuba Perks up as Venezuelan Foils Embargo," *New York Times*, August 4, 2006, A1.

100. "Hu Vows to Boost Ties with Cuba," *China Daily*, November 21, 2008, p. 1.

101. Julia E. Sweig, *Cuba: What Everyone Needs to Know* (New York: Oxford University Press, 2009), 251.

102. Ian James, "Cuba Trains Venezuela in Military, Communications," *Washington Post*, June 2, 2010, A12.

103. Jose de Cordoba and David Luhnow, "Bloc Lifts Cold War-Era Exclusion of Cuba," *Wall Street Journal*, June 4, 2009, A8.

104. Ginger Thompson, "U.S. Said to Plan Easing Rules for Travel to Cuba," *New York Times*, August 17, 2010, A4.

105. Elisabeth Malkin, "Cuba's Public-Sector Layoffs Signal Major Shift," *New York Times*, September 13, 2010, A1.

106. Juan M. del Aguila, "Cuba: Development, Revolution, and Decay," in *Latin American Politics and Development*, 7th ed., ed. Howard J. Wiarda and Harvey F. Kline (Philadelphia: Westview Press, 2011), 471.

107. Venezuela, World Factbook, Central Intelligence Agency, https://www.cia.gov/library/publications/the-world-factbook/rankorder/2173rank.html, accessed July 30, 2011.

108. Douglas Schoen and Michael Rowan, *The Threat Closer to Home: Hugo Chávez and the War against America* (New York: Free Press, 2009), 82–89.

109. David Stout, "Chavez Calls Bush 'the Devil' in U.N. Speech," *New York Times*, September 20, 2006, A1.

110. Mary Anastasia O'Grady, "The FARC Files," *Wall Street Journal*, March 10, 2008, A13.

111. Matthew Bristow, "Drugs Fade in Colombian Economy," *Wall Street Journal*, April 4, 2010, A7; and Bryan Bender, "Colombia Offers Lessons for US Aid Efforts Elsewhere," *Boston Globe*, April 16, 2010, A6.

112. Juan Forero, "Venezuela Acquires 1,800 Antiaircraft Missiles from Russia," *Washington Post*, December 12, 2010, A20.

113. Sergei L. Loiko, "Russia to Build Nuclear Plant in Venezuela," *Los Angeles Times*, October 16, 2010, A10.

114. Anne Flaherty, "US Downplays Iran Threat in Latin America," *Washington Post*, April 28, 2010, A12.

115. Michael Spence, *The Next Convergence: The Future of Economic Growth in a Multispeed World* (New York: Farrar, Straus, and Giroux, 2011), 203–5 and 265.

116. Simon Romero, "Venezuela, More Deadly Than Iraq, Wonders Why," *New York Times*, August 22, 2010, A1.

117. Jay Solomon, "Myanmar's Links with Pyongyang Stir Nuclear Fears," *Wall Street Journal*, December 18, 2010, A11.

118. International Crisis Group, "Myanmar: Major Reform Underway," Asia Briefing No. 127 (September 22, 2011), http://www.crisisgroup.org/en /regions/asia/south-east-asia/burma-myanmar/B127-myanmar-major-reform -underway.aspx, accessed November 3, 2011.

119. Thomas Barfield, *Afghanistan: A Cultural and Political History* (Princeton, NJ: Princeton University Press, 2010), 268.

120. *The 9/11 Commission Report: Final Report of the National Commission on Terrorist Attacks Upon the United States* (New York: W. W. Norton, 2004), 153.

121. Mary Pat Flaherty, David B. Ottaway, and James V. Grimaldi, "How Afghanistan Went Unlisted as Terrorist Sponsor, *Washington Post*, November 5, 2001, A1.

122. Benjamin and Simon, *Age of Sacred Terror*, 289–90.

123. Craig Whitlock, "U.S. Provides Backing to Syrian Opposition," *Washington Post*, April 18, 2011, A1.

124. James Glanz and John Markoff, "Internet Detour around Censors," *New York Times*, June 12, 2011, A1.

125. For the importance of democracy in creating peace, international order, and a bulwark against militant Islam, see Charles Hill, *The Trial of a Thousand Years: World Order and Islam* (Stanford, CA: Hoover Institution Press, 2011), 38, 160–61.

Bibliography

The 9/11 Commission Report: Final Report of the National Commission on Terrorist Attacks upon the United States. New York: W. W. Norton, 2004.

Aburish, Saïd K. *Saddam Hussein: The Politics of Revenge.* London: Bloomsbury, 2000.

Adams, James. *The Unnatural Alliance: Israel and South Africa.* London: Quartet Books, 1984.

Ajami, Fouad. *The Dream Palace of the Arabs: A Generation's Odyssey.* New York: Pantheon Books, 1998.

———. *The Foreigner's Gift: The Americans, the Arabs, and the Iraqis in Iraq.* New York: Free Press, 2006.

Albright, David. *Peddling Peril: How the Secret Nuclear Trade Arms America's Enemies.* New York: Free Press, 2010.

Albright, Madeleine. *Madam Secretary.* New York: Miramax Books, 2003.

Al-Khalili, Jim. *The House of Wisdom: How Arabic Science Saved Ancient Knowledge and Gave Us the Renaissance.* New York: Penguin Press, 2011.

Al-Rasheed, Madawi. *A History of Saudi Arabia.* New York: Cambridge University Press, 2010.

Alterman, Jon B. "Postscript: Libya as Harbinger? The U.S.-Libyan Rapprochement." In *Libya since 1969: Qadhafi's Revolution Revisited*, edited by Dirk Vandewalle, 239–48. New York: Palgrave Macmillan, 2008.

Axworthy, Michael. *A History of Iran: Empire of the Mind.* New York: Basic Books, 2008.

Badian, Ernst. *Foreign Clientelae, 264–70 B.C.* Oxford: Clarendon Press, 1958.

Baker, James A. III. *The Politics of Diplomacy: Revolution, War and Peace, 1989–1992.* New York: G. P. Putnam's Sons, 1995.

Baker, James A. III, and Lee H. Hamilton, co-chairs. *The Iraq Study Group Report.* New York: Filiquarian Publishing, 2007.

Baram, Amatzia. "The Iraqi Invasion of Kuwait: Decision-Making in Baghdad." In *Iraq's Road to War*, edited by Amatzia Baram and Barry Rubin, 5–36. New York: St. Martin's Press, 1993.

Barfield, Thomas. *Afghanistan: A Cultural and Political History*. Princeton, NJ: Princeton University Press, 2010.

Barker, Richard B. *Uncle Sam in Barbary: A Diplomatic History*. Gainesville: University of Florida Press, 2004.

Becker, Jasper. *Rogue Regime: Kim Jong Il and the Looming Threat of North Korea*. New York: Oxford University Press, 2005.

Benjamin, Daniel, and Steven Simon. *The Age of Sacred Terror*. New York: Random House, 2002.

Bermudez, Joseph S. Jr. *The Armed Forces of North Korea*. London: I. B. Tauris Publishers, 2001.

Bill, James A. *The Eagle and the Lion: The Tragedy of American-Iranian Relations*. New Haven, CT: Yale University Press, 1988.

Blackwell, Jacob C. *Southeast Asia: Background, Issues and Terrorism*. New York: Nova Science Publishers, 2010.

Bourne, Peter G. *Jimmy Carter: A Comprehensive Biography from Plains to Postpresidency*. New York: Scribner, 1997.

Brookes, Peter. *A Devil's Triangle: Terrorism, Weapons of Mass Destruction, and Rogue States*. Lanham, MD: Rowland and Littlefield, 2005.

Bush, George, and Brent Scowcroft. *A World Transformed*. New York: Alfred A. Knopf, 1998.

Bush, George W. *Decision Points*. New York: Crown Publishers, 2010.

Butler, Richard. *The Greatest Threat: Iraq, Weapons of Mass Destruction, and the Crisis of Global Security*. New York: Public Affairs, 2000.

Chang, Gordon G. *Nuclear Showdown: North Korea Takes on the World*. New York: Random House, 2006.

Chapulina, E. G. "The Barbary Corsairs." *Blackwood's* 328, no. 1982 (December 1980): 483–89.

Cheney, Dick, with Liz Cheney. *In My Time: A Personal and Political Memoir*. New York: Threshold Editions, 2011.

Chol-Hwan, Hang. *Aquariums of Pyongyang: Ten Years in the North Korean Gulag*. New York: Basic Books, 2000.

Cleveland, William L. *A History of the Modern Middle East*. 2nd ed. Boulder, CO: Westview Press, 2000.

Clinton, Bill. *My Life*. New York: Alfred A. Knopf, 2004.

———. "Remarks to Future Leaders of Europe in Brussels, January 9, 1994." In *Public Papers of Presidents, William J. Clinton, Volume I*. Washington, DC: Government Printing Office, 1994.

Cockett, Richard. *Sudan: Darfur and the Failure of an American State*. New Haven, CT: Yale University Press, 2010.

Cohen, Avner. *Israel and the Bomb*. New York: Columbia University Press, 1998.

Collins, Robert O. *A History of Modern Sudan*. New York: Cambridge University Press, 2008.

Combating Terrorism Center. *Al-Qaida's (Mis)Adventures in the Horn Africa*. West Point, NY: Combating Terrorism Center, 2007.

Corera, Gordon. *Shopping for Bombs: Nuclear Proliferation, Global Insecurity, and the Rise and Fall of the A. Q. Khan Network*. New York: Oxford University Press, 2006.

Crabb, Cecil V. *The Doctrines of American Foreign Policy: Their Meaning, Role, and Future*. Baton Rouge: Louisiana State University Press, 1982.

Del Aguila, Juan M. "Cuba: Development, Revolution, and Decay." In *Latin American Politics and Development*, 7th ed., edited by Howard J. Wiarda and Harvey F. Kline, 333–57. Philadelphia: Westview Press, 2011.

Dobbins, James F. *After the Taliban: Nation-Building in Afghanistan*. Washington, DC: Potomac Books, 2008.

Eberstadt, Nicholas. *The End of North Korea*. Washington, DC: AEI Press, 1999.

Ehrenfeld, Rachel. *Funding Evil: How Terrorism Is Financed—and How to Stop It*. Chicago: Bonus Books, 2005.

Falcoff, Mark. *Cuba: The Morning After*. Washington, DC: AEI Press, 2003.

Farouk-Sluglett, Marion, and Peter Sluglett. *Iraq since 1958: From Revolution to Dictatorship*. London: KPI, 1987.

Feith, Douglas J. *War and Decision: Inside the Pentagon at the Dawn of the War on Terrorism*. New York: Harper, 2008.

Fromkin, David. *A Peace to End All Peace: The Fall of the Ottoman Empire and the Creation of the Modern Middle East*. New York: Avon Books, 1989.

Gelman, Harry. "The Soviet Union in the Less Developed World: A Retrospective Overview and Prognosis." In *The Soviet Union and the Third World: The Last Three Decades*, edited by Andrzej Korbonski and Francis Fukuyama, 273–303. Ithaca, NY: Cornell University Press, 1987.

Gittings, John. *The Changing Face of China: From Mao to Markets*. New York: Oxford University Press, 2005.

Golan, Galia. *Soviet Policies in the Middle East: From World War II to Gorbachev*. New York: Cambridge University Press, 1990.

Goodarzi, Jubin M. *Syria and Iran: Diplomatic Alliance and Power Politics in the Middle East*. London: I. B. Tauris, 2009.

Gordon, Michael R., and General Bernard E. Trainor. *Cobra II: The Inside Story of the Invasion and Occupation of Iraq*. New York: Pantheon, 2006.

Haass, Richard N. *The Reluctant Sheriff: The United States after the Cold War*. New York: Council on Foreign Relations, 1997.

Hakakian, Roya. *Assassins of the Turquoise Palace*. New York: Grove Press, 2011.

Harik, Judith P. *Hezbollah: The Changing Face of Terrorism*. London: I. B. Tauris Company, 2005.

Harmon, Christopher C. *Terrorism Today*. London: Frank Cass, 2000.

Hassan, Hamdi A. *The Iraqi Invasion of Kuwait: Religion, Identity and Otherness in the Analysis of War and Conflict*. London: Pluto Press, 1999.

Henriksen, Thomas H. *American Power after the Berlin Wall*. New York: Palgrave Macmillan, 2007.

———. "The Rise and Decline of Rogue States." *Journal of International Affairs* 54, no. 2 (Spring 2004): 349–73.

Hersh, Seymour. *The Samson Option: Israel's Nuclear Arsenal and American Foreign Policy*. New York: Random House, 1991.

Hiro, Dilip. *Desert Shield to Desert Storm: The Second Gulf War*. New York: Authors Choice Press, 2003.

———. *The Essential Middle East: A Comprehensive Guide*. New York: Carroll and Graf Publishers, 2003.

———. *Neighbors, Not Friends: Iraq and Iran after the Gulf Wars*. London: Routledge, 2001.

Hoffman, Bruce. *Inside Terrorism*. New York: Columbia University Press, 1998.

Indyk, Martin. "The Clinton Administration's Approach to the Middle East." In *Challenges to U.S. Interests in the Middle East: Obstacles and Opportunities*. Washington, DC: Washington Institute, 1993.

Ismail, Salwa. "Changing Social Structure, Shifting Alliances and Authoritarianism in Syria." In *Demystifying Syria*, edited by Fred H. Lawson, 13–28. London: London Middle East Institute at SOAS, 2009.

Jaber, Hala. *Hezbollah: Born with a Vengeance*. New York: Columbia University Press, 1997.

Kagan, Kimberly. *The Surge: A Military History*. New York: Encounter, 2009.

Kaufman, Scott. *Plans Unraveled: The Foreign Policy of the Carter Administration*. DeKalb: Northern Illinois University Press, 2008.

Kawczynski, Daniel. *Seeking Gaddafi*. London: Dialogue, 2010.

Keddie, Nikki R. *Modern Iran: Roots and Results of Revolution*. New Haven, CT: Yale University Press, 2006.

Kepel, Gilles. *Jihad: The Trail of Political Islam*. Cambridge, MA: Harvard University Press, 2002.

Kroenig, Matthew. *Exporting the Bomb: Technology Transfer and the Spread of Nuclear Weapons*. Ithaca, NY: Cornell University Press, 2010.

Lake, Anthony. "Confronting Backlash States." *Foreign Affairs* 73, no. 2 (March/April 1994): 45–46.

Laqueur, Walter. *The New Terrorism: Fanaticism and the Arms of Mass Destruction*. New York: Oxford University Press, 1999.

Latell, Brian. *After Fidel: The Inside Story of Castro's Regime and Cuba's Next Leader*. New York: Palgrave Macmillan, 2005.

Lawson, Fred H. *Demystifying Syria*. London: London Middle East Institute at SOAS, 2009.

Lee, Chae-Jin. *China and North Korea*. Stanford, CA: Hoover Institution Press, 1996.

Lesch, David W. *The New Lion of Damascus*. New Haven, CT: Yale University Press, 2005.

Leverett, Flynt. *Inheriting Syria: Bashar's Trial by Fire*. Washington, DC: Brookings Institution Press, 2005.

Litwak, Robert S. *Regime Change: U.S. Strategy through the Prism of 9/11*. Washington, DC: Woodrow Wilson Center Press, 2007.

———. *Rogue States and U.S. Foreign Policy: Containment after the Cold War*. Washington, DC: Woodrow Wilson Center Press, 2000.

Lyons, Jonathan. *The House of Wisdom: How the Arabs Transformed Western Civilization.* London: Bloomsbury, 2009.

Mann, James. *The Rise of the Vulcans: The History of Bush's War Cabinet.* New York: Viking, 2004.

Marcum, John. *The Angolan Revolution: Volume II, Exile Politics and Guerrilla Warfare, 1962–1976.* Cambridge, MA: MIT Press, 1978.

Martinez, Luis. *The Libyan Paradox.* New York: Columbia University Press, 2007.

Mattes, Hanspeter. "Formal and Informal Authority in Libya since 1969." In *Libya since 1969: Qadhafi's Revolution Revisited,* edited by Dirk Vandewalle, 55–81. New York: Palgrave Macmillan, 2008.

Mazarr, Michael J. *North Korea and the Bomb: A Case Study in Nonproliferation.* New York: St. Martin's Press, 1995.

McDougall, Walter A. *Promised Land, Crusader State: The American Encounter with the World since 1776.* Boston: Houghton Mifflin Company, 1997.

Michaels, Jim. *A Chance in Hell: The Men Who Triumphed over Iraq's Deadliest City and Turned the Tide of War.* New York: St. Martin's Press, 2010.

Milani, Abbas. *The Myth of the Great Satan.* Stanford, CA: Hoover Institution Press, 2010.

Myers, B. R. *The Cleanest Race: How North Koreans See Themselves—And Why It Matters.* Brooklyn, NY: Melville House, 2010.

Nasr, Vali. *The Shia Revival: How Conflicts in Islam Will Shape the Future.* New York: W. W. Norton and Company, 2006.

Norton, August Richard. *Hezbollah: A Short History.* Princeton, NJ: Princeton University Press.

Pape, Robert A. *Dying to Win: The Strategic Logic of Suicide Terrorism.* New York: Random House, 2005.

Pillar, Paul R. *Intelligence and U.S. Foreign Policy: Iraq, 9/11, and Misguided Reform.* New York: Columbia University Press, 2011.

Pollack, Kenneth M. *The Persian Puzzle: The Conflict between Iran and America.* New York: Random House, 2005.

———. *The Threatening Storm: The Case for Invading Iraq.* New York: Random House, 2002.

Prados, John. *Presidents' Secret Wars: CIA and Pentagon Covert Operations from World War II through the Persian Gulf.* Chicago: Ivan R. Dee, 1996.

Primakov, Yevgeny. *Russia and the Arabs: Behind the Scenes in the Middle East from the Cold War to the Present.* New York: Basic Books, 2009.

Qassem, Naim. *Hizbullah: The Story from Within.* London: SAQI, 2005.

Rabinovich, Itamar. *The View from Damascus: State, Political Community and Foreign Relations in Twentieth-Century Syria.* London: Vallentine Mitchell, 2008.

Rabkin, Rhoda P. *Cuban Politics: The Revolutionary Experiment.* New York: Praeger, 1991.

Reiss, Mitchell. *Bridled Ambition: Why Countries Constrain Their Nuclear Capabilities.* Washington, DC: Woodrow Wilson Center Press, 1995.

Rice, Condoleezza. *No Higher Honor: A Memoir of My Years in Washington*. New York: Crown, 2011.

———. "Promoting the National Interest." *Foreign Affairs* 79, no. 1 (January/February 2000): 61.

Richardson, Louise. *What Terrorists Want*. New York: Random House, 2006.

Ronen, Yehudit. *Qaddafi's Libya in World Politics*. Boulder, CO: Lynne Rienner Publishers, 2008.

Rubin, Barry. "The Gulf States and the Iran-Iraq War." In *The Iran-Iraq War: Impact and Implications*, edited by Efraim Karsh, 47–64. London: Macmillan, 1989.

———. *The Truth about Syria*. New York: Palgrave Macmillan, 2007.

Rumsfeld, Donald. *Known and Unknown: A Memoir*. New York: Sentinel, 2011.

Ryan, Paul B. *The Iranian Rescue Mission: Why It Failed*. Annapolis, MD: Naval Institute Press, 1985.

Saad-Ghorayeb, Amal. *Hizbu'llah: Politics and Religion*. London: Pluto Press, 2002.

Safford, Frank, and Marco Palacios. *Colombia: Fragmented Land, Divided Society*. New York: Oxford University Press, 2002.

Salloukh, Bassel F. "Demystifying Syrian Foreign Policy under Bashar al-Asad." In *Demystifying Syria*, edited by Fred H. Lawson, 159–79. London: London Middle East Institute at SOAS, 2009.

Schoen, Douglas, and Michael Rowan. *The Threat Closer to Home: Hugo Chávez and the War against America*. New York: Free Press, 2009.

Seale, Patrick. *Abu Nidal: A Gun for Hire*. New York: Random House, 1992.

Shay, Shaul. *The Axis of Evil: Iran, Hezbollah and the Palestinian Terror*. New Brunswick, NJ: Transaction Publishers, 2005.

Shultz, George P. *Turmoil and Triumph: My Years as Secretary of State*. New York: Charles Scribner's Sons, 1993.

Sifry, Micah L., and Christopher Cerf, eds. *The Gulf War Reader: History, Documents, Opinion*. New York: Random House, 1991.

Simons, Geoff. *Colombia: A Brutal History*. London: Saqi, 2004.

Smith, Simon. "Piracy in Early British America." *History Today* 46, no. 5 (May 1996): 30–33.

Sofaer, Abraham D. *The Best Defense? Legitimacy & Preventive Force*. Stanford, CA: Hoover Institution Press, 2010.

Spence, Michael. *The Next Convergence: The Future of Economic Growth in a Multispeed World*. New York: Farrar, Straus, and Giroux, 2011.

Stark, Rodney. *God's Battalions: The Case for the Crusades*. New York: HarperCollins, 2009.

Staten, Clifford L. *The History of Cuba*. Westport, CT: Greenwood Press, 2003.

Stern, Sheldon M. *Averting "The Final Failure."* Stanford, CA: Stanford University Press, 2003.

Sultan, Khaled Bin, with Patrick Seale. *Warrior: A Personal View of the Gulf War by the Joint Forces Commander*. New York: HarperCollins, 1995.

Sweig, Julia E. *Cuba: What Everyone Needs to Know*. New York: Oxford University Press, 2009.

Taheri, Amir. *The Persian Night: Iran under the Khomeinist Revolution*. New York: Encounter Books, 2009.

Tanner, Stephen. *Afghanistan: A Military History from Alexander the Great to the Fall of the Taliban*. New York: Da Capo Press, 2002.

Tanter, Raymond. *Rogue Regimes: Terrorism and Proliferation*. New York: St. Martin's Press, 1998.

Teitelbaum, Joshua. *What Iranian Leaders Really Say about Doing Away with Israel*. Jerusalem, Israel: Jerusalem Center for Public Affairs, 2008.

Thucydides. *History of the Peloponnesian War*. Translated by Rex Warner. London: Penguin Books, 1972.

Tinniswood, Adrian. *Pirates of Barbary: Corsairs, Conquests, and Captivity in the Seventeenth-Century Mediterranean*. New York: Riverhead Books, 2010.

Tripp, Charles. *A History of Iraq*. New York: Cambridge University Press, 2002.

Vandewalle, Dirk. *A History of Modern Libya*. New York: Cambridge University Press, 2006.

———, ed. *Libya since 1969: Qadhafi's Revolution Revisited*. New York: Palgrave Macmillan, 2008.

Wehrey, Frederic, David E. Thaler, and Nora Bensahel. *Dangerous but Not Omnipotent: Exploring the Reach and Limitations of Iranian Power in the Middle East*. Santa Monica, CA: RAND, 2009.

Wheelan, Joseph. *Jefferson's War: America's First War on Terror, 1801–1805*. New York: Carroll and Graf Publishers, 2003.

Wiarda, Howard J., and Harvey F. Kline, eds. *Latin American Politics and Development*. 7th ed. Philadelphia: Westview Press, 2011.

Wiegele, Thomas C. *The Clandestine Building of Libya's Chemical Weapons Factory: A Study in International Collusion*. Carbondale: Southern Illinois University Press, 1992.

Wit, Joel S., Daniel B. Poneman, and Robert L. Gallucci. *Going Critical: The First North Korean Crisis*. Washington, DC: Brookings Institution Press, 2004.

Woodward, Bob. *Plan of Attack*. New York: Simon and Schuster, 2004.

Wurmser, David. *Tyranny's Ally: America's Failure to Defeat Saddam Hussein*. Washington, DC: American Enterprise Institute, 1999.

Wynbrandt, James. *A Brief History of Saudi Arabia*. New York: Facts on File, 2004.

Zatarain, Lee Allen. *The Tanker War: America's First Conflict with Iran, 1987–1988*. Philadelphia: Casemate, 2008.

Index

Abbasi, Fereydoon, 99
Abd Nasser, Gamal, 36, 147
Abdullah (prince), 157
ABM, *see* Anti-Ballistic Missile Treaty
A-bomb, *see* atomic bomb
Abu Nidal Organization, 18, 148, 156, 163, 174
Abu Salim Prison, 157
Abu Sayyaf, 53
Achaemenid Empire, 64
Additional Protocol, 90
Aesop, 3
Afghanistan, 13, 15, 57, 59, 80–1, 126, 183–5
   foreign policy toward, 56
   Iran and, 86, 87
   Red Army and, 154, 174
   resistance of, 157
   Soviet invasion of, 17
   withdrawal from, 101
Africa
   North Africa, 7–8, 120, 149, 151, 156
   piracy of, 8
   South Africa, 11, 12, 15, 153, 155
African Union (AU), 155
Agreed Framework, 113–16, 118, 127, 131
Ahmadinejad, Mahmoud, 63, 91, 93, 95–6, 102, 181–2
Ahmad Shah, 65
AIOC, *see* Anglo-Iranian Oil Company
air diplomacy, 53
Alawites, 161, 164
Albright, Madeleine, 3, 22, 47, 51, 79, 116
American imperialism, 21
American Power after the Berlin Wall, 1

Anglo-Iranian Oil Company (AIOC), 66
Anglo-Persian Oil Company, 66
anti-Americanism, 20, 68, 70, 71, 81, 183
anti-American states, 17
Anti-Ballistic Missile Treaty (ABM), 89, 165
anticommunism, 14–15
anti-Iranian sanctions, 76
anti-Zionism, 71
apartheid regime, 12
APEC, *see* Asia Pacific Economic Cooperation
Arab Cooperation Council, 36
Arab League, 37, 173
Arab Middle East, 4, 36, 147
Arab Muslims, 6
Arab Socialist Party, 161
Arab Spring, 4, 27, 61, 100, 146, 158, 187
Arafat, Yasir, 40
Asia Pacific Economic Cooperation (APEC), 129
al-Assad, Bashar, 161, 172, 185
al-Assad, Hafiz, 161
Assyria (empire), 30
Ataturk, Kemal, 66
atomic bomb (A-bomb), 11, 12
AU, *see* African Union
Austria, 102
authoritarianism, 16
axis of evil, 17, 44, 117, 119
ayatollahs, 17, 48, 69–70, 77–8, 85
Al-Azhar University, 95

Baath Party, 26, 32, 34, 48, 161, 163
Babylon (empire), 30
backlash states, 22

Baghdad, Iraq, 3, 31
  coercive diplomacy and, 40
  credit guarantees to, 35
  debt of, 34, 55
  military of, 43
  nuclear ambitions of, 44
  oil and, 39
Baghdad Pact, 32
Baker, James, 35, 37, 40, 42
Banco Delta Asia (BDA), 122–3, 130
Ban Ki-moon, 128–9
Bank Markazi, 97
al-Banna, Sabri Khalil, 18
Barbary Corsairs, 7
Battle of Marathon, 64
Bay of Pigs, 47, 179
bazaaris (merchants), 68, 70
BBC *China* (cargo ship), 152–3
BDA, *see* Banco Delta Asia
Beirut, 171
Belgrade, 23, 25
Berlin Wall, 1, 4, 30
bin Laden, Osama, 80, 83, 174, 175,
    183, 184
biological weapons (BW), 176
Black September, 174
Blair, Tony, 57
Blix, Hans, 53, 107, 108
Bogotá, 181
Bolivar, Simon, 179
Bolivarian Revolution, 180
Bolivia, 182
Bolsheviks, 9–10, 18, 64
Bolshevik Revolution, 87
Bolton, John R., 127, 136
Bosnia, 25
Brazil, 25
Brezhnev, Leonid, 149
Britain, 10
  Iran and, 65–8, 79
  Iraq and, 31
  Libya and, 146
  as nuclear power, 11
  Operation Desert Fox and, 52
  Spain and, 9
Burke, Edmund, 145
Burma Spring, 183
Bush, George H. W., 41, 77, 81, 107, 109
  Gorbachev and, 30
  Hussein and, 19, 34–7
  Iraq and, 38, 39

Bush, George W., 29, 43, 120, 153, 175
  Afghanistan and, 80
  axis of evil and, 17, 44
  Iran and, 89, 90, 91
  Iraq War and, 54–6, 58
  National Security Strategy of, 23
  North Korea and, 19, 117–19
  preventive war doctrine of, 30
  State of the Union address by, 81
Butler, Richard, 50
BW, *see* biological weapons

Camp David accords, 36, 53, 169
Carlos the Jackal, 174, 175
Carter, Jimmy, 70, 71–2, 112, 150
Castro, Fidel, 15, 16, 47, 176, 177, 178
Castro, Raul, 177–8
Cato, Marcus Porcius, 55
CCC, *see* Commodity Credit Corporation
Cedar Revolution, 167
cell phone networks, 187
CENTCOM, *see* Central Command
Center of Nonproliferation Studies, 25
Central Command (CENTCOM), 39
Chavez, Hugo, 53, 177, 178, 179,
    180, 182
chavismo, 180
chemical warfare (CW), 167
chemical weapons, 33, 152, 175
  Syria and, 167–9
Chemical Weapons Convention, 153, 167
Cheney, Dick, 55, 129, 135
China, 24, 53, 88, 100, 140, 141, 143
  North Korea and, 27
  US-China Economic Commission, 128
  see also People's Republic of China
Chinese Communist Party, 11, 114
Chinese Nationalists, 11
Chun Doo Hwan, 113
Clinton, Hillary Rodham, 137, 159
Clinton, William J. "Bill," 22, 29, 44–5,
    103, 112, 162, 184
  dual containment and, 47–9, 78–9
  North Korea and, 108–10
coalition of willing, 59
coercive diplomacy, 40
Cohen, William S., 55
Cold War, 1–2, 4, 5, 18, 25, 32, 54, 64,
    114, 161
  rivalry and, 13
  Syria in post-Cold War, 164–7

colonialism, 147
   American imperialism, 21
   French, 161
Commission on Intelligence Capabilities of
   the United States Regarding Weapons
   of Mass Destruction, 58
Commodity Credit Corporation
   (CCC), 35
communism, 20, 26
   anticommunism, 14–15
   fight against, 14
   outposts, 16
   Soviet Union and, 18–19
Communist Party, 154, 178
   Chinese Communist Party, 11, 114
competition, East-West, 13
Comprehensive Safeguard Agreement,
   168–9
Comprehensive Test Ban Treaty, 153
computer viruses, 187
Congress, 50, 92
containment, 27, 51, 62, 120, 122,
   142, 186
   dual, 47–9, 78–9
containment plus, 48, 54
Contras (guerrillas), 75
credit guarantees, 35
Crusades, 160–1
Cuba, 16, 20, 26–7, 173–6, 176–9, 186
   Bay of Pigs, 47
   Russia and, 15
   terrorism and, 19
Cuban missile crisis, 14, 16
Cuellar, Javier Perez de, 42
CW, *see* chemical warfare
cyber warfare, 187
Czech Republic, 25, 89

Damascus, 160, 164, 166, 172
Darfur, 174
Dawa Party, 86
defining rogues, 22–3
demagogues, 21
demilitarized zone (DMZ), 11
Democratic People's Republic of Korea
   (DPRK), 16, 24–5, 103–5, 114, 119
democratic states, 22
Deng Xiaoping, 114
denuclearization, 95, 96, 130, 155
Department of State, U.S., 18, 36
Desert One, 72

deterrence, 27, 48, 55, 120, 122, 154, 186
dictatorial rule, 19
dictatorships, 21, 34, 186
direct conflict, 186
dirty bombs, 126
DMZ, *see* demilitarized zone
Dominican Republic, 14
DPRK, *see* Democratic People's Republic
   of Korea
DPRK-Japan Declaration of 2002, 124
drug trafficking, 124
dual containment, 47–9, 78–9
dual-use, 33
Dubai, 87, 96

economic sanctions, 47
Ecuador, 182
EFPs, *see* explosively formed penetrators
Egypt, 14, 39, 53, 149
   Hezbollah and, 85
   Hussein and, 34
Egyptian Islamic Jihad, 85, 175
Eisenhower, Dwight D., 67
ElBaradei, Mohamed, 133
England, *see* Britain
enlargement, of democratic states, 22
Ethiopia, 124
ethnic violence, 172
European Economic Community, 151
European Union, 101, 151
explosively formed penetrators (EFPs), 86
Export Administration Act, 18

Facebook, 186
Fadh (king), 41
Faisal II (king), 31–2
FAR, *see* Revolutionary Armed Forces
FARC, *see* Revolutionary Armed Forces of
   Colombia
Farouk (king), 147
February 13 agreement, 130–3
female education, 69
FEW, *see* Fighter Wing Equivalents
Fifth Fleet, 83
Fighter Wing Equivalents (FEW), 111
Finland, 6
Firdos Square, 3–4
fire-and-forget foreign policy, 54
first-strike manifesto, 57
Foreign Affairs, 55
foreign buttressing, 186

foreign policy, 1, 48, 145
  Afghanistan and, 56
  anti-Iraq, 5
  fire-and-forget, 54
  of Iran, 72
  state terrorism and, 18
France, 10, 44, 46, 53
  colonialism of, 161
  as nuclear power, 11

Gates, Robert, 142, 145
Gaudeloupe, 9
Gauls, 6
Gaza Strip, 75, 85
GCC, *see* Gulf Cooperation Council
Geneva accords, 33
Glaspie, April, 38
Golan Heights, 162
Gorbachev, Mikhail, 30, 154
Grand Bargain, 93
Great Satan, 21, 68
Greeks, 5–6, 30, 64
Green Book (Qaddafi), 147
Green Movement, 95, 97, 99
Grenada, 14
guardianship of the jurist, 71
Guevara, Ernesto "Che," 15, 176
Gulf Cooperation Council (GCC), 82
Gulf of Sidra, 150
Gulliverization, 26

Hamas, 75, 82, 85, 87, 97, 162, 182
Hammurabi Division, 57
Hannibal (Carthaginian warrior-general), 6
hard power, 187
Hariri, Rafik, 166
Hekmatyar, Gulbuddin, 81
Hermit Kingdom, 105, 119, 123
HEU, *see* highly enriched uranium
Hezbollah (Party of God), 18, 19, 74–5, 87, 167, 169–70, 173, 182
  Damascus and, 165, 166
  Egypt and, 85
  Hussein and, 60
  Islamic Republic and, 79, 84
  Kataib Hezbollah, 86
  Marine Corps and, 41
  Syria and, 163
Hezbollah-Israel War, 84, 124
highly enriched uranium (HEU), 90, 91, 117
Hill, Christopher, 125, 129, 132, 135

Hispaniola, 9
History of the Peloponnesian War (Thucydides), 5
Hitler, Adolf, 10
hostis humani generis (enemies of all mankind), 9
House of Assad, 161, 165, 171
House of Saud, 83
Hu Jintao, 177
human rights, abuses of, 19, 134
Human Rights Act of 2004, 120
Hussein, Saddam, 23, 29, 30, 32–4, 43, 47, 88, 142, 164
  Baathist Party and, 26
  Bush, G. H. W., and, 19, 34–7
  Egypt and, 34
  Hezbollah and, 60
  military and, 73
  renegade regime of, 19
  resurrection of, 49–54
  statue of, 3–4

IAEA, *see* International Atomic Energy Agency
ICBMs, *see* intercontinental ballistic missiles
IDF, *see* Israel Defense Forces
imperialism, American, 21
India, 25, 100
  nuclear weapons and, 13
indigenous national liberation fronts, 14
infitada (Palestinian uprising), 57
interaction, 23–5
intercontinental ballistic missiles (ICBMs), 89
Internal Security Forces, 141
International Atomic Energy Agency (IAEA), 44, 88, 106, 168
International Criminal Court, 172
Iran, 1–2, 5, 23, 24, 63–102
  anti-Iranian sanctions, 76
  dual containment and, 78–9
  embassy takeover by, 71–2
  foreign policy of, 72
  history of, 64–6
  Iraq and, 32–3, 86, 91–4
  Israel and, 12
  long-range missile quests, 87–9
  modernization of, 65
  negotiations with, 95
  nuclear arms and, 25–6, 87–91

Obama and, 94, 96, 97, 98
oil of, 67
Persian Gulf War and, 77–8
presidential election of, 95
proxy movements in, 81–7
Russia and, 17
Saudi Arabia and, 65
September 11 and, 80–1
Soviet Union and, 17, 63, 65, 67
Syria and, 169–71
terrorism and, 19
Venezuela and, 181
see also Islamic Republic of Iran
Iran-Contra scandal, 75–7
Iran-Iraq War, 64, 73–4, 88
Iraq, 1–2, 16, 23, 24, 29–62
anti-Iraq foreign policy, 5
background of, 30–2
Baghdad, 3, 31, 34–5, 39–40, 43–4, 55
Britain and, 31
dual containment and, 47–9
economic isolation of, 48
Iran and, 32–3, 86, 91–4
Kuwait and, 37–40
natural resources of, 30–1
no-fly zones in, 45–7
nuclear arms and, 44, 58
Operation Desert Shield, 41–3
Operation Desert Storm, 43–5
Operation Iraqi Freedom, 59
Syria and, 164
terrorism and, 19
Iraq Liberation Act of 1998, 50
Iraq Study Group, 92
Iraq War, 4–5, 26, 54–6, 58–9, 61–2
IRGC, *see* Islamic Revolutionary Guards
Corps
IRGC-Quds Force, 86
Irish Republican Army, 18
IRISL, *see* Islamic Republic Shipping Lines
Ironside, William, 65
Islamabad, 13
Islamic Jihad, 162
Islamic Republic of Iran, 17, 32–3, 44,
63–4, 76, 81–2, 94
Islamic Republic Party, 70
Islamic Republic Shipping Lines (IRISL),
96–7
Islamic Revolutionary Guards Corps
(IRGC), 70, 171
Islamic Supreme Council of Iraq, 86

Israel, 14, 42, 81, 93, 94
Hezbollah and, 84, 124
Iran and, 12
nuclear weapons and, 11–12
Palestine and, 36
Israel Defense Forces (IDF), 98, 162
Italy, 146

jamahiriyya (state of the masses), 148
Jamaica, 9
Japan, 10, 39, 124–5
Nagasaki, 126
North Korea and, 112
Jefferson, Thomas, 7
Jewish Community Center, 84
Joint Declaration on the Denuclearization
of the Korean Peninsula, 108
Joint Statement of Principles, 122, 130
Jordan, 36, 40
Juan Carlos I (king), 182
juche (spirit of self-reliance), 105

Kang Seok-Ju, 117
Karine A (cargo ship), 81
Kashmir, 13
Kataib Hezbollah (Brigades of the Party of
God), 86
KEDO, *see* Korean Energy Development
Organization
Kelly, James A., 117
Kennedy, John F., 47
Kerzai, Hamid, 80
Khamanei, Ali Husseini, 77, 83, 90–1, 102
Khan, Abdul Qadeer, 90, 117, 128, 152,
168, 183
Khan, Ismail, 80
Khartoum, 174, 176
Khatami, Mohammad, 79, 90
Khobar Towers, 83–4
Khomeini, Ruhollah, 70, 71, 72, 78–9, 155
Khuzestan, 65, 72
Al Kibar, 132
Kim Dae Jung, 115
Kim Il Sung, 103, 104, 105, 108, 112, 113
Kim Jong Il, 109, 113–15, 119, 135,
141, 185
Kim Kye-gwan, 129
Kingdom of Kush, 174
Kingdom of Pontus, 6
Koizumi, Junichiro, 112
Korea, *see* North Korea; South Korea

Korean Central News Agency, 140
Korean Energy Development Organization
    (KEDO), 115
Korean Mining and Industrial Development
    Corporation, 130
Korean People's Army, 105
Korean War, 104, 110, 112, 131
Korean Workers' Party, 105, 134, 137
Kosovo crisis, 23, 25, 52
Kremlin, 14, 15, 16, 20, 55, 106
Kurdistan, 45–6
Kurds, 29, 31, 33, 43, 45, 50, 59
Kuwait, 19, 30, 32, 34–5, 43, 53, 73, 77, 82
    Iraq and, 37–40

Lake, Anthony, 22
Land of the Two Holy Places, 83
Latin America, 15, 181, 182
    see also specific countries
League of Nations, 10, 31, 161
Lebanon, 19, 60, 74, 75, 84, 86, 170
Lee Myung-bak, 136
Lefkowitz, Jay, 120
Lenin, Vladimir, 9, 18
lesser rogue states, 27, 145–88
liberation-technology movement, 188
Libya, 5, 16, 17, 27, 146–60, 186
    nuclear disclosures of, 153
    oil and, 155
    terrorism and, 19, 149–50, 151
    violence in, 148
    WMDs and, 152–4
Libyan People's Bureau, 150
light-water reactors (LWR), 109
literacy, 69
Luck, Gary, 111
luxury goods, 127
LWR, see light-water reactors

Macau Monetary Authority, 132
Machiavelli, Niccolò, 3
Madison, James, 7
Majles (national assembly), 65, 67
Malaysia, 96
Mandela, Nelson, 155
Maoists, 64
maritime terrorism, 7, 9
Marshall Plan, 13
Marxism, 15, 16
McChrystal, Stanley A., 87
Mecca, 52, 83

Medina, 52, 83
Medvedev, Dmitry, 181
al-Megrahi, Abdel Basset Ali, 156
MEK, see Mujahideen-e Khalq
Mesopotamia, 30
Middle East, 61, 121
    Arab, 4, 36, 147
    popular uprisings in, 99
    see also specific countries
Mikati, Najib, 167
military operations, 1
Milošević, Slobodan, 23, 52, 187
mineral wealth, 140
missiles
    Anti-Ballistic Missile Treaty, 89, 165
    Cuban missile crisis, 14, 16
    long-range quests, 87–9
    North Korea and, 23–4
    Taepodong, 24, 116–17, 124
Missile Technology Control Regime, 153
modernization, of Iran, 65
Monitoring and Verification Commission,
    UN (UNMOVIC), 53
Morgan, Henry, 9
Morgenthau, Hans, 145
Mossadeq, Mohammad, 67, 68, 70, 71, 95
Mosul province, of Iraq, 31
MPLA, see Popular Movement for the
    Liberation of Angola
Mubarak, Hosni, 36, 85, 100, 150, 175
Mugniyeh, Imad, 84
Muhammad (prophet), 64
mujahideen (Islamic holy warriors), 7,
    157, 174
Mujahideen-e Khalq (MEK), 89–90
Mukhabbarat, 48–9
Muslims, 70
    Arab, 6
    feluccas, 7
    Shia, 31, 43, 45–6, 59–60, 64, 71, 83
    Shiites, 17, 29, 64, 71, 73–4, 81–4, 161
    Sunni, 31, 43, 59–60, 64, 81, 84, 164
Muslim Brotherhood, 164, 165
Myanmar, 182–3

Nagasaki, 126
Nasrallah, Hassan, 85, 166
Nasser, Gamal Abdul, 147
Natanz facility, 89–90, 92, 98, 101
National Defense Commission, 113, 141
National Intelligence Estimate (NIE), 57–8

nationalism, 37
  Arab, 148
  Iranian, 67, 72
National Security Strategy, 23, 57
NATO, see North Atlantic Treaty
  Organization
natural resources, of Iraq, 30–1
Nazi Germany, 10, 66
Nicaragua, 182
NIE, see National Intelligence Estimate
9/11, see September 11, 2001
Nintendo warfare, 43
Nixon, Richard M., 69
Nixon Doctrine, 69
Nizar Hindawi, 163
Noel, Cleo A., 174
no-fly zones, 45–7
nonrogue states, 11–13
North Africa, 7–8, 120, 149, 151, 156
North Atlantic Treaty Organization
  (NATO), 8, 13, 23, 45, 80, 159
North Korea, 1–2, 16, 19, 20, 22, 23, 26,
  82, 103–44
  bargaining with, 111–17
  Bush, G. W., and, 19, 117–19
  China and, 27
  Clinton, W. J., and, 108–10
  emergence as rogue state, 106–8
  February 13 agreement and, 130–3
  history of, 104–6
  mineral wealth of, 140
  as missile-export central, 23–4
  Obama and, 136–42
  October 3 agreement and, 133–6
  Six-Party Talks and, 121–2
  two-simultaneous-conflicts dilemma
    and, 110–11
  see also Democratic People's Republic of
    Korea
North Yemen, 18
NPT, see Nuclear Nonproliferation Treaty
nuclear arms, 4–5, 11–13, 21
  denuclearization, 95, 96, 130, 155
  Iran and, 25–6, 87–91
  Iraq and, 44, 58
  Libya and, 153
  Syria and, 167–9
Nuclear Nonproliferation Treaty (NPT),
  88, 106, 109, 113, 130, 172
nuclear option, 97
Nunn, Sam, 127

OAS, see Organization of the American States
Obama, Barack, 89, 121, 142, 159, 171,
  172, 178
  Iran and, 94, 96, 97, 98
  Iraq and, 62
  North Korea and, 136–42
  Saudi Arabia and, 83
October 3 agreement, 133–6
October Revolution, 9
oil, 38–40, 66, 83, 97–8, 146, 164, 180
  Iranian, 67
  Libya and, 155
Omar, Mullah Mohammed, 183–4
OPEC, see Organization of Petroleum
  Exporting Countries
Operation Ajax, 68
Operation Desert Fox, 46, 51, 54
Operation Desert Shield, 41–3
Operation Desert Storm, 43–5
Operation Eagle Claw, 72
Operation El Dorado Canyon, 151
Operation Iraqi Freedom, 59
Operation Praying Mantis, 73
Operation Provide Comfort, 45
Operation Smoking Dragon, 122
Operation Staunch, 74
Organization of Petroleum Exporting
  Countries (OPEC), 53, 98
Organization of the American States
  (OAS), 177
Osirik nuclear facility, 44
Ottoman Empire, 31, 161
Ozal, Turgut, 40

packinko gambling parlors, 123
Pahlavi, Shah Mohammed Razi, 63
Pahlavi dynasty, 65
Pakistan, 118
  nuclear weapons and, 13
Palestine, 53
  Black September, 174
  infitada, 57
  Israel and, 36
Palestinian Liberation Organization, 18, 40
Panama, 37
Pan Am Flight, 17, 103, 151, 156, 158
parallel command, 41
Parthian Empire, 64
Party of God, see Hezbollah
Pashtunwali, 184
Pax Atomica, 106

Pentagon, 45, 110, 121, 159
People's Army, 141
People's Democratic Republic of Yemen, 18–19
Peoples' Liberation Army (PLA), 128
People's Republic of China (PRC), 11, 24, 104, 120
perestroika (restructuring), 154
Perry, William, 110, 116
Persia, 17, 64
Persian Gulf War, 42–3, 44, 52, 57, 77–8, 165
Peru, 181
Petraeus, David, 60
Philippines, 53
piracy, 8
Piracy Reporting Center of the International Maritime Bureau, 8
PLA, see Peoples' Liberation Army
Plan Colombia, 181
planes operation, 184
Poland, 25
Politics among Nations (Morgenthau), 145
Pollack, Kenneth, 56
Popular Movement for the Liberation of Angola (MPLA), 15
Powell, Colin, 39, 43, 54, 56, 58, 80, 107, 165
PRC, see People's Republic of China
Pretoria, 12
preventive-strike strategy, 175
proxy states, 14, 17
Public Authority for the Assessment of Damages Resulting from Iraqi Aggression, 39
Pyongyang, 16, 19, 23, 24, 25, 103–4, 106, 125, 127

al-Qaddafi, Muammar, 124, 146, 147–51, 153–5
    image of, 156
    political downfall of, 158–60
al-Qaeda, 53, 56, 59–60, 83–4, 100–1, 165–6
Qajar dynasty, 65
Qasim, Abd al-Karim, 31–2, 34
Quds Force, 171

Radio Free Asia, 118
Radio Free Iraq, 50
Rafsanjani, al Akbar Hashemi, 76
Reagan, Ronald, 15, 33, 72, 74–7, 106, 148–9, 150
realpolitiks, 81
Red Army, 13, 30, 66, 154, 174

repression, 186
Republican Guards, 38, 45, 50, 57, 78
Republic of Iraq, 52
Republic of Korea (ROK), 11, 15, 19, 103, 115
Republic of South Sudan, 174
Republic of Yemen, 19
reset policy, 172
Resolution 661, 41
Resolution 678, 42
Resolution 687, 46
Resolution 688, 45
Resolution 731, 151
Resolution 1559, 166
Resolution 1718, 127, 137–8
Resolution 1874, 139
Revolutionary Armed Forces (FAR), 176
Revolutionary Armed Forces of Colombia (FARC), 180–1
Reza Khan, 65, 66
Reza Shah, Mohammad, 68
Ricciardone, Frank, 51
Rice, Condoleezza, 55, 129, 130, 135
rivalry, 13
Riyadh, 170
Rodong Sinmum, 134
Roh Moo-hyun, 119, 120, 128
ROK, see Republic of Korea
Romans, 6, 64
Roosevelt, Franklin D., 10
Rubin, Barry, 171
Rumsfeld, Donald, 33, 55, 57
Russia
    ABM treaty and, 89, 165
    communist revolution in, 18
    Cuba and, 15
    Iran and, 17
    military of, 65
    October Revolution, 9
    Security Council and, 55
    trade with, 10
Russian Federation, 25, 53, 172

Sadat, Anwar, 149
al-Sadr, Moqtada, 86
Safeguards Agreements, 90
Sandinistas, 15
al-Sanusi, Muhammad Idris al-Mahdi, 146
al-Saud, Khaled Bin Sultan (prince), 41
Saudi Arabia, 31, 39–42, 53, 82–4, 101, 157
    Iran and, 65
    Obama and, 83
SAVAK, 68, 70

Schwarzkopf, Norman, 39, 41
seafaring states, 7–8
sectarian violence, 172
Security Council, 43, 47, 53, 58, 97, 101, 110, 159
    Resolution 661, 41
    Resolution 678, 42
    Resolution 687, 46
    Resolution 688, 45
    Resolution 731, 151
    Resolution 1559, 166
    Resolution 1718, 127, 137–8
    Resolution 1874, 139
September 2001, 11, 22, 30, 55–6, 80–1, 117, 183–4
Serbia, 23, 26, 52
SEZ, see special economic zones
shari'a law, 174
Shia, 31, 43, 45–6, 59–60, 64, 71, 83
Shiites, 17, 29, 64, 71, 73–4, 81–4, 161
Shultz, George, 150
Siemans, 98
Six Day War, 162
Six-Party Talks, 121–2, 129, 130, 133, 138, 141, 143
slant drilling, 37
slave trading, 7
smart sanctions, 54, 56
smart weapons, 187
socialism, 16
Socialist People's Libyan Arab Jamahiriyya, 148
Somalia, 8, 124
South Africa, 11, 15, 155
    apartheid in, 12
    atomic bomb and, 12
    postaparteid, 153
South Korea, 11, 121
    atomic bomb and, 12
South Yemen, 18, 173
Soviet Union, 2, 6, 9
    Afghanistan and, 17
    dissolution of, 22
    Iran and, 17, 63, 65, 67
    progeny of, 19–22
    terrorism and, 18–19
    see also Russia
Spain, 119, 182
    England and, 9
special economic zones (SEZ), 120, 128
Special Operations Forces, 166
Special Tribunal, UN, 166

Stalin, Josef, 9, 104
state organization, theory of, 147
states of concern, 22
"State Sponsors of Terrorism," 19
state terrorism, 18
street protests, 170
Stuxnet software code, 98, 99
Sudan, 27, 173–6
    terrorism and, 19
Suez Canal, 66
suffrage, 69
sugar, 27
Sumer (empire), 30
Sunni Arabs, 31, 43, 59, 60, 64, 81, 84, 164
sunshine policy, 115, 120
supernotes, 122
Supreme People's Assembly, 113, 141–2
Syria, 14, 16, 27, 82, 132
    chemical and nuclear weapons, 167–9
    Hezbollah and, 163
    historical overview of, 160–2
    Iran and, 169–71
    Iraq and, 164
    post-Cold War, 164–7
    terrorism and, 19, 162–4
Syrian Arab Republic, 160

Taepodong (missile), 24, 116–17, 124
Taiwan, 11, 25
    atomic bomb and, 12
Taliban, 80, 183, 184
Tanker War, 73, 76
Team Spirit (military exercises), 107, 108, 111
Tel Aviv, 12
terrorism, 17–18, 21
    Libya and, 19, 149–50, 151
    maritime, 7, 9
    Pan Am Flight 17, 103, 151, 156, 158
    September 11, 22, 30, 55–6, 80–1, 117, 183–4
    Soviet Union and, 18–19
    Syria and, 19, 162–4
Terrorism and Communism (Trotsky), 18
theory of state organization, 147
third universal theory, 147
Thucydides, 5–6
Tolstoy, Leo, 26
tourism, 85
trade, 23, 24, 140
Treasury, U.S., 96–7, 122–3
Treaty of Friendship and Cooperation, 154
Tripoli, 146, 149, 150, 152, 155, 156, 159–60

Trotsky, Leon, 18
Tudeh Party, 67, 68
Turkey, 25, 39–40, 66
turnkey program, 152
twin pillar policy, 69, 71
Twitter, 186

ulema (community of the clergy), 70
UN, *see* United Nations
UNDP, *see* United Nations Development
    Program
Union of Soviet Socialist Republics (USSR),
    10, 15, 17, 106–7, 114, 154, 185
United Nations (UN), 11, 40, 42, 46, 103, 139
    Special Tribunal, 166
United Nations Development Program
    (UNDP), 123
United Nations Special Commission
    (UNSCOM), 47, 48, 50
United Socialist Party of Venezuela, 180
UNMOVIC, *see* Monitoring and
    Verification Commission, UN
UNSCOM, *see* United Nations Special
    Commission
uranium, 88, 152
    highly enriched, 90, 91, 117
US-China Economic Commission, 128
USS *Cole*, 184
USS *Pueblo*, 105
USSR, *see* Union of Soviet Socialist Republics
USS *Stark*, 35
USS *Vincennes*, 73

Vandals, 6
velayat-e faqih, 71
Velvet Revolutions, 19
Venezuela, 27, 53, 173–6, 179–83
Versailles peace conference, 161
Versailles Treaty, 10
Vietnam War, 11, 16, 69
Vikings, 6
violence, 172
    in Libya, 148
    see also terrorism
Visigoths, 6
Vulcans, 55

wars
    Cold War, 1–2, 4, 5, 13, 18, 25, 32, 54,
        64, 114, 161, 164–7
    Hezbollah-Israel War, 84, 124
    Iran-Iraq War, 64, 73–4, 88
    Iraq War, 4–5, 26, 54–6, 58–9, 61–2
    Korean War, 104, 110, 112, 131
    Persian Gulf War, 42–3, 44, 52, 57,
        77–8, 165
    Six Day War, 162
    Tanker War, 73, 76
    Vietnam War, 11, 16, 69
    World War I, 31, 65
    World War II, 10, 102
    Yom Kippur War, 167
Warsaw Pact, 106, 114
weapons of mass destruction (WMD), 23,
    32, 44, 47, 57–9, 119, 167
    Libya and, 152–4
Weimar Republic, 10
Wen Jiabao, 125
Westernization, 69, 147
white paper, 57
White Revolution, 69
Wilhelm II (Kaiser), 10
Wilson, Woodrow, 66
wireless communication, 187
WMD, *see* weapons of mass destruction
Wolfowitz, Paul, 55
working groups, 131
World Food Program, UN, 103
World Trade Organization, 92
World War I, 31, 65
World War II, 10, 102
"World without Zionism"
    Conference, 93

Yemen, 18–19, 40, 119, 173
Yemen Arab Republic, 18
Yom Kippur War, 167
YouTube, 186
Yu Myung-hwan, 118

al Zarqawi, Abu Musab, 59–60
Zinni, Anthony, 51
Zoroastrian region, 64